Persuasive Writing

PERSUASIVE WRITING

HERMAN HOLTZ

McGRAW-HILL BOOK COMPANY

New York   St. Louis   San Francisco   Auckland   Bogotá
Guatemala   Hamburg   Johannesburg   Lisbon   London
Madrid   Mexico   Montreal   New Delhi   Panama   Paris
San Juan   São Paulo   Singapore   Sydney   Tokyo   Toronto

1 2 3 4 5 6 7 8 9 0   DOCDOC   8 7 6 5 4 3

ISBN 0-07-029627-8
ISBN 0-07-029630-8(PBK)

LIBRARY OF CONGRESS CATALOGING IN PUBLICATION DATA
Holtz, Herman.
Persuasive writing.
1. Communication in management. 2. Persuasion
(Rhetoric) I. Title.
HF5718.H64 1983   808'.042   82–17977
ISBN 0-07-029627-8
ISBN 0-07-029630-8 (pbk.)

Book design by Christine Aulicino

*To many more individuals than I can name,
from whom I've absorbed whatever I know
about writing in general and
persuasive writing in particular.*

CONTENTS

AUTHOR'S PREFACE

WE HUMANS SPEND a great deal of our time and energy persuading each other. Politicians seeking your vote are trying to persuade you, as are salesmen and saleswomen seeking your orders. Your children try to persuade you to give them money for the movies, while you are trying to persuade them to get better marks in school or rake up the leaves. Perhaps you have been working on your employer for a promotion or a raise, or perhaps you've been talking to friends and other "contacts," seeking a better job.

Last week the program chairman of a small, local organization persuaded me to be a luncheon speaker next week. There is no fee, but I permitted myself to be persuaded because I believe it a worthy cause, and I feel honored to be of service to my fellow professional writers—perhaps even as an act of noblesse oblige.

I have persuaded others to review my books in their publications and give those books a plug, if they found them worthy. Sometimes I have persuaded someone to write a foreword for one of my books, for the same reasons that I am speaking free next week: a worthy thing to do, and a much-appreciated gesture of graciousness, although there are usually some indirect benefits also.

Persuasion is based on a great many things: appeals to vanity—it is flattering to be asked to speak and assured that you are especially asked because you are so great to listen to or you have such important ideas to impart; guilt—you owe it to others who are less privileged or less gifted to donate just a bit of your time or money, perhaps both; greed—the publicity will be great for you, and make you more in demand than ever; or any of many other motivations.

Sometimes the "persuasion" is more than persuasion: it may

even be close to coercion—the fear of consequences if you refuse—delicately put, of course. Or some other tactful suggestion that refusal would be not only immoral and perhaps ungracious and even ungrateful, but that acquiescence is definitely in your self-interest—as the Godfather might say, an offer you can't refuse.

Some 6,000 advertising agencies devote their full time and energies to promoting the arts of persuasion, constantly seeking better, more effective ways to be persuasive in print, on radio and TV, and via whatever hybrid media may exist or impend in the future. But some 13 million business enterprises in the United States also seek to persuade: all seek to persuade others to become their customers; many seek to persuade banks to favor them with capital advanced at favorable interest rates; many others seek to persuade the rest of us to invest in their enterprises by buying their stocks and bonds; and many also seek to persuade the best of us to become their star-performer employees, especially when they need specialists who are not in abundant supply, such as computer experts.

Over the past few decades we have been hearing, ever more insistently, that far too few executives, managers, and professionals know how to write well. Their reports are not only pompous monuments to the cult of purple prose, but are totally obfuscatory, defying even the arts of cryptographic analysis. And the same illnesses mark their other writings—general correspondence, memoranda, and—worst blow of all—their sales proposals, so vital to the prosperity and even the continued existence of the enterprise.

In consequence, a great many books, articles, training programs, lectures, and other efforts to solve the problem have been written. And along with these have been the books of scholars who regard modern usage as a perversion of the English language, equivalent morally to denying the existence of God or the sanctity of motherhood. And some of these defenders of the language have enjoyed themselves greatly, while also enriching themselves, by tracking down the most humorous malapropisms, spoonerisms, and other delightful slips of those who are considerably less than faultless in their command of the language. These are the kinds of slips they find tickling their ribs:

A technical writer who was a better engineer than he was a writer wished to explain that in a particularly sensitive piece of equipment there were redundant circuits so that should the main circuit fail for any reason, a duplicate of the circuit would be automatically switched on. The writer managed, somehow, to refer to the "duplicity" of the circuits.

In another case of a technical-writing task, the writer wished to explain the method by which numbers had been assigned to wiring terminals in a multiterminal switching apparatus. He managed to introduce the subject under the heading: The Assignation of Terminal Numbers.

All of this is amusing, of course, even if a bit pedantic. However, the faults and weaknesses of most business and professional people as writers have little to do with their vocabularies, whether large or small, or even with their mastery of grammar, spelling, punctuation, and other mechanics of using the language. What is truly of consequence is not whether the writer is less proficient in vocabulary than he or she believes himself or herself to be, nor even whether the writer knows a dangling participle from a split infinitive or a gerund from a verb. What is of consequence is whether the writer is capable of thinking the matter out coherently, deciding what the main point or points is or are, and organizing the writing to march to the objective in an orderly way, bringing the reader along.

That latter consideration of bringing the reader along is what many people like to refer to as "communicating." Unfortunately, that word is one with so many meanings it is almost without meaning. Everyone puts his or her own interpretation on the word. For example, when someone says, "What we have here is a breakdown in communication," it may mean either 1) the other guy won't do things my way or 2) he refuses to believe or agree with what I say. That is, he doggedly refuses to be convinced or persuaded by my argument, and he absolutely insists on receiving something other than what I am sending. The fault is, of course, not mine: I speak and write with utmost clarity, and my messages are unmistakable. The fault lies with the receiver, not with the sender.

Not surprisingly, the receiver has the opposite view. He or she firmly believes that the fault lies with the sender, not with the receiver. The sender is not logical, not persuasive, not clear.

Some people believe, evidently, that communication is a unilateral action: you send out a clear message, and that is communication. If you happen to have a boob on the other end who is incapable of receiving your clear message, that's beyond your control.

But that's what's wrong with using the term, and why I have always felt most uncomfortable with it: I fear that anyone who receives that word, when I send it, may very well not be receiving the message I sent. And I think that if there is any validity to the idea of communication, it can only be said to have taken place when the sender has taken measures to be sure that the message received is the same message as the one that was sent.

And this is where we get down to what writing is really all about: sending messages in a clear way that will arrive at the reader's brain with the same meaning they had when they left your brain. Your skill as a writer, at least in the business and professional worlds, has nothing to do with style, rules of language usage, elegance, fluency, or anything else, other than sending intelligence that will be received as intended.

And along this line, what shall we infer when the messages are so badly garbled that what is received does not in any way resemble what we sent? Shall we condemn the boob of a reader who obviously can't understand plain English? Or shall we have a look and see whether what we sent *can* be misunderstood—garbled in the translation, as they say about some messages sent in Morse code. And the simile is not selected casually, for *translation* is what all writing must undergo in its conversion from symbols on a page to words "heard" and images "seen" in the receiver's brain.

You can hardly persuade someone to do anything if the someone does not *understand* your message. And the someone cannot understand your message if you have failed to first conceive and organize a clear message, and then select the right symbols for transmitting the message. The preponderance of evidence is that the chief reason for failed communications is failure to decide first *exactly* what the message is to be: far too often a sender taps out only a general and often rather vague idea and unconsciously hides the lack of clarity behind a cloud of meaningless verbiage in what is an effort to conceal the fact that he or she really either has nothing to say, or is quite unsure of exactly what it is that he or she wishes to say.

Translate and decipher those clouds of purple prose, and the truth fairly springs at you from the page: translated into simple English, the "gobbledygook" becomes apparent as an exercise in futility, either saying that which is painfully obvious and does not merit being said again, or that which is a total non sequitur, and has no apparent significance or meaning relevant to anything of immediate interest. It is rare that bad writing conceals anything that is worth the energy necessary to translate or interpret—even to *decipher*—it.

It is not by coincidence that the world's best minds—minds such as those of Bertrand Russell, Carl Sagan, and Winston Churchill—have produced many volumes of brilliantly clear and simple prose. True thinkers never write badly; only the muddle-minded do so. Nor should that come as a surprise to anyone, for the logic is inescapable: you can write only what you think, and your writing is then inevitably a reflection of your thought processes. If you are to persuade anyone with your writing, you must certainly be able to communicate your ideas clearly. But to do that, you must think out your ideas, know precisely what you wish to express so that *it is first clear in your own mind.*

That, however, does not mean that orderly logical presentations are automatically persuasive in themselves. Quite the contrary, logic and reason rarely persuade. We humans are emotional creatures, and we are much more often illogical and irrational than we are logical and rational. Persuasion is primarily a matter of emotional appeal. And yet, logic and reason play a part, and in practice persuasion does depend on logic and persuasion to support and reinforce—to justify and rationalize—the emotional motivator.

The art of persuasion is the art of understanding and satisfying human emotional needs. For, oddly enough, even that logic and reason so essential to accomplishing persuasion is designed to satisfy an emotional need. Unless that latter emotional need is satisfied, the persuasion will probably never come about. You will learn, as we proceed, that complex as human nature and our society are, the most basic principles of persuasion are quite simple:

1. A basic emotional appeal to cause the subject(s) to *want* to be persuaded
2. The need to be offered plausible rationalizations
3. The reassurance that being persuaded is a wise decision

Obviously, if we are going to persuade others through written instruments—letters, brochures, proposals, commercials, advertisements, and whatever other forms our writing takes—we must use salesmanship and persuasive methodologies, but we also must be able to deliver our messages in the clear: even the best strategy of persuasion will not succeed if we fail to put our message across. Therefore, we must discuss here not only how to write persuasively, but how to write in general, how to write *well,* that is, which means how to write *clearly* (content and presentation, not style). But even here we are discussing persuasion because "understanding" is not itself entirely a logical or reason-based process. Conventional wisdom tells us that as humans, we come to believe things after we understand them. For example, we believe that all matter is made up of tiny particles called "atoms," and that these are made up of even tinier particles. We believe that because we understand it. Or do we? Do we believe because we understand, or do we "understand" because we believe? After all, who has ever seen an atom? Our most powerful electron microscopes cannot reveal an atom to us directly, much less the electrons, protons, and neutrons that we *believe* make up the atoms. In short, our entire "understanding" of the nature of matter rests on something we accept on faith, something we *believe* but have only indirect evidence for.

Communication itself, then, rests on persuasion. People will "understand" us when we persuade them to believe what we say. The art of persuasion and the art of communication are inseparable and perhaps indistinguishable from each other. The art of writing persuasively *is,* perhaps, the art of communicating with writing.

HERMAN HOLTZ
Silver Spring, Maryland, July 1982

Persuasive
Writing

1

THE GENTLE ART
OF PERSUASION

One surefire way of persuading others is to tell them what they want to hear. They'll always believe that.

THE MOST BASIC PERSUASION PRINCIPLE

IT'S A RARE HUMAN—probably a nonexistent one—who is not at root selfish. Being selfless is unnatural, and those who lead lives of apparent selflessness are gaining satisfactions from doing so, or they would not do it. This is not to derogate or sneer at those who dedicate their lives to helping others, nor is this an effort to play amateur psychologist, but only a logical reasoning of the most basic motivation that impels human behavior: self-interest.

Abraham Maslow once hypothesized a hierarchy of human needs that motivated all of us, including such needs as to love and to be loved; to gratify our own egos; to be respected; to be secure; etc. In a sense, perhaps all of these are really drives for security, both physical and mental or emotional security. However, even if this is the case, it is far more useful, for our purposes, to break security down into some specific terms that have direct application to our needs, in conceiving if not a science of persuasive writing, at least the beginnings of an organized methodology.

SOME EXAMPLES OF HUMAN NEEDS

Here are a few of the things most of us want or think we want (frequently, we change our minds after we get something we thought we wanted, because it is quite true that the anticipation of something desired is often far greater than the realization achieved):

Love	Someone to love
Financial gain	Job advancement
Recognition	Status
Independence	Security

And here are a few of the factors that drive us to do or refrain from doing certain things:

Guilt	Embarrassment
Fear	Greed
Hate	Love

At least one publisher has assured me that the two factors that are most influential in selling books are fear and greed. Perhaps that explains the great success of a book called *How to Prosper During the Coming Bad Years,* for the title covered both fear and greed. Several other books of the same genre, often referred to as "gloom and doom" books, have also done well, even making best-seller lists, but the one with both fear and greed in the title outdistanced all others by far.

Greed appears to be a most powerful motivator all by itself. Bookstore shelves are loaded with titles promising to make the reader rich beyond dreams of avarice, through wheeling and dealing in real estate, mail order, and a thousand other entrepreneurial enterprises. Some have made more general promises, maintaining that the reader can think his or her way to unparalleled success by "positive thinking," "dynapsych," and other such methods. And only recently I was lectured all of a Sunday afternoon on the virtues of "est," a sensitivity training named for its founder, in an effort to persuade me to subscribe to and undergo a weekend course in the experience. (My friends could not tell me just what it was, however.)

Even when the promises of rewards are ludicrously extravagant, readers believe because they want desperately to believe. If you want badly enough to believe, your reason will surely desert you and leave you to the mercies of your own irrational emotional drives. Nothing, apparently, can dissuade people from believing what they want badly enough to believe—what they *need* to believe—nor will reason and logic ever persuade people to believe what they do not want to believe—what they *need* to doubt, disbelieve, discount, reject.

It is this human failing that makes possible Ponzi schemes, schemes in which investors are paid unreasonably large dividends out of the investment of the most recent group of suckers. When the pyramid runs out of enough new investors to continue paying out the dividends, the swindler decamps with whatever he or she has—several million, frequently. (Charles Ponzi had many imitators duplicating his scheme and making his name synonymous with this swindle.) In one case a few years ago, a swindler entrapped and victimized even supposedly sagacious bankers in such a scheme, linked to a fanciful story about importing industrial-grade wine (which, experts assured newspaper reporters later, does not even exist). The lure of exorbitant profits caused even conservative bankers to take leave of their reason.

Ironically, those swindlers and con artists often fall victim to that same greed that motivates their own victims and persuades the latter to believe in the exorbitant profits promised. More than one such swindler has lingered a bit too long, after his or her scheme had begun to collapse, overcome by the temptation to steal just a few more dollars before the law and exposure shut him or her down, and the law has then caught up with the swindler. And sometimes these swindlers have even managed to persuade themselves to believe that their pyramids can go on forever as legitimate businesses, which demonstrates not only the powerful influence of greed, but how easily people can be persuaded to believe what they want to believe, even when the belief defies logic, reason, and their own experience.

Another phenomenon of human credulity is the overpowering influence of anything we believe "everyone knows" or "they say." Many of us will unhesitatingly accept and believe totally illogical ideas simply because these ideas appear to be commonly accepted by many others. We accept the idea that physicians are almost gods, and it is almost sacrilegious to question the wisdom or ability of a physician, as it is to have less than total respect and even reverence for anyone of the clergy. By the same kind of unreasoning acceptance we require ourselves to believe in the innate goodness of motherhood, the propriety of insurance, and the infallibility of the FBI.

To some degree, this fear motivation—the fear of being thought a fool, of being embarrassed, of being sneered at, of nonconformance—drives us to accept what society in general appears to accept. An advertisement that had as its headline DO YOU MAKES THESE MISTAKES IN ENGLISH? ran successfully for many years. The copy promised to teach the prospect how to use our language properly and so avoid being embarrassed by making grammatical mistakes and being thought uneducated and boorish. The familiar "ring around the collar" TV commercials pursue the same objective of motivating the prospect to fear being embarrassed and to avoid it by using the advertised product.

Fear is probably as powerful a motivator as greed, but not nearly as versatile in application to situations where persuasion is required. Insurance is sold most often through fear, as is anything calling for preventive measures. Exterminating services, for example, especially the extermination of or preventive treatment for termites, is sold most often through appeals to fear. Employees are "persuaded" to do whatever the boss wants through fear, especially if the boss is reputed to be rough and tough, given to firing people abruptly. Locks, burglar alarms, smoke detectors, fire extinguishers, and a great many other devices and services are sold with fear as the prime motivator.

Guilt can be used, too, especially in selling such things as insurance, IRA and Keogh plans, savings accounts, and even such items as those just listed—alarms, locks, and safety devices. Even if the prospect is not motivated by fear directly, he or she may be motivated by guilt, by being convinced that to fail to do what the persuader is urging is to be guilty. That is what is behind such appeals as the statement that you owe it to your loved ones, etc.

You may be sure, then, that nothing is more basic as a motivator in general than is self-interest. What is less obvious and often masks the fact that all motivation is related to self-interest is that *Homo sapiens* is an infinitely variable species, and there is no way of getting a truly representative sample. That is, we can make certain generalizations about people, but the generalizations hold up only if they are never used to predict the behavior of any given individuals or even group of individuals.

WHAT IS "SELF-INTEREST"?

Humanity is made up of individuals, despite the fact that humans often behave like sheep and permit themselves to be herded and guided as though they were truly without the ability to think for themselves. And because humans do definitely behave as individuals when they are not being sheep, human notions of what constitutes self-interest are almost as varied as are the faces and bodies of the approximately 4 billion individuals on this planet. Not surprisingly, what some individuals consider to be in their own interests appears irrational to others, who have entirely different ideas of what their own interests are.

For example, someone recently asked me for permission to use some of my writings on government marketing as the basis of a small brochure he wished to print and give away with a new newsletter he was launching. Although he proposed to write new materials, based on my earlier work, rather than use my material in its original form, he offered to pay me a reasonable fee. Legally, he has no obligation to do this, as long as he does not use my original writings, but only the information contained in them. Therefore, I thought his offer entirely reasonable, and perhaps even generous, and I accepted. My wife, however, had serious doubts that I had acted wisely, evidently thinking that I should have refused or demanded much more money. She obviously perceived our interests differently here than I did, perhaps because she does not understand the legal aspects of the transaction. You must know the facts to guage your self-interests accurately.

A business associate publishes a bimonthly tabloid he calls the *Consulting Opportunities Journal.* He receives enthusiastic support from a local consultant who has no pecuniary interest—no direct one, in any case—but believes that the publication helps his business indirectly because he publishes a series of specialized books for sale to consultants. Another individual, in the same position, might consider the tabloid to be harmful competition, instead of a supporting factor.

In that respect, some entrepreneurs believe that all competition is harmful to them. But there are others who believe that competition is the best thing that can happen to them because the combined effect of everyone's advertising and sales promotion creates a much larger market than anyone can create through his or her own efforts alone.

These are fairly obvious rationales, easily understood, whether you agree with them or not. The individuals have used what is, to them, logical analysis to decide whether something is beneficial or harmful to their own interests. But there are far more subtle influences—emotional influences, principally—at work also, some of them far more difficult to understand.

I once had a friend explain to me that the alternator in his car had burned out, and he'd had it replaced by a mechanic who explained to him that the belt driving the alternator was too tight. That, according to the mechanic, forced the alternator to run at too high a speed, which caused the damage.

I tried to explain to my friend that while too tight a belt might put excessive pressure on a bearing and do damage, it would not change the speed at which the alternator rotor turns because the pulley ratio was fixed, and was not affected by the tightness of the belt. At that, he flew into a rage and demanded indignantly to know whether I presumed to know more about it than his automobile mechanic. Somehow, he found it in his self-interest to defend the mechanic against me. He perceived his own prestige as being involved here, and obviously feared that if my argument was valid, his mechanic was guilty of some degree of incompetence—he did not understand basic gear and pulley ratios, as a mechanic should. And if his mechanic was less than completely competent, he—my friend (who was not feeling very friendly toward me at the moment)—had been taken in. Therefore, to avoid feeling guilty or foolish at being taken in by an absurd theory, he became enraged and decided that it was I who did not know what he was talking about. It was his only defense: I had stupidly left him no other.

That is not an atypical reaction to logical deflation of nonsense arguments. Again and again I have noted that rage and hostility are almost automatic reactions when you respond to an illogical position with irrefutable logic. A person who has taken a firm position and defended that position vociferously feels his or her honor and dignity now tied up—invested—in that position. To destroy the position is to humiliate the individual, and if there is no logical rebuttal to your argument, the only recourse is rage and irrational rejection of your proofs, no matter how valid they are. Or, to put this into more direct terms, if you wish to preserve your relationship with someone else who has taken a position you can easily destroy with logic—*don't*. You cannot truly win an argument by polarizing the positions; at least, if you do win, it will be a Pyrrhic victory: you'll lose more than you win.

It is always in one's self-interest to avoid being humiliated, made to feel inept or impotent, or otherwise caused to "lose face." No, it is not only in the Orient that "face" is important; it is a matter of great importance in the West, too, and has even been a factor in major wars of history.

Losing face has at least three degrees of severity, depending on the circumstances. Here they are in ascending order:

- Being made to feel foolish or inept in some manner, in private exchange
- Being made to feel and appear foolish in the presence of strangers
- Being made to feel and appear foolish in the presence of others whose opinions are of special importance, such as superiors at the office or friends and family members

Of course, what makes an individual feel inept, impotent, incompetent, or in some manner "put down" varies a great deal from one individual to another. It has a great deal to do with the individual's perceptions and basic characteristics. For example, I have noted that in dealing with people, some of them my peers, some my subordinates, and some my superiors in the organization hierarchies, a wide range in their sensitivities. These are the two extremes I've seen:

Ultrasensitive. Some individuals must be handled with the utmost tact because they are quick to see an attack or a put-down in the most innocent of remarks. For example, when I was consulting with a computer firm having serious problems in writing its technical manuals (I had been called in to help), I asked one of the staff writers what I thought was a perfectly innocent question: who was/were the person/persons I should talk to to get technical details about the circuitry in this new computer? The reaction was immediate hostility, with the challenging demand to know whether I thought that he, the staff writer, was incompetent?

In fact, he happened to be a journalism major who didn't know a transistor from a transponder—he had no reason to know, nor did anyone expect him to. It was only with great difficulty that I managed to persuade this gentleman that I was merely asking for help in finding the right design engineers.

Of course, the problem was this staff writer's perception. He had been hired by the company as a technical writer, but without the expectation that he could write technical explanations without the help of the engineering staff. However, when it proved necessary to bring in a special consultant who was both writer and engineer, that was a perceived put-down in itself. And when I asked who understood the technical details, that was a confirmation of the writer's growing self-doubt. So it was not too surprising that he felt increasingly frustrated and reacted with anger.

Circumstances made this individual ultrasensitive in this situation. But there are those individuals who are haunted by general self-doubts, who will find reason to suspect a put-down in all circumstances and situations. I once reported to such an individual, and my biggest problem on that job was to do the best work I could do without providing my boss what he thought was a good reason to believe that I was trying to "show him up" by being better at everything I did than he was at anything he did. He actually accused me of making him feel inferior, in this manner, as though my abilities were a personal affront and perhaps a deep-rooted plot against him.

It requires a great deal of care to get along with such people without offending them because they do have such deep-seated feelings of inadequacy. It is wise, in dealing with ultrasensitive types, to think over your choice of words before speaking, and to avoid confrontation and dispute completely, if you hope to persuade them to anything at all.

Thick-skinned. There are many people at the opposite extreme, almost totally insensitive or what we often call "thick-skinned." At first glance, it might appear that such people are easy to deal with and to persuade because they do not take offense readily nor feel humiliated or put-down. But they present another set of problems, nevertheless. Here is one case, to illustrate:

One of my subordinate managers in an organization of which I happened to be the general manager was in hot pursuit of the affections of one of our female employees. She came to me with the complaint that he wouldn't "let her alone." I therefore spoke to the manager in question, pointed out that the woman did not return his interest and wanted to be "let alone." I spoke to him in a friendly and casual "man-to-man" fashion, with a kind of "don't waste your time" tone to my remarks.

The young woman complained to me again, reporting that my talk with the man had done no good. So I spoke to the man again, a bit more bluntly this time, telling him rather directly that I disapproved of office romances in general, and especially objected to his trying to force his attentions on anyone. I ordered him to "leave the girl alone," in fact.

I had a third complaint from the woman. My manager was still harassing her with his efforts to develop a romantic relationship. And this time I handled the matter a bit differently: I entered his office, thrust my finger at him, showing my anger quite plainly, and told him, "One more complaint from that girl, and you are fired!"

That did it. He finally got the message. But in retrospect, I should have known better than to try to persuade him to any action I wanted by tactful or diplomatic phrasing: I knew him to be insensitive to others' feelings because I knew how his subordinates felt about him. (I kept him on the job because he was bright and got the job done; I could give him difficult tasks that others had failed at, and he would accomplish them successfully.)

With such people, tact and diplomacy—all subtleties—are a waste of time. These people simply do not understand anything that is not absolutely blunt. It is almost literally true that some people with these characteristics can't be insulted—at least, it takes a great deal to make them feel offended. They are blunt and tactless with others, and are more puzzled than anything else when they are themselves treated in any other way. In fact, some of them will regard with suspicion any attempt to be tactful, diplomatic, or even kind in dealing with them.

We all fall along the spectrum marked by these extremes, although the majority of us fall somewhere between the extremes. But there are many others who have one characteristic that is dominant, as far as understanding them and being able to determine how best to persuade them. Here are a few of those types:

The suspicious nature. Perhaps closely related to the ultrasensitive individual is the person who tends to be suspicious of everything and everyone. These individuals tend to believe that every invitation to participate in something, or every effort to interest them in something is a prelude to somehow victimizing them, to taking advantage of them. These are the people who would not buy dollar bills for ninety cents each, even if you were able to give them a good reason why you were selling money at a discount and permitted them to examine the crisp, new dollar bills to satisfy themselves that they were genuine. In fact, the more you did or offered to do, in an effort to persuade them, the more suspicious they would become: the degree of effort to persuade them is itself regarded as evidence of your eagerness to victimize them!

The impulsive one. Impulsive people are frequently easy to sell: they become enthusiastic quickly and buy without much contemplation. The problem is that often the item doesn't stay sold: the buyer is soon back to return it. Experienced sellers of merchandise have learned this, and they tend to be suspicious, or at least uneasy, when a sale comes too easily—when a buyer agrees and yields to a sales argument for an item of substantial cost without very much persuasion.

The know-it-all. Some individuals quite evidently have a compulsive need to appear to know everything about everything. All too often, they are completely wrong-headed about things— they know so many things that aren't so—but they insist on making pronouncements, rather than venturing opinions. Ergo, they polarize their positions instantaneously, making it most difficult to disagree with them without arousing their instant hostility. On some occasions I have found myself sharing a platform with such an individual, and I have had to think most carefully about everything I say, or I will unwittingly turn a panel discussion into a public debate. However, such individuals, properly handled, are often easily persuaded, surprisingly enough.

The gullible one. Some people are trusting souls; they are quick to believe everything they hear, often on the flimsiest kind of evidence or allegations that are offered as evidence. They are often the good souls of the world, reluctant to believe that anyone would deliberately deceive another person or take unfair advantage of anyone. They can be either quite bright or not so bright:

intelligence and gullibility appear to be in no way related to each other. (In fact, if anything, people of higher intelligence appear to tend more toward gullibility, while those of lesser mental capacities appear to tend more toward having suspicious natures.)

The self-conscious one. That characteristic we often refer to as "self-consciousness" is probably akin to the ultrasensitivity discussed earlier, in that it is another manifestation of a profound sense of insecurity. Those people we regard as being self-conscious are embarrassed by minor incidents, such as discovering that some article of clothing fits improperly or has become torn in some manner. Anything which draws attention—or which the individual even *fancies* is drawing attention—is a cause for deep embarrassment.

These are just a few of the thousands of characteristics that are dominant in individuals. Some are obvious or readily apparent characteristics, such as a hearty manner or a shy and retiring one; some are not readily apparent, such as great sensitivity or dogmatic attitudes. The important thing to know is that there are these many characteristics among your fellows in this world, and that these are both obstacles and aids to persuasion, depending on a variety of conditions and circumstances.

The effects of these characteristics on your efforts to persuade can be quite surprising, often directly contrary to that which you might expect. For example, you might expect the shy and sensitive person to shrink from undertaking a course in public speaking, but you may be entirely wrong. Some people undertake such studies without the slightest notion of ever speaking publicly, but because they believe that the training will assist them in overcoming the handicaps of their shyness. And you might expect that the bluff, dogmatic, know-it-all is going to be a tough one to sell. But, handled well, such an individual can be a pushover to be sold or persuaded to something or other.

So it is necessary to understand first that these various characteristics exist and often dominate people, and second that these characteristics are decisive in the individual's perception of self-interest. And with that understanding established, we can begin to see why that which persuades one person does not persuade another. Example:

Only yesterday I spoke at the luncheon meeting of a local group, the Association of Editorial Businesses. These are people who furnish writing, editing, typing, and related services to clients in government and industry. They are all writers and editors, small firms, even self-employed individuals, in some cases. Because they are located in the Washington, D.C., area, they had asked me to tell them something of how to pursue and win government business. Of course, the subject of proposal writing, a necessity in government marketing, arose.

Unfortunately, another speaker remarked to this group that they should not offer their government prospect the best possible proposal because that would require them to offer the agency the most expensive project and therefore be doomed to failure. This speaker was wrong on two counts, one of which was failing to perceive that it was a fundamental mistake to counsel writers and editors to produce less than their best work. It is a rare writer or editor who would agree to deliberately offer less than his or her best writing and editing. Of course, that was probably not what he intended to say, but it was what he did say, and in so doing he managed to turn the entire audience against him from that point on. He aroused their hostility with his thoughtless phrasing, when what he intended to recommend was that they propose something less costly than the most ambitious project. (Even that is a rather dicey thing to recommend.) He "lost" his audience at that point.

Take careful note that self-interest is whatever the individual judges it to be—not what you, I, or any other individual believe it is—but what "the party of the first part" perceives it to be. Take note, too, that the perception is based far more on emotional considerations than on rational ones, and that sends an immediate message: do not attempt to use pure reason in an effort to dissuade the prospect from whatever his or her biases—perceptions of self-interest—happen to be. If the perception is not rooted in logic, it can't be changed by logical argument.

EMOTIONAL NEEDS ARE A FIRST CONSIDERATION . . .

Many of these perceived self-interests are emotional *needs*. The self-conscious individual needs to feel more secure, and that includes the need to avoid or be spared any situation that is likely to cause embarrassment or in any way lessen the individual's sense of security. The dogmatic know-it-all is also highly insecure, and will fiercely resist any effort to disprove or invalidate any of his or her positions, for that is an attack on his or her sense of security. The highly sensitive person needs to be reassured, as often as possible, that he or she commands respect, is loved, has ample prestige, and is in no way less worthy than is anyone else; failing to get *positive* reassurance, he or she assumes the opposite.

On the other hand, it is relatively easy to persuade these people, once you understand their emotional needs. What you must do is satisfy those needs in some manner.

... BUT REASON HAS A ROLE TO PLAY, TOO

Most of us perceive a need to be logical, despite our emotional drives. What most of us do is to permit our emotional drives to crystallize basic positions, and then rationalize those positions so that we can deceive ourselves into believing that we are entirely rational beings. All persuasion, therefore, is generally based on both the emotional and logical appeals, designed to satisfy both the emotional need and the need to rationalize and thereby justify an action. In most cases, both elements must be present, if a persuasive effort is to succeed.

Examine any professionally produced materials designed to persuade, and you will find both these elements, but the main theme is always an emotional appeal, and the backup is rational. Lyndon B. Johnson defeated Barry Goldwater handily at the polls with a fear campaign, based on portraying Goldwater as someone who was sure to "shoot from the hip" and thus embroil us in a war in Viet Nam, while he (Johnson) would keep us out of war. Johnson succeeded in emulating Eisenhower in presenting something of a father image to the voters, another emotional appeal. Jimmy Carter took an entirely different tack: he offered himself as someone from outside the Washington power structure, suggesting strongly that those who were "insiders" in Washington and national politics were out of touch with the average citizen, but he was one of us common folk. He appealed to our great desire to believe that the President understood, sympathized with, and responded to the problems and needs of the common citizens of this country.

Of course, in each case the emotional theme was such that a persuasive rationalization was possible. It was possible to find "evidence" that Goldwater was a shooter from the hip because it could be readily shown that he was a rather blunt and outspoken man, who said what was on his mind. And he was also a reserve officer of the air force, reinforcing the argument that he was, at heart, a military man. Carter simply capitalized on the fact that he was, indeed, an outsider, as far as Washington political and bureaucratic circles were concerned. However, he cleverly turned that condition, which might easily have been deemed a liability and exploited as such by his opponent, into an asset, co-opting any possible effort to discredit him on the basis of inadequate and insufficient political experience.

In advertising, finding those arguments is referred to as "positioning." And in the simplest terms possible (we'll come back to this subject again and examine it more closely), *positioning* is finding the reason a customer should buy what you are offering, because you must tell the prospect why he or she should buy. And knowing ahead of time that you must provide these two elements, emotional appeal and rationalization, you must consider the two together, and frequently the rationalization dictates the emotional appeal. That is, it is of no avail to make an emotional appeal for which you cannot offer a sensible rationalization, for there is also the important matter of credibility: you cannot expect the prospect to be a cretin and accept any argument you offer, no matter how infantile you find some TV commercials to be.

Imagine, if you will, what might have happened had Goldwater's campaign staff concentrated on showing their candidate as someone who would always tell us the truth, perhaps à la Harry Truman, who was widely regarded as a most honest man. And, as we later learned, they might have found some good ammunition for attacking Johnson's capacity for truthfulness.

Or what might have happened to Jimmy Carter's campaign had he used some theme other than the one he did, and permitted his opponent to focus attention of the voters on how little qualifying experience he really had, especially as compared with Ford, who had spent most of his life in Washington law-making activity?

In both cases, it appears that the losing candidate's campaign strategists failed to make an analysis to determine what would be their candidate's greatest strength, vis-à-vis an emotional appeal that could be rationalized credibly, while simultaneously attacking a weakness of the opponent. Or if they did make such analyses, they came up with the wrong conclusions. Despite Ford's unpopular pardon of Richard Nixon and his blunder on national TV on the state of eastern Europe vis-à-vis the USSR, it is still somewhat incredible that this likable and seasoned veteran of Washington, who was an incumbent President, should have lost the election to an unknown interloper with a relatively unimportant constituency. Ford's persuasive strategies were obviously faulty. And four years later, Mr. Nice Guy, Ronald Reagan, committed an incredible series of gaffes and blunders, was frequently ridiculed in the press and by his opponents, and still won overwhelmingly, largely because he was so likable. No one wanted to believe that this genial, smiling fellow could do any serious wrong. He was so obviously a well-meaning friend of the common man, a white knight who would battle the federal dragon in our behalf and vanquish the monster so we could all be prosperous and happy again. And even if a great many respected economists attacked his economic premises and theories, we were willing to accept his "Trust me."

Such is the power of emotional appeal: even when the rationale is so weak as to be almost nonexistent, if the emotional appeal is strong enough, we'll buy the argument and the assurances. We'll believe what we want to believe, if we want to believe it strongly enough. But at the same time, we still, each of us, have our egos, we do still have some degree of sophistication, and we do not want to feel as though we are complete fools. We do require some logical evidence to rationalize our conclusions and permit us to believe that our decisions or conclusions (which are, of course, also decisions) are reasoned and arrived at independently after weighing the "facts."

Note that that itself is also an emotional need, that need to assure ourselves that we are intelligent, independent adults, and that we reason and draw reasonable conclusions therefrom. While there are some instances where we are quite ready to accept ideas based on someone's authority as an expert, there are other situations where we would be quite incensed at being asked to do just that. If an ordinary salesperson delivers a rapid, high-pressure sales pitch and says something such as, "Take my word for it," taking his or her word for it is probably the last thing in the world most of us would do. Quite the contrary, most of us would be offended at the obvious inference to be drawn that the salesperson must think we are uninformed boobs.

The difference between the two cases is that most of us would not challenge a recognized authority in a specialized field (Einstein on relativity?), but we would usually resist allowing a total stranger to set himself or herself up as an "instant authority" on anything. At least, we would not allow an obvious "slick," fast-talking salesperson to try to force us to accept him or her as an authority. With a certain amount of tact and an effective persuasive technique, a salesman might have indeed persuaded us to take his word for it. But he certainly could not bring that about by speaking down to us, in the condescending manner of virtually demanding that we accept as fact whatever he says is fact. That naive and trusting very few of us are today.

2

SITUATIONS REQUIRING PERSUASIVE WRITING

Despite radio and TV, by far the vast bulk of our communications are in writing—correspondence, newspapers, magazines, reports, books, proposals, and other products of the pen.

IT IS NOT ONLY ADVERTISING and sales literature that must attempt to persuade the reader to some belief, although perhaps such material is the outstanding "for instance." In fact, all writing must be persuasive, if it is to be effective at all: a reader must always be persuaded to believe whatever the writer is offering as information. Even in the case of fiction, the reader is asked to "suspend disbelief" and be caught up in the illusion of reality that the writer is attempting to create.

It is much more so in the case of writing what purports to be factual information, and even more so in the case of what is clearly the writer's own opinions—arguments for or against something.

We live in an age of skepticism. Many of our taken-for-granteds no longer are. We once believed that reporting in newspapers and news magazines was objective and factual. Most of us have learned otherwise; we know that news is usually slanted, to at least some degree, to suit the bias of the publisher and the advertisers. The once unassailable "argument" offered of seeing it "in black and white"—in print, that is—is rarely heard today, to demonstrate that something must be so. It's an argument that today would be more likely to draw an amused stare and disdainful rejoinder than any agreement that seeing something in print is evidence of validity.

Despite this, the one common business situation that calls for a great deal of written materials, all of which are designed to persuade, is the marketing/sales situation. Business begins with marketing and sales, and business success depends entirely on the success of the marketing/sales efforts. However, there is almost an infinity of marketing/sales situations and, therefore, of kinds of written products and of considerations.

GENERAL SALES SITUATIONS

Sales and marketing situations or requirements can be divided into classes or categories along several lines, such as these:

Direct selling versus indirect selling
Selling tangibles versus selling intangibles
Selling services versus selling goods
Small-tag sales versus big-tag sales
Selling a new product (or service) versus selling a new brand

Of course, any given sales situation may also be a hybrid or variant of any of the above basic situations. A given situation, for example, may be both a big-tag and intangible sales challenge, or a sales effort may include the selling of both goods and services.

The above discriminations involve also the typical degree of difficulty in making the sale, which is a chief reason for making the discrimination. It is generally easier to sell something for a few dollars (small-tag sale) than something which means virtual investment (big-tag sale) for the customer. It is generally easier to sell a tangible item than to sell an intangible one. It is usually easier to sell a new brand than a new product. "Usually," in most of these cases, but not always; there are exceptions. However, let's talk first about the typical situations and conditions and consider the exceptions later.

DIRECT VERSUS INDIRECT SELLING

That fellow who offers you a special kitchen tool or record album on late-night TV is in direct sales. He is generally selling something he manufactures or imports directly to the consumer, without going through the distribution levels of jobbers/wholesalers, distributors, and retailers. He is his own retailer, and he "cuts out the middleman" in his mode of operation. Part of his sales argument is that he saves you money because there is no "middleman" taking a profit. Another part, generally, is that the product he is plugging is not available elsewhere. (There are some exceptions, with late-night TV sales promotions sometimes promoting items found in your local stores. These are not "direct-sales" efforts.)

Frequently, one of the biggest problems in this kind of selling is that the item being promoted is new and unknown or relatively unknown to the average consumer. It's always difficult to sell revolutionary, new items, especially when the price tag is fairly high. The food processor is a good example of this. Now they are well-known and available everywhere, some models at rather low prices. But they were introduced at very high prices and sold by direct sales because that was probably the only way they could be sold effectively at the time.

Another way direct sales are pursued is by the department-store demonstration, where the demonstrator gathers an audience and proceeds to put on something of a show. Still other ways include selling by mail, selling by demonstration and sales booths at fairs and conventions, and by having salespeople make direct house calls on prospects sometimes from leads, sometimes by "cold canvassing" of houses at random.

Typical direct-sales organizations are Fuller Brush Company and Avon, whose sales representatives—they are really retail dealers who sell by direct methods—do most of their selling in the prospect's home. There are many other such organizations, usually less well-known, such as Mary Kay cosmetics and Stanley, a Fuller Brush competitor.

There are many other direct-selling methods. Direct-selling specialists are blessed with active imaginations, are usually fairly aggressive—the most successful ones are generally highly aggressive—and are "positive thinkers." Some of them sell general merchandise by auction techniques at farmer's markets and country fairs, and they can usually be counted on to put on a good show and entertain their audiences. They are often showmen, in fact.

Public speakers are also often direct-sales specialists. For every Art Buchwald and Henry Kissinger, who can charge thousands of dollars for a single appearance and speech of an hour or so—whether they even happen to be good speakers or not—there are dozens of relatively unknown public speakers, who speak for a few hundred dollars and who sell their special manuals, books, and reports at the back of the lecture hall. While Gerald Ford and Jimmy Carter will book all their speaking eagements via a prominent speaker's bureau, such as Harry Walker or the American Program Bureau, these others tend to win most of their speaking engagements by selling themselves directly to the colleges, associations, and others who book them. So they are direct salespeople in both regards—selling their appearances, as well as their own publications.

Perhaps what characterizes direct selling even more than the fact that it avoids the lengthy chain of distribution levels is the fact that it is aggressive: it is based on pursuing customers actively, as contrasted with waiting for customers to present themselves, asking to be sold. It may go directly to people's homes, it may go to wherever people congregate, or it may do something to provoke a congregation of people, but it then works aggressively to try to close sales. Of course, there are many variants of this basic idea, and those aggressive and imaginative individuals who specialize in this field constantly invent new ways to reach prospects directly. So there are no absolute rules to distinguish the direct-sales operation from what might be considered to be more conservative and more conventional sales methods.

SELLING TANGIBLES VERSUS SELLING INTANGIBLES

There are no absolute rules for discriminating between tangibles and intangibles. Or perhaps it would be more accurate to point out that "tangible" and "intangible are all not absolute definitions or descriptions; there are degrees of each. Technically, a tangible item is one you can see, touch, feel, taste, smell, sense physically in some manner; an intangible is something you must use your imagination to visualize. An automobile, a carrot, a book are tangibles; an insurance policy, a service contract, an investment in stocks are intangibles. In practice, and especially in terms of selling, such distinctions do not hold up at all. Let's consider why.

For most of us, the idea of something being intangible may depend in large part on how familiar we are with it. Those who play the market—buy and sell stocks—regularly don't find stock-market investments intangible at all. The whole thing is so familiar to them that they are quite at ease in making their transactions and need not strain their imaginations at all to visualize any given stocks, bonds, warrants, commodities, buying short or long, or any other investment item or maneuver. Of course, there are those who confine themselves simply to buying and selling, and who are quite unfamiliar with such maneuvers as selling short, and who find the idea of arbitrage quite intangible itself.

For most of us, we accept the idea that automobile insurance is an absolute must, even if we live in a jurisdiction that does not mandate that we have such coverage. The idea and the insurance itself is not at all intangible, as far as we are concerned as customers.

On the other hand, as far as some shoppers are concerned, meat and potatoes are quite tangible enough, when they are shopping at the supermarket, but artichokes and lobster tails may not be, either because they are unfamiliar foods or because they are too expensive to become familiar foods. Or the buyer of a small, "economy-model" automobile may find that much more "tangible" than an expensive luxury model. (Bear in mind that we are not talking about dictionary definitions or technical meanings of words, but about the practical implications of the terms in considering how we must attempt to bring about a sales persuasion. This will become much clearer, after a while, when we discuss what people *really* buy.)

SELLING SERVICES VERSUS SELLING GOODS

The services-versus-goods sales problem closely parallels the intangibles-versus-tangibles sales problem, in that services tend to be regarded (and, in fact, to be) intangible, while goods tend to be totally tangible. Yet, what has been said about tangibles versus intangibles is largely true here, too. We all accept the need for service to our automobiles and TV receivers, and treat such purchases as the purchase of tangibles. But we are less familiar with and receptive to many other services, such as resurfacing the drive-way or learning how to speak publicly. In general, the selling problems are those of selling tangibles versus selling intangibles.

SMALL-TAG VERSUS BIG-TAG SALES

The difference here is quite obvious. The only question is this: What do "small-tag" and "big-tag" mean in terms of actual dollars? And here again, if we reflect, we discover quickly that there are no absolute scales, but only comparative or relative ones. That is, to some people and in some situations a small-tag sale may be one of a hundred dollars or even several hundred, while others might consider that to be a rather large tag to pay. The definitions, then, depend on 1) the individual customers and their economic status and attitudes, and 2) the situation itself, wherein what might be a big tag in other circumstances becomes a small tag in the present circumstances. For example, to illustrate the latter idea, most of us probably do not spend a $100 or $200 casually, but give at least some reflection before making a decision. However, if we are buying an automobile that costs quite a few thousands of dollars, we might not ponder more than a moment on some accessory that costs $150. By association and comparison, it has become an insignificant sum.

On the other hand, some of us spend $10 or even $25 spon-taneously, casually, without more than a moment's reflection, whereas there are many people to whom even $2 represents a sum of money to be spent only after consideration. However, despite this truth—and it is an unfortunate truth—purchases run-ning to such sums as $5, $10, $20, and others on that general scale must be considered to be small-tag sales, and items running to hundreds of dollars and more must be considered at the low end of the big-tag sales spectrum.

In terms of selling prospects when sales involve such small, medium, and large sums, the consideration is principally twofold:

How much effort is required to achieve such sales?

How much effort is justified or worth undergoing to achieve such sales?

In the jargon used by some salespeople, selling the big-tag item is not a one-call sale, and that expression sums up the selling problem in such a way that it may be more significant to rephrase the two questions just hypothesized, in this manner:

How *many* efforts (sales calls or presentations) are necessary to achieve the sale?

How *many* efforts (sales calls or presentations) are justified or worth undertaking to achieve the sale?

If you are selling $10 items, to carry the reasoning out in practical terms, you would hardly find it worthwhile to make several sales calls on a prospect to close the sale. On the other hand, if you are selling a $5,000 item, you can hardly expect to close the sale in a single call, in most cases. And that is at the heart of the problem when dealing with big-tag sales.

SELLING A NEW PRODUCT VERSUS SELLING A NEW BRAND

This is perhaps the trickiest and most interesting problem in sales persuasion. In both cases, there is almost automatic customer resistance to be overcome because customers almost automatically resist anything totally new, especially when the price is fairly substantial—that is, when more than a small sum is at risk. That is the heart of the problem and the reason for customer resistance: the risk. The amount of risk determines the amount of sales resistance the customer will exhibit and, of course, the amount of resistance you will have to overcome, if you are to make the sale. Madame might risk $3 or $4 on a new cosmetic item, for example, just to try it out or out of curiosity, but $30 or $300 is another matter entirely. Her curiosity is rarely that great, and you will have to appeal to something more persuasive than curiosity to close that sale.

Risk, of course, is always the customer's assessment, and this is a point that is commonly missed by salespeople and others: all appeals must be based on the customer's perceptions. (Technically, they are not yet customers; they are prospects. However, for convenience, I'll refer to all prospective buyers as customers.) To be a successful persuader in any situation, you must be able to perceive the proposition from the viewpoint of the "persuadee" (if you will permit me that coinage), for that is the only viewpoint or perception that counts. No matter how confident you are that the new product works well and is not a risk of any kind, financial or otherwise, the customer may perceive it far differently. Suppose, for example, that you are offering milady a new hair dye, but she is fearful of using an unknown product on her hair, regardless of price. After all, such products have sometimes done damage to people's hair. Unless you understand this perception, this reason for fear, you can never persuade this customer to try your product.

THE CUSTOMER'S PERCEPTION

This consideration does not apply to fears or perception of risk only. It applies to all situations in which you are trying to persuade anyone to believe or do anything at all. People will resist your arguments, your appeals, and your blandishments for their own reasons and in terms of their own perspectives and views—even biases or prejudices. The consideration applies also to the opposite of fears and resistance—to positive motivations. For some people money is by far the greatest motivator, while to others it may have little appeal. Take the "upwardly mobile" careerist, for example: he or she is often a technical/professional specialist of some kind, who changes employers very two or three years, always managing to better his or her position in the process, in terms of salary. To this person, career success is represented by money primarily. But there are many others—those working in banks are generally considered to be typical—to whom salary is less important than titles and relative rank. Some would much rather have an impressive title and a handsomely appointed office than a substantial raise in salary. But there are others who have still other motivations. Some people hate to work indoors, and prize a job that allows them to be outdoors or traveling a good bit. Some of us like working in a somberly quiet atmosphere, while others prefer a noisy bustle of activity around them.

Peter Drucker made the point some time ago that too many of us don't know what business we're in. That somewhat cryptic observation was a wise one because it addressed this problem of whether we do or do not understand our customers' perceptions. It's become an exceptionally trite platitude to observe that America's railroads thought they were in the railroad business, instead of recognizing that they were in transportation, and that they suffered because of that. And the term "horse and buggy" has become an idiom denoting that which is so out of date and obsolete as to be an anachronism. This is what Drucker was driving at, in his own unique style of expression. However, despite the fact that the syndrome of not understanding what business you're in is very well established and very well-known, most of us are still guilty of that failing. We are still trying ineffectually to define and understand what businesses we are in.

Let's take that railroad-business problem, for example. True enough, the railroads were in the "transportation" business. But what does that say? Does that define or identify the railroad business *from the customer's viewpoint?*

No, it does not. People shipping goods by railroad and people engaging in travel by rail don't think of railroads as selling "transportation," nor do they consider what they are buying to be something called "transportation." Let's consider, first, what the shipper of freight is buying when he consigns his shipment via some railroad line.

First of all, the shipper may not even consider whether his shipment is going to travel by rail or not. He may simply call in a freight service of some kind that picks up his consignment in a small truck and carries it off to transfer to a boxcar, or perhaps an over-the-road trailer. The shipper may have simply sought out the most convenient service: someone who picks up shipments at his door in the shortest possible time. Or he may have bought the least-expensive method for *delivering his shipment to a customer.* (For that is the true concept, in most cases: getting the goods delivered to the customer.) In one case, perhaps the consideration was speed, and he opted for the fastest method, whereas if speed is not important, he is likely to choose the least-expensive method.

In short, what most shippers are buying, as far as their motivation is concerned, is the best means for delivering the goods to their customers, consonant with whatever requirements may exist for schedule, cost, or related services (such as pickup and delivery at each end). They don't think of it as "transportation" or "railroad" business, but only of how to carry out their own self-interest goal of making delivery to their customers.

The individual who travels personally by train is interested in *getting somewhere personally.* The question of "transportation" doesn't enter into it; only *getting there* counts, but getting there under certain conditions. If the customer has opted to travel by train, there are two or three possible considerations important in deciding how to travel: costs, schedule convenience, amount of time required to get there, convenience of terminus served by the carrier vis-à-vis the desired destination. In short, the customer wants to buy what is to him or her the best way to get wherever he or she wishes to go. And "best" can mean different things to different travelers, or even to the same traveler at different times and under different conditions.

And so the railroads, had they but known it, were and are in the two businesses of helping businesspeople make deliveries to their customers (or to their distributors and dealers, which is the same thing) and of helping individuals go where they wish to go. If you are a railroad operator and wish to persuade businesses to patronize you and buy your services as a hauler of freight, show them how you can help them better than others, through beneficial costs and services. If you wish to attract passengers, show them that you can help them get to their destinations more conveniently, more comfortably, more safely, at lower costs, and/or under whatever other conditions and benefits you can offer as inducements.

Here again, there are many possible motivators, and you must find the right ones if you are to succeed in being persuasive. But it must begin by identifying "what business you are in," even if you are not literally in a business or trying to persuade someone to become your customer. "What business you are in" can be translated more freely as why the other party should do whatever it is you want the other party to do. If, for example, you are trying to persuade someone to hire you, the "business you are in" is whatever benefits there are to the other party in becoming your employer—*why* should he or she hire you? What can you do for him or her? How will hiring you serve the other's self-interest? Unless you can can up with some reasonable and believable answers to those questions, you don't know "what business you are in."

Let us take my own case, since it is one with which I am somewhat familiar. In addition to writing books in general, I have written several about marketing to the government, since I am something of a specialist in that field. I also lecture and conduct seminars on the subject, especially on how to write effective proposals. And I do some consulting, principally, again, in helping others develop proposals that win government contracts. What business would you suppose this represents?

For a long time, I thought I was being quite sophisticated and sagacious in considering myself to be in the "information" business, and I loudly proclaimed my profound insight into this fundamental truth to anyone who would listen. But when I tried to incorporate that as an example in my own lectures and seminars,

I discovered that I was making the same mistake the railroads did when they decided that they were in the transportation business: I was broadening and generalizing what I do, but I was still defining my business from *my* viewpoint, not from my customers' viewpoint. That is, I was in the business of selling information, but my customers were buying help in winning government contracts. Abandoning my excursion into ego-land (I felt so late-twentieth-century, smart-modern, in being in the "information" business!) and thinking of my customers' needs and aspirations finally enabled me to see the truth for the first time.

What difference does this make? you may be asking yourself. What does it matter what the seller thinks, as long as the buyer gets what he or she wants? It makes a substantial difference in selling, in persuading others, to know what they want. When I ceased and desisted in my efforts to sell "information" and began to sell help in winning government contracts, the coefficient of sales success began to soar immediately. I began to truly "communicate"—to strike a nerve in my sales efforts when I began to sell my customers what they wanted to buy instead of what I wanted to sell.

The mistake many of us make is to assume that a customer will perceive the benefit—the self-interest—in what we offer. If a steak house offers "prime aged beef," it is with the assumption that the customer will recognize a benefit in being served "prime aged beef." But how many customers know that steaks must be aged, to be properly tender? And how many know what "prime" means in grading beef? And even if they did know these things, to how many customers will those terms translate into mouth-watering temptation for one of the restaurant's fine steaks?

The late Elmer Wheeler, often acclaimed as America's greatest salesman, was most often quoted for saying, "Sell the sizzle, not the steak." That quotation summed up his sales philosophy: make the basic appeal an emotional one, and explain the benefit or self-interest to the customer.

A well-known story about Wheeler is that he was challenged once by the proprietor of a general store to help him (the proprietor), get rid of a large stock of long underwear, when such underwear was going out of style. Wheeler responded, we are told, with a successful campaign in this manner: he created a large display of the underwear in the store with a sign that said, "They don't itch."

That latter story tells us something: always give a customer a good reason for buying what you offer, even if it is a negative reason. People are often motivated by the wish to avoid certain things even more than by the desire to gain or achieve things. That is, the benefit may well be the avoidance of something.

Take the philosophy of Ron Popeil, chairman of Ronco Teleproducts, for example. He has built a multimillion-dollar enterprise, principally in kitchen gadgets sold by late-night TV and similar promotions, after having started earlier doing in-person demonstrations with a great deal of success. Asked what he looks for in selecting the products he chooses to sell, he says that he is interested in one thing only before he decides to take a second step: he wants to know what problem the item solves. If it does not solve a problem that he believes to be a common problem, he drops the idea immediately. To illustrate this, one of his most successful devices was the Splatter Screen, that screen which fits over a frying pan and prevents the hot oil from splattering on the cook's hands and clothes. The Pocket Fisherman and the Buttoneer were also great successes, as was a device that scrambles an egg while still in its shell. Of course, what Popeil is saying when he explains that he wants to know first what problem the new device solves is that he wants to know what persuader he can use on customers. He has to judge whether the problem is common enough to constitute a large-enough group of potential customers, and whether it is serious enough to make it likely that a large percentage of those prospects will be motivated by the desire to solve the problem. If the answers to those questions appear satisfactory, the next step is to judge whether the device will solve the problem effectively and whether it will solve the problem at a price people will pay.

In most cases, Popeil is selling new items, and must face the typical resistance to new items, therefore, the need for demonstration and for low enough price so that the risk is not great. The writing he needs for his sales effort is a TV commercial, which is both verbal and visual. His business is a prime example of direct selling, and he deals in small-tag sales of new products that are highly tangible. Note that each of the five general sales situations is covered in a description of Popeil's business.

On the other hand, selling subscriptions to one of the new services that reduces the cost of long-distance telephoning, such as Sprint, is a somewhat different kind of situation. First of all, while it is not exactly a big-tag item, it does ask the customer to make a commitment to pay some minimum sum each month. Secondly, it does ask the customer to undergo some risk by trying out a new service. Or, if you wish to consider that it is not a new service because we are all familiar with long-distance telephoning, it is at least a new brand because we are all familiar with the Bell System. It is a service, not a product, and it is an intangible, in at least that sense. The benefit offered is that of reducing costs of a service we use more or less regularly, and the sellers of the service pursue both the positive benefit of reducing costs and the negative—fear—benefit of avoiding high costs. So far, at this writing, all the advertising for these new systems has been on the basis of lower costs, whereas the established Bell System people have been engaged in an extensive campaign of emotional appeals designed to persuade that we can now afford to talk with our geographically distant loved ones by using the company's special, low rates of off-peak hours. Obviously, this campaign is in head-to-head opposition to the newer systems. Which campaign is the more effective is impossible to say, but it is likely that the Bell people's campaign is highly effective. However, note that this campaign is focused on urging subscribers to make the distance calls during off-peak, lower-rate hours, but this in no way ensures that the subscribers will not do the calling of distant loved ones by using the other systems! That is, the Bell advertising campaign may be aiding their competitors because while it is an argument for calling long distance, it offers no arguments for using the Bell System completely for the calls, relying on the *implied* message that Bell System rates are low enough in off-peak hours to offer the same benefits as do the new systems.

Bell has the advantage, of course, because it is the established, well-known, accepted system. And because the new systems are trying to sell against very tough competition, offering if not a new service, at least a new brand of a familiar service, they find that it is not usually a one-call sale. A single presentation does not close sales. Rarely does a customer call or write and say, "Please sign me up for your service and send me the bill." Instead, calls and letters are requests for more information, and the new systems in their advertising ask only that prospects call or write for detailed information.

This is a significant point because it strikes at the heart of what persuasive efforts are all about: the specific, direct objective of the effort. On the one hand, as in the Ron Popeil example, the presentation has as its objective a sale. In the latter case, the objective is to arouse the prospect's interest enough to elicit a call or letter requesting more information. That is in recognition of the fact that at least two steps or two presentation efforts are going to be needed to make the sale, typically, and even more are often needed.

PERSUASION OFTEN REQUIRES
AN ENTIRE CAMPAIGN

Persuasive effort must be geared to the level of difficulty, and must be designed in recognition of the need, in many cases, to achieve persuasion in successive stages, rather than in single quantum leaps, as one makes a long journey with a series of objectives, leading finally to the final or main objective. A most common reason for failure in persuasive efforts is that of trying to accomplish too much in a single effort. Persuasion must often be accomplished through being organized into entire *campaigns.*

Very likely you have been subjected to more than one of these campaigns yourself, although you may not have recognized what was happening. First, you received a package of literature, which probably included a sales letter, a brochure, a slick-paper, multicolored foldout or "broadside," an order card, and a return envelope. Perhaps you read it before you threw it away, perhaps not. But soon after, you got another package of literature, again attempting to interest you and probably making some kind of "special offer."

This campaign may have gone on for several months through a half-dozen such mailings, and perhaps after the first two or three mailings, you began to get a variety of "special inducements" and other blandishments. There may have been "free trials," free samples, and other efforts to arouse your interest before the mailer gave you up as a prospect. You may be sure, unless that company was totally amateurish, that they kept most careful records and made careful analyses. They know how many sales they close on a given mailing, and how many mailings are required before writing off a new prospect. Their records tell them what percentage of prospects respond on the first, second, third, and fourth mailings, how many respond to each kind of special inducement, and what is the *specific* objective of *each* individual mailing.

They know the value of persistence, repetition, and escalation. In fact, it is demonstrated over and over and is well-known to those experienced in sales campaigns that frequently—perhaps most of the time—a given population of prospects produces *better* results *each time* a sales presentation is made to them, to some peak, which may not be reached until the third, fourth, fifth, or even later repetition in the series. And even then, the series is by no means over. Frequently, the campaign continues to produce near-peak results for some time after the peak has been reached.

In short, persuasion cannot always be achieved in and by a single effort, but may have to achieved by stages, based on the levels of difficulty. Consider, for example, how an effective new-car salesman might operate in several stages:

1. Induce the prospect to come in and look at the new models. Just to pass the time, satisfy curiosity, no obligation, of course.
2. Try one out. Drive it around the block. No obligation, of course.
3. Let me have a look at your present car. Yes, I know you're just looking and aren't ready to trade yet. Just curious. No obligation. Just want to show you what we can do for you when you are ready.
4. Let me show you the kind of deal we can now offer you, now that I've looked over your present car. No obligation, of course. Just an example for when you are ready for your next car.
5. Suppose I could put you in that new car for only $*xxx* per month—what would you say to that? Well, how much could you handle without strain?

Note the gradual escalation of objective of each effort, persuading customer to a series of steps, none of which represents commitment by itself, but which are gradually conditioning the customer to a final stage where commitment becomes conceivable, perhaps acceptable. The success of the campaign depends on selecting a series of objectives that are achievable individually. It is axiomatic that few new-car sales are made to people who came into the showroom to buy a new car; almost all new-car sales are made to prospects who are "just looking." And I can personally vouch that I bought my first new car while "just looking." I truly had no intention of buying a new car that evening, but a resourceful salesman conditioned me to the idea through a series of presentations, leading me to something I'd had absolutely no intention of doing an hour or two earlier.

Conducting such a campaign of escalating persuasive presentations may take only an hour or two in an automobile showroom, or it may take several weeks or months, when conducted by mail or other more remote means. But philosophically, the two are identical: both are based on setting the "ante" (objective) low initially, and raising it steadily, until it reaches the level of the main goal of the entire campaign. There are several factors to consider, to understand why this is effective and works, when a direct effort to achieve persuasion in one leap will not work:

1. There is the general effect of repetition. What one's mind may rebel against on first contact because it is alien tends to become less distasteful or objectionable, as repetition makes it more familiar, and we have had time to absorb it and become somewhat conditioned to the idea.

2. If carefully designed, a campaign sets its original target relatively low, asking the prospect to agree to something that is relatively easy to agree to, such as try before you buy, or try with an ironclad money-back guarantee, or ask for more information. None of these objectives represent much risk or much of a threat, and so are not met with the resistance the main objective would probably generate.

3. No matter how cleverly we analyze our target population—the prospects, that is—they are all individuals and are all individually motivated. So if we conceive several motivators—benefits—likely to appeal to this population of prospects, we are still dealing in mathematical probabilities, not absolute certainties. If we have, for example, three good motivators, we need to offer them all. But offering them all in the same presentation rarely works as well as offering them one by one. That is, offering them all at the same time dilutes the impact overall of the entire presentation, and a presentation is almost always far more effective if narrowly focused on a target—on a benefit or compelling reason to buy. Ergo, the advantage of making three successive presentations, each focused on a different benefit. In effect, in addition to the overall advantages of repetition and escalation, each of these is actually addressed to a different component of that prospect popu-

lation, that component for whom this benefit has the greatest appeal.

4. The foregoing does not mean that the other benefits are dropped completely in each of the presentations, but that the other benefits are soft-pedaled or low key, while the prime benefit is featured and focused sharply. Take note of how this is done in TV advertising campaigns, where the advertiser often has two or three different commercials, each focusing on a single major benefit, while not completely neglecting the others.

This latter concept is especially important when persuasion is attempted through a general dissemination to the public at large, rather than to a chosen and selected target. For example, if you are trying to sell beer, you must offer it to the world at large. If yours is a "light" beer, you feature that, knowing that among the entire world of those reading, listening to, or viewing your advertising, you are reaching, first of all, only those who have an interest in beer and, secondly, only those beer drinkers who have an interest in light or low-calorie beer. However, you may be able to reach some of those who do not drink beer only because of the caloric content by stressing the low-caloric content of your beer. But the general truth is that for some kinds of persuasion, you have to send your message to the entire world and structure it so that you signal those who ought to be interested that they should listen to, read, or watch your message.

This works even when you have chosen a more select group than the entire world of readers, listeners, or viewers. Suppose you are trying to sell woodworking equipment and tools, and you choose to advertise in *Popular Mechanics,* under the reasonable assumption that a greater percentage of *Popular Mechanics* readers are good prospects than would be the percentage of *Wall Street Journal* readers. Still, not all those *Popular Mechanics* readers are interested in woodworking and tools. Even then, you structure your messages to attract the attention and interest of those interested in woodworking, to let them know that your message is for them.

It can get even more specialized than that. Suppose that you can find a publication that addresses only those interested in woodworking, or get a mailing list of those who are woodworking hobbyists. Even then they are not all good prospects because some may already own items similar to those you sell and others may simply not be interested or specialize in some manner such that your items are really of no interest or value to them.

Ideally, you would want to send your appeals only to those who have a distinct need or use for the items you sell and who do not now own such items. And, of course, can also afford to buy those items from you. That's an ideal essentially impossible to attain, existing only as a hypothesis. The more closely you can approach it, if you can, the more effective your persuasive efforts will be and the more efficient your campaigns overall. But everything in this world is a trade-off: you must always sacrifice something to gain something else. If you succeed in raising the efficiency and incidence of success in your persuasive efforts, it will be as a result of narrowing your potential market considerably, and so the end result may be actually less than if your overall efficiency was lower! I know personally of one case, for example, where a firm won fully 50 percent of the market for a machine they manufactured. Unfortunately, as it turned out, the entire market consisted of only six companies in the entire world, so even if they had won 100 percent of that market they would not have had a major marketing achievement.

OTHER SITUATIONS CALLING FOR PERSUASIVE WRITING

Obviously, persuasive writing has a place in virtually all sales and marketing situations generally, for they are all exercises in persuasion per se, by their innate functional requirements. But there are many specialized situations, too, calling for special written presentations, some for sales purposes directly, others for other purposes.

CUSTOM PROJECTS

Custom projects undertaken for customers generally require the preparation and submittal of special sales proposals. These proposals can vary enormously, from one situation to another, with the most elaborate and demanding those required by the federal government for major projects. But even relatively small projects, such as the remodeling of or the construction of an addition to a private residence, are likely to call for a proposal of some sort. (Such projects are almost always competitive, and customers want to read and compare proposals, and make a selection from among them.)

MAJOR EQUIPMENT SALES

Making a major equipment sale, such as the heating and air-conditioning plant for a large home or other building, or any comparable sale, is generally large enough to cause the customer to want to review several competitive proposals, as in the case of a custom project. The equipment may be standard equipment as manufactured, it may be built to custom specifications, or it may be standard equipment but assembled into a custom system—that is, an assemblage and configuration of equipment that is custom, although none of the equipment is custom made. Again, the proposals required may be relatively simple, or they may be quite extensive to prepare.

STUDY AND OTHER REPORTS

A custom project may entail or consist primarily of some sort of study or survey, sometimes as a preliminary to further work, whose nature is determined by the initial study. But even when the study is a complete project in itself, it invariably requires some sort of final report and, frequently, a series of progressive reports. Perhaps it is not readily apparent that such reports must be persuasive in nature, but experience soon proves that customers must be persuaded, quite often, to accept what the report presents.

Sometimes such reports are written for or must be reviewed by those in superior positions, and in such cases those superiors are the "customers" who must be persuaded to accept what the report offers. A bit of experience in these matters soon demonstrates the need to be persuasive, even in writing reports. (In some cases, reports are themselves proposals, or direct preliminaries to proposals that will be based directly on the reports.)

JOB HUNTING

The need to be persuasive in job hunting is obvious, and the written instruments commonly demanded and in use today are resumes and letters. Even secretaries and, in many cases, blue-collar workers must present resumes to be considered for employment.

GENERAL CORRESPONDENCE

An author named Ralph Charell wrote a best-selling book that explained how he wrote successful letters of complaint when he felt that he had been mistreated in some manner. But a great many individuals do not know how to go about doing this. Several individuals have set up successful part-time enterprises at home writing letters for others, for a fee, especially letters to persuade someone to do something or other. A TV broadcaster in Washington, D.C., Paul Berry, runs a TV feature on our local channel 7, called "Seven on Your Side," which helps viewers with their problems, most often entailing the writing of letters to persuade someone to refund money or otherwise adjust a legitimate complaint.

In both business/professional and personal situations there is an almost continuous need to be persuasive in writing letters generally, to persuade the other party to either do or accept something. (If you reflect on it for a moment, you will realize that all persuasion is exactly that—to persuade others to do or to accept something, and in some cases to both do and accept.) To put this into a proper reference frame, it is the exception rather than the rule when anything written does not have to be persuasive. The difference is a matter of degree—*how* persuasive we must be—rather than of kind. And that, in turn, means how much resistance we must overcome in being persuasive.

THE MESSAGE SENT VERSUS THE MESSAGE RECEIVED

An example was used earlier of the efforts of several new companies to enlist subscribers to a service offering lower long-distance telephone costs, and the advertising of the Bell Telephone people designed to counter this service. The point was made here that the Bell advertising aims to persuade viewers to do more long-distance calling of loved ones during off-peak hours at the lower rates offered then, but it does not stress using the Bell System, evidently assuming that the viewer will infer that portion of the sales message. Perhaps the strategy dictates that that not be stressed, for fear of planting the idea of using competitive systems and thereby causing Bell advertising to work in behalf of the competition. In any case, it is virtually impossible to do other than guess at how many people are motivated by the Bell advertising to do more long-distance calling, but turn to other systems to do the calling at lower rates.

The problem is an old one: sending a message that is clearcut and plain enough, as far as the sender is concerned, is no guarantee that it will be the same message as that received by the receiver. Here again we have the problem of the other's perception, which is often far different from ours, unfortunately, for a variety of reasons.

Fortunately, the advertiser tested the commercial in a theater first, for he learned that the visual had effectively drowned out the narrator's resonating command. What the test audience heard was, "Break the chain-smoking habit," which was hardly the message a cigarette manufacturer wanted to transmit to customers.

What the copywriter had neglected to consider here was, first of all, that visuals generally have greater impact than do words, especially when the visual is of a most familiar object. A reader or listener must *translate* words into an image, whereas a visual is already an image. But the copywriter had also neglected to consider that "chain smoking" is such a common and familiar expression that associating smoking with a chain was all but certain to impart that idea, no matter what the narrator said or how commanding his voice.

We must never lose sight of the fact that *most people are poor readers.* Not only those who have not had advanced formal educations, but most people, even highly educated people with advanced degrees. Why is this so? Well, there are undoubtedly many reasons and possible explanations, and most of it far beyond the scope and purpose of this book. But let us consider it briefly for whatever benefit we can derive from even a partial appreciation of this phenomenon. (For it is a phenomenon that highly educated people read not much more effectively than those of far less educational achievement.)

One reason, probably the principal one, is that we live in an atmosphere where many things compete for our attention—newspapers, magazines, books, TV, radio, movies, children, cocktail conversation, and numerous other distractions. At the same time, we live in a most complex society, and we are under the pressures and influences of all the complexities and crosscurrents of our business, professional, social, and personal lives. It requires distinct effort to truly concentrate on anything, and it is rare that we concentrate on anything as trivial as a commercial or newspaper account of some distant event of only passing importance. We even invest time and money in learning something called "speed reading," so that we can become more accomplished at reading rapidly and picking up main themes, while skimming extraneous detail. We actually make a special effort to do at least some of our reading more superficially in the hope of gaining time without losing any more of the meaning than we already lose in reading slowly. At the least—and advocates of speed reading will oppose these arguments, I am sure—those of us who do undertake speed reading courses admit to feeling a need for help in reading.

In any case, there can be no doubt that a large portion of our written messages are garbled in the translation from sender to receiver, in passing from a writer's brain to a reader's brain. And it is not a matter of short direct sentences and short, monosyllabic words, either; it's far more complicated than that, and all the millions of words printed in books and spoken in lectures and classrooms in almost-frantic efforts to improve the situation have worked almost zero improvement. There is at least tacit agreement that the approach to solving this lies more in the direction of improving writing skills than of improving reading skills, but this is rarely truly implemented, strangely enough, because most effort to solve the problem focuses on how to write, rather than on how to understand the reader's viewpoint. That is, we appear to agree that it is primarily a failure of the writer when the reader does not understand what the writer means, and yet we devote all our effort to trying to understand the writer's problems in writing, rather than the reader's problems in reading.

To write so that you can be understood is not enough, as one of my own editors of many years ago once counseled me; you must write so that you cannot be misunderstood. He said no more, leaving it to me, obviously, to translate that sage observation into something that would make a useful working tool out of a bit of editorial wisdom. And I pondered long and worked hard taking that advice much to heart and trying to bring the concept to life.

A first effect was to do my self-editing through a more perceptive eye: I began to study everything I wrote to judge whether what I said could be reasonably interpreted to say more than one thing—to say something other than that which I intended it to say. And I soon discovered that ambiguity is not a characteristic of the writing necessarily, but may well be a characteristic of the reading. The author has a most difficult time editing his or her own work for possible ambiguities, for obvious reasons. Perhaps it is crystal clear that when you say that the earth is an oblate spheroid you are saying that it is approximately round, but slightly flattened at the poles, somewhat like an orange. It's crystal clear if you happen to know the meaning of those two words, *oblate* and *spheroid.* If the reader has happened to read somewhere that our space-age satellites have revealed to us that our earth is actually pear shape, rather than round and flattened at the poles, that reader may be led to believe that *oblate* means pear shape! So there is a double hazard, in that not only may the reader fail to understand your meaning, but he or she may fail to learn that he or she does not understand, and may gain a false impression, in effect achieving an ambiguity that the writer may have felt confident could not possibly exist.

Were we to get into general semantics, we would begin to investigate such matters and learn that our problem, in this case, is that most of our readers have a *referent* for such words as *orange,* but not for such words as *oblate* and *spheroid.* So the problem becomes at least partially one of referents: to be completely unambiguous, crystal clear, and understood perfectly by most, if not all your readers, you must confine yourself to words for which your readers have good referents. Combine that with short, direct sentences; a clear style; and scrupulous avoidance of idiom, and you probably will have relatively little difficulty in sending the message you intend to send. But note that to do this, you must be oriented entirely to your reader's perceptions—to *their* referents. So we come full circle: writing "clearly," so that message received is the same as message sent, is writing from an understanding of the reader's views and orientations. We'll have to consider that as we proceed to study ways and means of being more persuasive in everything we write, for at least one-half the problem of persuasiveness in writing is the problem of being understood. But there is yet one final consideration: Who is the reader?

A READER PROFILE

In creating technical manuals for Department of Defense projects (these manuals are generally for installation and maintenance people), the question of "reader profile" always arises. It is a must that the reader be defined, in specifying the manuals and planning their development. This is particularly true here because the manuals cover technical materials, and it is essential that the technical level of the coverage be suitable—compatible with the prior technical training and technical knowledge of the reader.

Unfortunately, this consideration does not apply equally to the definition of the reader's reading skills, vocabulary, and other matters pertaining to the reader's general ability to receive messages as sent, without misinterpretation or other garbling. However, if we are to solve the problem of sending messages that are not misinterpreted or misread, we must consider, among other things, the reader profile so that we always know what business we're in when we write.

3

THE DIFFERENT WRITTEN INSTRUMENTS OF PERSUASION

Business and society in general run on paper, and by far most of the many forms of paper are effective only insofar as they carry out some primary mission of persuasion.

IF ANYONE DOUBTS that we have truly experienced a paper explosion, let him or her work in the offices of any busy company, but especially in the marketing and technical/professional departments of a high-technology firm. Here are some of the products of the pen one would find being generated on an almost continuous basis there:

Proposals	Product/service brochures
Press releases	Reports
Specification sheets	Advertisements
Journal articles	Direct-mail packages
Speeches	Newsletters
Sales letters	General correspondence
Capability brochures	Magazine articles
Professional papers	Books

In many cases, persuasion is the direct, admitted objective of the product; in others it is a less-obvious objective, but still an objective. Let's consider some of these items—why they are written, what they are intended to accomplish.

PROPOSALS

The very word *proposal* has more than one meaning, as translated into a written product. In the commercial world a proposal traditionally was a quotation of price, specifications of goods/services to be delivered, and contract terms required. It was, in fact, often called a "sales proposal."

A number of factors have changed that concept considerably, but none more than the mammoth purchasing of our federal government over the years following World War II, especially in areas of high technology, such as aircraft, electronics, computers, rockets, missiles, spacecraft, satellites, and related procurements of modern times.

The principal influence has been not only high technology per se, but the constant pressure by federal agencies to push the state of the art—to conduct continuous research and development and produce more and more sophisticated devices. The Department of Defense, NASA, and several other federal agencies have been the driving forces behind the rapid development of modern miracle machines—computers, radar, aircraft, satellites, space vehicles, incredible miniaturization in electronics, and literally thousands of other new developments.

The reason this pressure for constant technological progress affected the art of proposal writing is this: for a large portion of government purchasing—about 85 percent of all federal procurement dollars, in fact, which means about $120 billion at current rates of spending—price is of far less importance in a procurement than is the capability of the contractor. That is, a low bid is not significant if the low bidder can't do a good job of developing a better aircraft or more reliable space vehicle. Therefore, the government must rely on establishing the technical/professional abilities of the bidder first, and consider price second. Thus, when a federal agency asks for proposals to supply some item that requires technical skills, facilities, and other resources, the proposal must discuss these matters in great depth as a completely separate consideration, without reference to cost. The government then evaluates the proposals submitted, decides which represent the best offers in terms of abilities and plans, and only then do the government procurement officials turn to a study of the costs.

In modern times, most large government procurements make it necessary for those organizations winning contracts to subcontract portions of the work. In the billion-dollar BMEWS (Ballistic Missile Early Warning System) project, for example, the prime contractor (RCA) let some 300 subcontracts for a variety of support projects. Prime contractors go through a similar process of asking those bidding for subcontracts to submit proposals, from which the prime contractor will select winners and make awards. And, of course, the prime contractor tends to emulate the federal system as closely as possible.

There are also fifty state governments and local governments for 3,042 counties, 18,862 cities and other municipalities, and 16,822 townships which have purchasing offices. Too, there are 15,174 local school districts and 25,962 special districts which have purchasing offices. And there are many agencies of federal, state, and local governments that do much of their own purchasing, independently of the government's centralized purchasing function. All of this, government and private-sector purchasing of goods and services that require evaluation of the vendor's qualifications, adds up to an astronomical number of proposals written every year—literally in the millions, with at least several hundred thousand of them representing substantial writing effort, all of it designed to be persuasive.

BROCHURES

All organizations, public and private, profit and nonprofit, large and small, and responding to many other descriptions and definitions use brochures of many types and for many reasons, most of them persuasive. Here are some of the common types of brochures and their uses or purposes:

General sales brochure. This may be a little 3- × -9-inch leaflet, describing a company or its offers briefly, handed out freely. Or it may be, at the opposite extreme, a slick manual, bound by any of several means used today (plastic spine, perfect or glued back, side-stitched with heavy staples, sewed, etc.), with expensive color illustrations, and used as a virtual testimonial to the organization and its leaders. Or, of course, it may and most often does fall somewhere between these extremes.

Product brochure. This is a brochure written to describe a given product or line of products, intended to be persuasive, of course, as a specialized sales brochure, focusing sharply on the product or line's merits.

Announcement brochure. This is usually a sales brochure, but is generally low-key and specialized, announcing a new product, new service, new offices or facilities, or otherwise using something new as an excuse for printing it and asking customers to read it.

Capability brochures. The capability brochure is a special one, used generally by organizations seeking contracts to provide custom services and/or custom products. These brochures, which generally are by their nature rather substantial in size, describe the organization, its specialties, its experience, its staff, and whatever else is deemed helpful in demonstrating the firm's technical and professional abilities. For firms offering such services and seeking such contracts with government agencies, for example, such a brochure is a must in marketing activity.

SPECIFICATION SHEETS

"Spec sheets," as they are informally referred to by those familiar with them, are "sheets"—they may be one side of one page or may be several pages—presenting the details that specify a product's characteristics. This is to distinguish the product's true characteristics from the general, usually extravagant claims made in general advertising. By unwritten agreement—by tacit understanding, that is—the spec sheet is factual and reliable, where the advertising is admittedly hyberbolic, dealing in superlatives and metaphors. For example, the slick multicolored advertising brochure about a stereo system may claim "concert-hall quality of reproduction" and use many superlatives to claim absolute audio fidelity. The spec sheet, however, will report actual, physical characteristics of the system's response—the actual curves may be reproduced, but whether they are or not, figures will be presented to report the system's response at various frequencies, usually in decibels. Those who know how to read such data will know just how good the quality of the system is.

The spec sheet will also provide much other information—weight, physical dimensions, typical circuits, types of components, and other such items—which may not be of great concern or have a great deal of meaning for the lay customer, but are highly significant data to the technically knowledgeable customer. It is usually in connection with technical products sold to technically trained customers that spec sheets are used. For example, the engineer-buyer of parts for his or her company will not buy components without seeing spec sheets and studying them to verify that the components are what he or she wants and can use.

Characteristically, spec sheets are reliable, but—! Spec sheets usually are reliable to the extent that the truth of their claims can be demonstrated, but they push their claims to the extreme limits of truth. For example, in one case the U.S. Army Signal Corps asked an electronics firm to make a military version of a commercially distributed oscilloscope, an electronic test instrument, matching the oscilloscope's characteristics. The manufacturer's spec sheet for the 'scope was supplied, along with one of the commercial instruments. The contractor had great difficulty in making his "carbon copy" 'scope exhibit the same characteristics as the commercial version. His first effort came very close, but did not quite attain the characteristics claimed for the commercial 'scope. It developed, finally, that some rather minute differences in components—the contractor was using components that met military standards—was responsible, and the problems were solved, in the end. But it was only with great difficulty, because the original manufacturer did, indeed, press his claims to the nth degree, staying within the bounds of truth by a fraction of a millimeter.

Spec sheets, then, provide the truth behind the "Madison Avenue" claims of the brochures and advertisements, and are expected to be truth, but may and usually do push truth to the edge of the cliff.

ADVERTISEMENTS

There is not a great deal to be said about advertisements at this point, although we'll delve deeply into advertising later. Advertising utilizes many media—radio and TV, print, billboards, direct mail, signs, and a few odd and assorted others, some of which we'll discuss individually here. Advertising is openly and admittedly an effort to persuade, and has no other purpose in life at all. At the same time, some advertising has as its direct objective the closing of sales or the creation of demand, some seeks only to arouse some general interest (for example, to introduce a new name, such as when Standard Oil became Exxon), some is "institutional" advertising (such as General Electric or Hughes Aircraft running advertisements to let the public know about their work in the space programs), and some seek to elicit inquiries for follow-up by other means. These are some of the ways in which advertising can be used. (Advertising is always intended to be persuasive, but not always aimed at making sales directly.)

PRESS RELEASES

Also called "news releases" and simply "releases," press releases are efforts to get free advertising, generally referred to as "publicity," or "P.R." P.R. stands for public relations and the specialists in that field are sometimes referred to as press agents.

In many respects, a release is more effective than a paid advertisement simply because it is not a paid advertisement, but is "editorial matter" in the magazine or newspaper in which the information appears. This is offset, to some degree, by the fact that an advertiser has total control over the material appearing in his paid advertising, but rather little control over what appears, if anything, as a result of his releases. Paid advertising attempts to persuade the reader to do something—order an item, request more information, or even simply recognize that the advertiser is an important and reliable organization. A press release must accomplish two acts of persuasion: first, it must be such as to persuade editors to use it—print the information it contains—and second, it must persuade the reader to do or believe something or other.

A press release offers news, if the word *news* is used rather liberally. It may report changes of personnel or promotions in an organization. It may report the presentation of a new product. It may report a technological breakthrough in the laboratories of an organization. It may report a merger or divestiture. It may report any of a myriad of other events, which may or may not be news and, even if news, may or may not be of interest to many people.

Editors are not fools. They are well aware that press releases are bids for free advertising, parading as editorial matter of general interest. That does not mean that they will not use the release, although a great many releases do wind up consigned to "the circular file" (wastebasket). But that is the challenge—to create releases that will somehow persuade editors to use them and provide the publicity they were written to gain. (In Chapter 8, we will discuss ways and means of accomplishing this.)

REPORTS

There are probably as many kinds of reports written in business operations as there are kinds of brochures, perhaps even more. Some are almost blatantly obvious advertisements, some are disguised, to at least some degree, and some are not intended to affect sales and marketing, although they do inevitably have persuasion as an objective to be achieved. Let's look at a few of the more frequently encountered types of reports:

Annual reports. Most corporations produce annual reports and corporations with stockholders must produce such reports. In small corporations such a publication may be little more than a few typed sheets bound with a staple in the upper left-hand corner, presenting the factual (or factual-appearing) data which accounts for what the corporation has done in the previous year. Of especial interest to stockholders are the several accounting reports, showing such important matters as profit and loss, proprietorship, and other such things. Characteristically, however, annual reports are expensive, slick publications in which corporate managers explain to stockholders how well their corporation has been managed during the year just elapsed, what investments have been made, what great plans exist for the future, and why the red ink is really not red ink at all, but is something that will pay out in future years.

In short, an annual report is one in which the corporation's managers—the officers of the corporation, that is, especially the President, Chairman of the Board, and other top people—attempt to persuade the stockholders that they have been doing a fine job of running the corporation, ought to be perpetuated in office, and should be supported and encouraged to go on doing what they've been doing and plan to do in the future.

Quite often, the managers have bad news for the stockholders—losses instead of profits, declining sales, white-elephant divisions that have to be dumped, expensive projects that have gone sour, the need to bypass the payment of dividends this year, and other distasteful items. The need for persuasion, in such circumstances, is acute, especially since the numbers that glare so starkly from the glossy pages have been prepared by certified public accountants who must, in fact, certify them and swear to them. (The numbers can be made somewhat more palatable to the uninitiated by certain euphemistic devices, but the knowledgeable stockholder knows how to read an annual report and is not easily deceived by euphemisms and other persuasive stratagems.)

Progress reports. Projects and other ongoing efforts, especially when they are special custom efforts and/or are long-term efforts, generally require that progress reports be prepared and submitted on some regular basis, such as monthly or quarterly. The recipient of the report wants to be assured that satisfactory progress is being made, all problems encountered are being solved, that the budget and schedule are being adhered to. Too, in the event that problems have shown up, the recipient wants to be kept informed about progress in eliminating or solving the problems.

The writer of the report has analogous goals, of course, and wants to assure the recipient, who may be a superior or a customer, that all is well, all is being coped with satisfactorily, and all will end well.

Obviously, as in the case of an annual report, the reporter tries to soften bad news as much as possible, and at the same time to paint his or her own work and abilities in the best light. However, there may be other objectives, given different circumstances in each case. In one case, the series of progress reports may be calculated to prepare a client or superior for final results that are not those originally expected. As in the example used earlier about the car salesman, wherein it was shown that some persuasion could be accomplished only by a series of steadily escalating efforts and objectives, a series of a dozen or more monthly progress reports may be employed in exactly this manner, so that the final report will prove acceptable. That is, it may be necessary to break the bad news gradually, over many months, to persuade the customer or superior to accept it. In any case, progress reports and final reports on projects are inherently persuasive in nature.

Financial reports. Some of the routine financial reports prepared by accountants are those called "P&L"—profit and loss—statements and balance sheets. There are many others that can be and are prepared to reflect the condition of the enterprise and to assist managers in making wise decisions. Some of these reports serve only the purpose of aiding managers perceive factors that should be considered in making decisions or that will guide decision making. Others serve this purpose, to some degree, but are principally final reports on the overall condition of the enterprise, and are prepared principally for owners as feedback on how their business is doing. (For example, these are the kinds of reports that appear in the corporation's annual reports.)

There is a problem with such reports in interpreting what the figures mean, in terms of their overall significance. For example, suppose a P&L reveals that the company lost money again, for the third year in a row. But suppose that another kind of report showed that the loss was not an actual operating loss on the year's business, but was caused by residual effects of the previous year's problems—that is, that the business is now turning an operating profit and will show an actual profit as soon as last year's disaster has been completely liquidated. This means that it is sometimes necessary to generate reports to explain and understand the significance of other reports. Profit of itself, for example, may be far less significant than return on investment (ROI), so it is essential that ROI reports be generated.

Financial reports are also often needed to bolster managers' arguments, when they are urging some course of action and meeting with opposition in their companies. A manager trying to get approval from the Board of Directors, for example, must present some pretty strong arguments, especially if the recommendations are going to require substantial investments or entail risks. Financial reports are almost invariably a must in such situations, if the manager urging the action is to have any hope of prevailing.

Research reports. Anyone engaged in research and development of any kind must produce research reports. These are, in fact, progress reports, and if they are reporting on projects that are supposed to produce a useful end product of some kind, the need to be persuasive and convince the reader of the need for continued support is great indeed. On the other hand, if the effort is pure research, the report must persuade the reader that the research is being conducted logically, methodically, in accordance with sound principles of research practice, and that results are being sensibly evaluated and analyzed. The writer is inevitably tempted to present himself or herself and the work in the best possible light, even when no particular end result is demanded, other than information or knowledge. In many respects, research and study reports are very much the same as progress reports. (Study reports are almost identical to research reports, for all practical purposes, except that they may cover surveys instead of laboratory work.)

PROFESSIONAL-JOURNAL ARTICLES

Those in the professions usually find it desirable to publish in professional journals. Such journals are dedicated to the advancement of knowledge in, and status of, their fields—law, medicine, dentistry, engineering, and others—and encourage scholarly articles of interest to members of their professional societies, who read the journals. For the individual who writes such articles and has them published, the achievement is one that adds to the individual's prestige and personal reputation in the professional field.

Such journals are circulated among one's professional peers, of course, since they are typically publications of professional societies, read only by one's peers. The objective in writing such articles, then, may be a sense of professional duty and pride, but it also may be, and often is, ego gratification, since publishing in professional journals is generally recognized as truly an accomplishment and is therefore prestigious. To realize the accomplishment, the author of such an article must generally manage to persuade the editors of the journal that the article is scholarly, highly professional, and presents information of great value, not otherwise known in the profession. The result of this is a special writing style, which is itself somewhat ponderous and jargon ridden, but presumably makes its own contribution to persuasion.

TRADE-JOURNAL ARTICLES

Every field, professional and other, has its share of trade journals—magazines, usually, but sometimes newsprint tabloids, too. TV repair shops may subscribe to *Electronic Technician,* for example, while a department store operator may subscribe to *Mil-*

itary Market or *Sew Business,* and a radio station owner may subscribe to *Broadcast.* Such journals are published by private, for-profit publishers, usually have a somewhat limited circulation as compared with magazines appearing on the newsstands, and carry a great deal of advertising and a number of articles in each issue.

In some fields, such journals are highly "professional" in that they carry highly technical articles, often quite abstract and having usefulness to a quite-limited audience. In other fields, such journals are quite broad in their appeal, and even a layperson would have no difficulty in understanding the articles (although the layperson may not be at all interested!).

There is a certain amount of prestige in being published in some of these, especially those that closely resemble the professional journals. In some cases, such journals may be read by people with whom you might do business, and having your articles published there or getting your press releases used there may represent useful advertising for the writer. Therefore, trade-journal articles may have to be persuasive to carry out their missions.

MAGAZINE ARTICLES

Much of what has been said for trade journals will apply to some popular magazines. For example, it may be useful for the TV or radio repair shop owner to write articles for such newsstand electronic magazines as *Popular Electronics.* Of course, the same thing applies to press releases vis-à-vis popular magazines of general interest. For many, this represents free advertising, which is even more important and more valuable than that achieved with trade journals because the popular magazines normally have much wider circulation.

SPEECHES

One of the most effective ways to get publicity, for certain callings (such as consulting and other professions wherein commercial advertising is impractical, for one reason or another), is by making speeches before various assemblages. Writing a speech is a special problem in writing, and it is best to write your own speeches, if at all possible. One reason for this is that the speech you write for someone else may sound fine when you deliver it, but may either trip up someone else's tongue constantly or may simply not fit the other person's speaking style. Many well-written speeches are discarded simply because the individual for whom they are written is not comfortable with them.

Opportunities to make speeches exist at every meeting of any organization whose existence has relevance for what you do or offer, at national conventions and conferences, at seminars, at trade shows, and at many other gatherings, social and business. "Relevance" does not mean that the group is one of people in your own field. You may have things to say that are of interest to almost everyone, although you may have to "slant" your presentation differently for different audiences. One gentleman I know has a speech he has used for years about the evolution of modern educational technology, and he has presented it to a great many different kinds of groups, such as writers, editors, educators, professional specialists, and others, managing to relate the material to his listeners' interests without making substantial changes in his address, simply by how he introduces his subject.

Persuasiveness in speaking publicly has certain, special considerations, which we'll probe when we discuss the subject in detail later.

SALES LETTERS

The sales letter is normally part of the direct-mail package, although there are many situations in which the sales letter is used by itself, which is why we discuss it as a separate topic here. It has the open purpose of either making a sale directly or of persuading the reader to some course of action that is designed to lead to a sale. It might, for example, urge the reader to visit the showroom and look at the new automobiles or new TV sets. It might urge the reader to make application for a credit card or open an account. It may invite the reader to send in a request for a sample or to accept something on a trial basis. In any case, it has as its direct purpose persuading the reader to some course of action or belief.

So much is true for sales letters sent out by for-profit organizations as part of their regular marketing/sales programs. However, there are other cases in which letters are used to persuade and in which the senders might not regard the letters as "sales letters," nevertheless they are used exactly as sales letters are.

One such case is the letter sent out by a political candidate, seeking to persuade readers to support the candidacy with their votes. But politicos not currently running for anything also use the mails often to keep their public images fresh and in focus.

Letters sent out by those soliciting contributions for one purpose or another are also sales letters, in that they urge the reader to do something and to "buy" their arguments and their causes.

Letters sent out by many organizations, seeking support of various kinds for various causes—petition against nuclear energy, write your Congressman and demand that he or she vote for/against the next SALT treaty, join a huge protest meeting on the mall next week, pray for peace—are all sales letters, in essence, even if they are trying to sell only ideas.

DIRECT-MAIL PACKAGES

The sales letter is a centerpiece of the direct-mail package, as a rule, although often eclipsed by the weight of other enclosures and inserts in the package. Typically, a direct-mail package includes the sales letter, a brochure or broadside of some sort, an order form, and a response envelope. Frequently the package includes even more—sometimes as many as a half-dozen different items, in a kind of scattergun approach, apparently in the belief that if enough arguments and persuaders are fired in the direction of the addressee, something ought to work. And if that isn't enough, many direct-mail packages also are sent off in a fairly large envelope, the outside of which is covered with various other sales messages, often in two or three colors.

Of course, not all such packages are necessarily sent to persuade addressees to buy merchandise or services; they may be barrages of persuasive missiles fired by political candidates and "causes" of all kinds, soliciting votes, money, and other kinds of support.

NEWSLETTERS

Newsletters may be divided into three general categories, as far as origin and basic objectives are concerned. Many associations publish newsletters for their members, and the most basic purpose is to maintain "visibility," especially in the case of organizations so large and widespread that many members don't get to meetings, conventions, and other events regularly. Where this is the case, an association newsletter enables members to keep in touch with their association and with others in the association. But it also serves as a means to communicate with members, to solicit their votes and their support of association activities, and to promote the association generally. In some cases, advertising is accepted, which aids the association financially.

Private companies and other organizations, such as nonprofit government and community groups, sometimes publish newsletters also. The for-profit company primarily uses its own newsletter as a sales/marketing tool, and nonprofit organizations and government agencies use their newsletters for purposes not much different: to polish their own images and prove the worth of their activities.

By far the bulk of newsletter publishing, however—and there are some 30,000 newsletters published, by best estimates available—is by private interests seeking profits as newsletter publishers. Some of these are fairly large organizations, often publishing an entire string of newsletters, while many are very small organizations and even one-person enterprises, operating from private homes, as a tiny (but perhaps profitable) cottage industry.

The latter class of newsletter is a special case. By comparison with other kinds of publications, the subscription rates are very high, and are justified only because the newsletters are so specialized and bring the reader information not readily available elsewhere. The publisher must persuade the reader that the slender newsletter is worth the price because the information it contains is worth the price. Therefore, it is essential that information be highly concentrated in a newsletter—many use telegraphic style, dropping most articles and other nonessential words—and no trivial information included. Theoretically, at least, a good newsletter is all important information, with not a line wasted on trivia.

HOUSE ORGANS

The term *house organ* is one applied to an in-house magazine usually, such as some major corporations and many government agencies have published. Sometimes also called "company publications," these include such journals as *Ashland Now* (Ashland Oil Co.), *Caterpillar World* (Caterpillar Tractor Co.), and *The Enthusiast* (Harley-Davidson Motor Co.) House organs are intended for company employees or for customers, and often for both. As such, they are sales/marketing aids and they are also part of what is often called "corporate communications," which refers to the corporation's public relations and relations with both customers and employees.

Obviously, then, such magazines seek to persuade the employees that the company is a first-class employer and that the employee should be loyal and support the company as much as possible. It further attempts to persuade employees to do whatever is in the company's best interests, as well as seeks to persuade customers to patronize the company as much as possible.

House organs can be quite slick or professional. Gemco/Memco's *Gemco Courier* is a monthly, with a claimed 5.5 million circulation. Shopsmith's *Hands On* is bimonthly, with a 1 million circulation. These and others use process-color photo-spreads, print on slick paper, pay free-lance contributors well for their work, and carry lots of promotional materials for their own businesses, of course, as you would expect. There aren't as many of these publications around as there once were because of today's high costs, but there are still a considerable number of them.

BOOKS

Many large and successful corporations have hired free-lance authors to do biographical books about the corporation's beginnings and history, and especially about its founder. Such a book was done not too long ago, for example, about Willard Marriott, Sr., of the huge Marriott Corporation. Perhaps such books are ego trips by the founders of such companies, or perhaps they are truly useful sales/marketing efforts. In any case, such books have been done, are being done, and will continue to be done as company-sponsored efforts. Whatever the purposes, they are intended to offer persuasive arguments for and against something, or to create a favorable public image, which is the same thing, in the end.

MISCELLANEOUS MOTS

There are a number of other ways in which persuasive words find their way into print and into the hands of those intended to be the persuaded. Here are a few:

Reprints from publications. This is something of a favorite device, and it is generally rather effective. The reprint may be of an article written by or about someone (or about the organization), published earlier in a magazine or newspaper. When the article is such that it supports the company's or individual's image and/or other purposes, it is usually easy to have the article reprinted and distributed freely in mailings and by other means.

Reprints from/of reports. Sometimes a report produced by, for, or about the organization serves the company's purposes in one way or another. Frequently, then, the company makes arrangements to have the report reprinted in quantity (in whole or in part, if the report is quite lengthy and not all of it relevant) and made available for distribution freely.

Advertising novelties. Aside from the garden-variety advertising novelties, such as matches and calendars, there are many truly novel ways to get your good (persuasive, that is) words before those you wish to persuade. For example, when "Murphy's Law" was a well-known and amusing idea, one entrepreneur had a placard made up that listed those "laws," along with his business identity and a suitable message, and he distributed these widely among people who gleefully tacked them up on their walls and otherwise displayed them freely. And you might wish to consider making up reprints from your own advertisements, when appropriate, for general distribution.

Seminars and handouts. Many entrepreneurs offer free seminars as marketing promotions. (Evelyn Wood recruits students for speed-reading courses in this manner.) Those attending seminars should be given handouts, and this is a good way to get helpful literature into willing hands. However, it is not necessary to run your own seminars: many other people conduct seminars, for which they charge substantial attendance fees, and will welcome your participation as a speaker, especially if you offer your services free or at a nominal honorarium. And that isn't all of it. Usually at such seminars, especially if you speak for little or no fee, you are welcome to distribute your literature, either as part of the standard handout package or by stocking a literature table often provided at such sessions. It is precisely for this reason—to reach prospects with literature and possibly direct conversation—that many specialists and entrepreneurs speak at seminars without fee.

Planted articles.   There are some journals, especially those directed to "opportunity seekers" and others looking for ideas and leads for small business enterprises, who give their publications away free or at nominal subscription rates, and depend entirely on advertising revenues for their income. In fact, many of these have a few subscribers but give away several times the number they are paid for so as to get enough circulation to justify adequate advertising rates. Many of these use "planted" articles, which they accept from only those who advertise with them, so that the "article" is really a thinly disguised advertisement. In fact, such "articles" produce so much better results than the paid advertisements do, in many cases, that some advertisers buy advertising space only to get the editorial space then made available to them!

Public service contributions.   The U.S. Small Business Administration (SBA) publishes a great many books, booklets, pamphlets, monographs, and brochures, many of them distributed free. Many of these, particularly those given away free to anyone who asks, are written without charge, as a public service by individuals. The articles identify the authors and their respective organizations, in attributions or credit lines. Writing such pieces—and they are relatively brief, running to a few thousand words, typically—therefore results in 1) some publicity for the author and the author's organization and 2) another opportunity to reprint something—this time an SBA (official) publication—for promotional distribution.

SIMILARITIES AND DIFFERENCES

Among the myriad of written products possible there are many basic similarities, and yet there are many differences. Nothing is ever a panacea for everything—every ill, every need. Each need calls for its own best remedy, and each remedy is suited better to one situation or need than to any other. For example, the sales-promotional instruments that are effective in selling hair spray are almost totally ineffective in selling legal services, for a variety of reasons.

A major consideration, first of all, is image. Every business and every profession acquires a certain image associated with the profession in general. Or, in some cases, the industry or profession may acquire more than one image. At the same time, the various practitioners, whether they are individuals, small companies, or major corporations, each acquire their individual images. And these images determine, to quite a large extent, what "business you are in," because they (the images) reflect the customers' perceptions. It is therefore possible to find yourself victimized unfairly by an unfavorable image associated with your business or profession or, of course, the reverse may be true: you may be the beneficiary of a good image in the public consciousness. In either case, you must still work at developing a proper personal image among those with whom you do business or hope to do business—your own public.

Your image is a significant factor, unless you are relatively unknown and truly do not have an image. Those who find your personal manner charming, for example, will tend strongly to be charitable in their estimate of your professional abilities or how you deal with customers. Of course, in such case, it will be far easier to persuade them to accept what you say.

The reverse is true: if you have managed to acquire a reputation as a trader who is so sharp as to border on the merciless or even unscrupulous, your motives are always likely to be suspect. Or if you have a gruff manner with your clients and manage somehow to make them always feel a bit inferior or disadvantaged in some manner, they will find it easy to be skeptical of anything you say.

Persuasiveness of your writing is, then, not entirely a matter of how skillfully you have constructed the material; it is strongly affected and influenced by these other factors. And even if you are an unknown quantity to those who read what you write, some general impression shines through, between the lines of your writing, and creates at least the beginnings of an image.

TV commercials are an example of this. I personally find some of them so offensive that I resolve not to patronize the advertiser and use his product. And this is not merely because I think the copy is in bad taste, although that is a factor, but is often simply because the copy is so banal or so infantile that I am insulted. The advertiser appears to have utter contempt for my intelligence, and so has managed to offend me deeply. And, of course, I may or may not represent a minority opinion, but whether I do or not, I am one of many who react in the same manner.

H. L. Mencken, "the sage of Baltimore," was reported to have declared most emphatically that "no one ever went broke underestimating the intelligence of the American public." Unfortunately, some advertisers appear to be taking Mencken's hyperbole literally, and even if that does not prevent bad advertising from achieving some success, it certainly impedes that advertising from being as successful as it might otherwise be. If you can somehow manage to feel respect for your readers, no matter what you are writing, you'll find the results vastly improved over writing cynically, with contempt for your readers.

SITUATIONS AND NEEDS DICTATE METHODS

Whether you choose to launch a direct-mail campaign, write and deliver speeches, run print advertisements, or undertake any other kind of campaign of persuasion is not entirely arbitrary. Some of these methods are far more appropriate to and effective in one situation than they are in another. Therefore, a large consideration in your persuasiveness is in choosing the right instrument. Sales letters and print advertising, for example, are simply not effective in selling legal services to any but a certain, small group of prospects. More subtle methods are required for such persuasion needs, such as articles published in respectable professional journals, use of reprints of such articles, speeches, and discreet P.R.

On the other hand, media advertising is probably the most effective way to sell appliances, automobiles, and many other commodities that require reaching mass audiences. Here are some of the basic factors you must consider in deciding what written instruments are best suited to your needs:

Image. Physicians, lawyers, consultants, and many other professional classes must be extremely careful to advertise indirectly. The consideration for such people is this: to conduct your professional work successfully, your clients must have great faith in you. Blatant, highly commercialized advertising methods tend strongly to cheapen your image—make you appear to be an ordinary huckster—and make it far more difficult to generate that confidence your clients must feel in you. Therefore, any advertising professional people do usually must be such that it does not appear to be advertising at all, but merely professional activities, such as making speeches and writing articles. (Even though lawyers may advertise today, by far the majority choose not to, for the very reasons listed here.)

Types of prospects. This factor is closely linked to the one of required image, and very much the same considerations apply. Even if you are seeking a job, as an individual, image and the type of organizations you wish to appeal to must dictate how you structure your resume, any letters you use, and any methods you pursue in your job prospecting.

Selectivity of appeal. If you are selling TV receivers or bath oil, you usually wish to reach and appeal to virtually every adult in the country (or even in the world), as a prospect. But if you are selling Rolls-Royce automobiles or deluxe $3,000 TV receivers, you would logically want to be far more selective, since it is obvious that only some relatively small proportion of the total population represents true prospects. This may very well be a case where a direct-mail campaign might be your initial step in developing sales leads to follow up. Or, if you do wish to use print advertising to help develop leads, you would seek out publications that have a somewhat limited appeal and reach those whom you believe are true prospects for what you wish to offer—perhaps *Fortune* magazine or the *Wall Street Journal,* although even these might not be exclusive enough to pursue leads for selling Rolls-Royces.

The selectivity factor might also be in terms of occupations of prospects, rather than economic class. If you are trying to persuade individuals to subscribe to a newsletter devoted strictly to trial practice, you would probably decide that lawyers would be your only suitable prospects. But if your newsletter concerned corporate law only, you would seek out a certain, special class of lawyers. Again, you would have to decide where and how to best reach these prospects.

What you want prospects to do. It seems rather obvious that what you want the reader to do is an important factor in selecting the manner of delivering your persuasive effort. If you want your reader to visit your establishment for a demonstration, it is not too likely that you can accomplish that with a small print advertisement. The possibility is excellent that you must make a fairly lengthy presentation to bring that about. That indicates a probable need for a sales letter, possibly as part of an entire direct-mail package. (One basic reason for using direct mail, in many situations, is simply that you need several thousand words to explain your entire proposition and furnish all the motivators, and this is far too expensive to do in print advertising or on TV.) On the other hand, if it is near the end of the year and you want people to visit your automobile showroom, you may be able to get enough prospects without even mentioning automobiles by simply running a small ad or TV commercial inviting everyone to stop in and get a handsome new calendar free.

The image you must overcome. Suppose that you have an image problem, not of your own making. Automobile dealers, for example, have the image of being high-pressure sales operations, which causes some people to be reluctant to visit, unless they are seriously thinking of buying a new car. (Many people are afraid that they cannot resist sales pressure, and work at avoiding it entirely.) The simple device of offering something for nothing, without even mention of what you sell, may help bring reluctant prospects through your doors. Other motivators may be a pledge to permit visitors to browse at their leisure, with the promise that no salesperson will approach them until asked for help, or a general assurance that there will be absolutely no pressure to buy.

The inherent nature of the persuasion problem. If you need to mount a campaign because you are selling what you know is not a one-call sales item, a direct-mail campaign may be the best way to carry this out, as described earlier. Somehow, while being an unknown quantity is a negative factor in the beginning, the repetition makes the customer more comfortable as time goes on. By the time the customer has seen your advertising materials the third or fourth time, you have begun to become something of an old shoe. Somehow, since the customer has now seen your name and read your literature several times over several months, the customer begins to feel as though you've been around for many years, you're solid and dependable, and it's safe to do business with you.

That's one of the reasons small businesses often adopt what they hope are impressive names. A neighborhood TV technician in Philadelphia called himself "The Great Northern TV Service."

To his delight, a great many customers sincerely believed that they had known about his company for many years because the name sounded as though they *should* have known of him. Certainly, where there is some element of risk, such as in TV service, and especially given the general image the public has of TV service technicians, "The Great Northern TV Service" is far more reassuring than is "Joe's Neighborhood TV Service" or "Joe, the TV Man." (One man calls himself "Honest Herb's TV Service," and has that painted boldly on the side of his panel truck, arousing much derisive laughter, as he veers around the neighborhood streets on his calls.)

Miscellaneous considerations. One man built a radio repair service, in the pre-TV days, and later a TV repair service in the same manner, by the simplest of persuasive strategies: he was totally low-key and low pressure in his entire approach. He built his entire promotional campaign around a 4- × -6-inch card, which he both mailed out and had distributed under front doors and under the windshield wipers of thousands of cars parked on the streets and in supermarket parking lots. The card did not say a great deal—it was more white space than copy. The key line was across the top in the boldest type, and was the heart of the sales strategy. It said this: SAVE THIS CARD. YOU'LL NEED IT SOMEDAY. That was followed by a few lines of copy, which explained that he offered TV and radio service, listed an address and telephone number, and promised that all work was guaranteed.

He distributed this card once a week for a month, then once a month for several months, and then only intermittently, as by then he was quite busy and didn't wish to become much busier.

The second key, after the common-sense admonition to save the card, was the understatement. He didn't make extravagant claims of any kind, but only promised competent and guaranteed service. It's a technique that works quite effectively, in many cases. The reason is that the advertiser shows complete *self*-confidence, which tends to inspire the customer's confidence. However, the repetition—distributing the card frequently, over a period of months—also inspired the customers' confidence, as the advertiser assumed an aura of solidity and permanence over those months. More than one customer remarked to him, in fact, when they called on him for service, "I threw the cards away, at first, and then my set broke down. But I knew there would be another card coming along pretty soon, and sure enough, there was another one the next day." Or: "I didn't take your advice and save your card, but when my set broke down, I asked my neighbors, and got your number from one of them. I knew some of them would save your card."

In general, an appeal to 5,000 prospects repeated three or four times will produce more results in the end than an appeal made once to three or four times those 5,000 prospects, so great is the cumulative effect of repetition in persuading prospects.

This consideration applies in virtually every arena of persuasion, and not only in sales and marketing per se. Once, for example, having interviewed a number of prospects for a position, I was still pondering which of several acceptable candidates I would choose from those I had interviewed. One of those candidates called me several times, to inquire pleasantly whether I had reached a decision and when he might expect to hear from me. Finally, after several calls, he said some such thing as, "What are you gaining by waiting? I could be at work, producing good results for you right now."

That convinced me that I was procrastinating to no useful end, and I put him to work. Later events proved that I had made a poor choice, but the point is simply that almost any of those candidates could have moved me to similar action for them, had they persisted in pursuing the job.

There is one other factor that ought to be noted in this case: my base motivation was emotional, not logical. The gentleman made me feel that I was being deficient as a manager in not making a decision without further delay, which was damaging to my ego, or would have been, had I delayed longer. I did not wish to be an indecisive manager, of course, and it was that, rather than any logical process, that pushed me to immediate decision.

Logic—reason—has its place in the persuasion process, but it's far from being the dominant feature or first cause. Quite the contrary, logic is generally used by customers to rationalize an emotion-based decision. Persuasion campaigns based on pure reason inevitably must fail, because:

1. It is rare, indeed, that you can prove your product or service to be superior to your competitors' products and services. They probably are not superior, but even if they are, it is nearly impossible to prove that.

2. Customers are not really moved by alleged superiority of product or service, even if you do have incontrovertible evidence. They are motivated by emotional factors, such as convenience, perceived benefits, feeling of comfort with and confidence in the supplier, and feelings of security in general.

3. An all-too-human failing is that of forcing ourselves to believe what we want to believe, so that even when we fondly believe we are being rational we are swayed by emotion. However, since we know intellectually that we *ought* to be rational, we have an emotional need to believe that we are being rational. It is essential, therefore, that logical, reasonable arguments be presented to your reader *after* the emotional appeal is firmly established and the customer is now looking for the rationalization of the rightness of the emotionally based decision already made!

In computers, the Number One company is Number One by a huge margin, so that one of its leading competitors, who was Number Two at the time, expressed the wish that it could become a "better Number Two" in the coming year. They and other competitors of Number One worked diligently at proving that their computers were technologically superior to those of the leader— more sophisticated, better designed, better engineered, and so on. And the leader did not even bother to attempt refutation because refutation was neither necessary nor would it have helped anything. The leader just went on quietly providing the best service of any company in the business and keeping its customers feeling comfortable and secure in their dealings with their computer company.

In most cases, arguments about quality, if based on logical appeals, are non sequiturs: they are simply not at all germane. Take note what successful insurance companies sell. It hardly needs saying that there is extremely little difference between what one insurance company provides and what another insurance company provides: despite their claims, you can get virtually the same policies from one that you get from any other. So the most successful insurance companies are not selling better policies; they sell emotional factors. Some sell what is supposed to be a comforting pat on the back, assuring you verbally that they are looking after you. But at least one sends that message graphically, by holding out two hands, palms cupped together, and assuring you that "you're in good hands" with them. Another promotes its image as a solid and dependable insurer, standing behind you, by using a symbol of stability and permanence, the Rock of Gibraltar, even urging you to buy yourself "a piece of the rock." These are about as emotional as any appeals can be, designed to instill confidence in the companies more than anything else.

CREDIBILITY IS
A FIRST REQUIREMENT

Credibility is not an absolute characteristic of the written product. It is a complex idea, affected by several factors, some of them rather complex in themselves. It does not result automatically from skillful writing, and yet writing that does not achieve it may as well not have been written at all.

WHAT, IN FACT, IS CREDIBILITY?

FEW THINGS ARE inherently either credible or incredible. They are usually made credible or incredible by the manner of their presentation, although the authority or reputation of the presenter (or source) may also be a factor, and even a decisive factor. There is, as already noted, the factor of what the reader wishes to believe, as one major factor. However, there is also the role that logic and reason must play: few of us are so irrational that we will believe everything on pure authority, even when it emanates from "high sources" or other origins usually deemed trustworthy. But, as Bertrand Russell once pointed out in one of his philosophical essays, there are everyday truths and Sunday truths: many of us tend toward a kind of double standard when it comes to what we will and will not believe, or try to persuade ourselves to believe. Take the matter of UFOs—unidentified flying objects—for example: there are those who "believe in" them and those who do not. Unfortunately, we usually fail to define what we mean by "believing in" UFOs, so that when someone admits to having such a belief we don't know whether that means believing that there are flying objects that have so far defied identification or whether it means a belief in an extraterrestrial origin for such objects. Many who find the idea of UFOs as alien space ships intriguing are likely to believe in them *wishfully*—because they want to believe. But those who are adamantly opposed and vociferously challenge any belief in UFOs are sometimes also thinking wishfully, because the idea of alien space ships is terrifying to them, and it is much more comfortable to disbelieve the notion and dismiss it as an absurdity. Therefore, calling those who profess a belief to be "cranks" is defensive, and perhaps more an effort to persuade themselves than to refute others.

Credibility is therefore often what a reader would prefer to believe or disbelieve, rather than a quality of the material. It is not possible to assign credibility as an absolute figure of merit to any written product; credibility is as much a product of the nature or class of reader as it is an intrinsic quality of the writing. But let's try to understand why one reader will find something entirely credible, while another reader will find it completely incredible.

CONDITIONING AND PREPARATION FOR BELIEF

As a boy I read science-fiction magazines, long before man had even invented television, let alone space ships and ICBMs. My older brother was fond of having hearty laughs at my expense, with constant jests at my eccentric habit of reading such "crazy stuff" and believing in such absurd notions as sending pictures through the air and vehicles to other worlds than Earth. I found these notions entirely credible, and so was gratified when they came about; my brother found these ideas incredible and was baffled when they came about. The difference between us was primarily that I was prepared to believe in such things, while he was not. But strangely enough, because I acquired a scientific education and have precise, detailed knowledge of how TV works, I am more amazed by it than my brother is. He accepts it with a shrug as an inevitable triumph of technology. I accept it with astonishment at the ingenuity of man. And perhaps I would have found the idea of "pictures through the air" unbelievable then, had I known that it would require painting lines on the screen 15,750 times every second, among other electronic marvels, to make it work.

The conditioning of the reader is a critical element in how credible or incredible the reader will find the material. A reader may be biased for or against a belief, or may be completely neutral, when reading your material. If biased against, there is little chance you will bring about conviction; if biased for, there is little chance you can fail to persuade; and if neutral, it is up to you and your material whether it persuades or not. But there is one major factor that is a function of how the writer writes.

GENERALYSIS

Philosophers sometimes cluck their tongues over the obscenity of the waste of food in this country, while so many others in the world are hungry. The problem, they assure us, is simply one of an improper system of distribution. Install a better system and we can banish hunger with our enormous surpluses of crops and other foods. The details? Trivial, of course; we can hire experts to work out the mere mechanics of the system needed.

An employee came to me with a complaint that our organization was an inefficient one and should be improved. I replied that I tended to agree, and I suggested that I would welcome a concrete, detailed reorganization plan from this employee. He was incredulous. He indignantly advised me that I should be content with being fortunate enough to have been given his idea without charge; the details of putting it into practice were up to me.

In some years in technical publications, including serving that industry as editor and, later, as manager, I found that problem also prevalent among technical writers: many could only generalize in their writing, and could not provide the details. After a while it became obvious to me that it was necessary to distinguish clearly between a manuscript on such technical matters as installation and maintenance of equipment that reported what ought to happen and a manuscript that explained to the reader how to make it happen. That, in fact, was the essence of what was wrong with a great many technical manuals already published. A manual might, for example, explain that a certain measurement in a given piece of equipment ought to be 85 volts, but fail to tell the reader what to do if the measurement were other than 85 volts—what to do about it and what higher or lower readings might signify.

The same shortcoming was often to be found in theory manuals, manuals that were supposed to educate the reader in how the equipment operated. The manual might offer the explanation that a Hartley oscillator is more suitable to the needs of the circuit than any other type, but then go on without any explanation of that, asking the reader to accept the author's assurance that this was a fact.

This proved to be so common a failing among writers that I came to regard it as a virtual disease, which I was ultimately to call "generalysis," a coinage of my own, I must confess. And the pervasiveness of generalysis, deplorable though it is in such areas as technical manuals, is even more evident in some other areas, notably that of written marketing and sales materials. Generalysis is an obstacle to the effectiveness of technical manuals, but it is a fatal disease when it infects proposals, brochures, and sales letters. "Arguments" and "explanations" that really say "just take my word for it" are simply not at all persuasive, with only rare exceptions. Even the President of the United States cannot avoid eventually explaining himself to the public if he wants to be believed, as a few of our more recent Presidents have discovered.

Ultimately, I found in writing proposals that the amount of detail offered had a profound effect upon credibility: customers were persuaded far more by proposals that furnished a great deal of detail than they were by those proposals that offered unctuous generalizations and glib promises, along with all the "Madison Avenue" that necessarily goes hand-in-hand with this approach to persuasion. The overall impression a reader gets then is that anyone can generalize, and the ability to generalize proves nothing. But it takes know-how to plan and explain plans in detail, and the detail tends to prove—is, at least, strong evidence—that the writer is truly authoritative and has "done the homework." Ergo, a detailed presentation is almost without exception far more credible than one that only generalizes.

THE ELEMENTS OF CREDIBILITY

The essence of all this is that there are several elements making up that characteristic we call credibility: the reader's built-in (inherent) biases or prejudices, any special conditioning preceding or part of the presentation, the characteristics of the presentation itself.

Built-in biases are all but impossible to overcome, at least by direct, frontal assault. Arguments are unlikely to persuade a Republican to become a Democrat or a Harvard graduate to agree that Yale is a superior school. If bias can be overcome at all, it will not be by pure polemics, no matter how skilled.

An inherent bias may be weakened by events preceding the presentation or by the presentation itself, if an adequate *emotional* influence is at work. Bear in mind that bias is ordinarily an emotion-based factor and if it can be defeated at all, it will have to be through emotional influences. Life is full of examples of such conversions—alcoholics who become teetotalers, individuals who become religious zealots, and drug users who become evangelists against drugs. So it is not impossible to overcome bias, although it is admittedly difficult, and it usually requires a deeply felt experience for someone to cast off a bias or to replace it with another bias, which is what happens more frequently, as in the examples just cited.

THE FUTILITY OF LOGIC AS AN ARGUMENT

One common mistake some make in argument is to rely on logic and reason to make their points. This, of course, flies in the face of all experience: the least effective argument for shaping anyone's beliefs or attitudes is logic, even when the subject is more or less neutral, and especially when the subject is already biased in another direction or in opposition to what you are trying to "sell" (*sell* being used in a broad sense of persuade or convince, rather than the literal sense of exchange for money).

A more common mistake than this, however, is to press the issue when you are attempting to persuade someone who is biased or, at least, tends strongly to another position or belief than the one you advocate. The uninitiated debater presses on to the point at which the argument has become polarized. At this point, the other party has defended his or her position so strenuously that he or she is now emotionally committed and cannot retreat, even if your logic is overpowering, without a humiliating loss of face. Were you to press on beyond this point, especially if you presented evidence so overpowering that your opponent recognized the weakness of his or her position from a logical viewpoint, you still would not win the argument, in most cases. The usual result of this situation is the arousal of deep hostility on the other's part, for you have indeed brought about his or her humiliation. It may be good polemics, but it's poor human relationships, and it rarely accomplishes your purpose if you are trying to bring the other to agree with your own point of view. Even the most logical and reasonable of us will abandon logic and reason for irrational bias when we are sufficiently aroused. (And nations are no more rational in this than are individuals, as witness the ceaseless procession of wars.)

These principles are as pertinent to written presentations as they are to in-person exchanges. In writing, you must know to whom you are writing—who the intended reader is, that is—as well as what you are trying to accomplish by your presentation, and you should have a good idea of what kinds of mental sets or attitudes you are going to encounter and have to cope with successfully. You can polarize the position of a reader just as you can polarize positions in a personal encounter. Read some newspaper columnist with whom you disagree violently, and see how swiftly he or she can polarize your position and provoke you into thinking up arguments to defend your position, rather than seeking to learn logical truths about the matter. For that is what happens: the individual driven into an emotional and logical corner now seeks to defend a position, and sometimes defending that takes the form of attacking the party holding a much-hated view.

There is, of course, no chance that your presentation will be credible to someone who has become an antagonist, no matter how logical your reasoning, no matter what evidence you present. All your logic and evidence will be rejected totally by someone who ardently wishes to disbelieve what you say.

ONE WAY TO COPE SUCCESSFULLY WITH BIAS

There are no sure cures for bias, only sure ways to deepen the bias and turn it into hostility. Assuming, however, that you have managed to avoid polarizing your reader's position by avoiding putting him or her on the defensive, there is a way that *may* bring about a metamorphosis of your reader's opinion, a way that often works. It is based on a gradual conditioning of the reader, with the aim of enabling the reader to have a change of mind— or, at least, a partial change of mind—without having the feeling of surrender or of having been bested, or even of having been wrong. If you can manage to give your reader a desire to believe

you—that is, a benefit derived from believing you—without at
the same time being forced to accept a punishing blow of any sort,
you can often bring around even the reader who started with a
bias against you. To pull this off, you must somehow manage the
following things:

Do not be dogmatic in the tone/style of your writing.

Present all sides of the matter, as fairly and as objectively as
possible.

Find and make clear some benefit to the reader in agreeing.

Don't ask for an immediate decision; encourage taking time
to consider.

All the above are important in any effort to change another's
attitude, but the latter is especially important, particularly when
you are dealing with someone already biased. Few people are able
to overcome a bias instantaneously; it requires time to adjust one's
thinking (and "thinking" really means emotional bias, rather than
intellectual conviction). But given the above conditions of a reasonable set of arguments, giving due consideration to all sides of
the matter, presenting reasonable views and evidence, offering
some benefit in agreeing, and permitting the other ample time to
adjust to a new idea, the change often comes about.

I once worked for a man who insisted that despite the size
of his company—it operated a number of branch offices and did
over $50 million in annual sales, employing several thousand peo-
ple—all requests for salary increases had to be approved personally
by him. That is, as a manager of one of the branch offices, I had
to forward to him at the home office all the forms on which I
proposed increases for my staff, whereupon he was supposed to
review and approve or disapprove my requests. However, he rarely
disapproved or approved; he simply stalled.

I never learned whether he stalled to find out if the manager
felt strongly enough to put up a fight for his staff or to save
whatever could be saved by delaying the increases as long as possible, although I suspected the former was the case. However, I
learned that a request was never approved until and unless I took
some follow-up action. I learned also to employ the strategic approach outlined in preceding paragraphs—the gradualism to avoid
confrontation and polarization. Instead, I allowed the requests to
repose on his desk for a couple of weeks, and then followed up
with a polite inquiry as to when I might expect approval, knowing
what the answer would be: he "hadn't had a chance to look at

them yet." And then, a week or two after that I took the action that would get me results, the action that would make my strong feelings about the *need* for the raises credible. For example, in one case I sent the boss a note telling him that he could forget those requests for increases because all the people involved had grown impatient and were submitting their resignations to me. He approved all the increases immediately. (He now believed that the raises were, indeed, necessary.)

This brings up another point: you must know exactly what it is that you wish to prove, what *credibility* means, that is. In the case cited here, my employer had to learn and believe that 1) I was determined to have those raises approved and I would not let the matter drop, and 2) the raises were, indeed, necessary and I was not being frivolous in requesting them. But for me to have predicted that the people would resign when I first asked for the approval of the increases would have been regarded as a threat or, at the least, as an alarmist attitude on my part. It would have been only my opinion that they would resign. But when several weeks had passed, and I said that they *were* resigning, that was accepted as factual *reporting,* and I got prompt action.

In fact, I used several variants of that approach, since we went through the ritual every time I wanted raises approved. No matter what I wanted that required his personal approval—raises, furniture, a new lease, or whatever else we had to spend money for—I had to undertake a similar campaign of that gradualism, until I adjusted his thinking to acceptance of the fact that what I asked for was necessary, I intended to press until I got it, and it would be harmful to the company's interests to deny me what I had requested.

It is possible, therefore, to overcome a reader's biases and prejudices if you do so on that basis of gradualism and allow, even aid, the other to adjust to the idea slowly. Nor does this necessarily mean that the process must entail more than one written communication. It is possible to do this in a single communication—a letter, brochure, resume, or other—if handled well.

THE CHARACTERISTICS OF
THE PRESENTATION ITSELF

Aside from the special problems of biases and prejudices, there are the problems of how information and arguments are presented. We've already touched briefly on that writer's disease I call "generalysis," in which writers "protest too much" in an apparent effort to compensate for the lack of specific information. Or perhaps they have the mistaken notion that superlatives are arguments and the reader will believe you if only you are vociferous enough and insistent enough, possibly along the same lines of reasoning pursued by some proposal writers, who believe that the customer evaluates proposals with a scale: the one that weighs the most is the best.

Even the totally unbiased, open-minded reader is skeptical of claims that are obvious exaggerations, or that *appear* to be obvious exaggerations. Suppose, for example, that you want to report in your resume that during your career you've written over 2 million words of engineering reports. You're going to have to put some evidence of it in your resume, beyond your mere assertion. Here, for example, are some ways to claim or report that accomplishment in your resume, which might elevate a reader's eyebrows but not evoke an immediate snort of skepticism:

Average of three 25,000-word engineering reports each year over past twenty-six years—approximately 1,950,000 words

Seventy-eight engineering reports since leaving college, totalling 1.95 million words.

Write about three engineering reports every year, which usually run about 25,000 words each, and have been doing so for over twenty-six years, for total of 1.95 million words, to date

The last statement would be most credible because it provides the most detail in explaining the total figures. An employer reading that in a resume would be likely to be impressed, but would have no reason to doubt the claim, since it appears to be reporting or documentation. And because it is written in such matter-of-fact language and tone, it is unlikely that anyone would question the truth of it, although an employer reading that in a resume might want to discuss it.

In my own case, for example, because I can make the claim of having written and led or directed the writing of many technical proposals, which produced over $120 million in government contracts, it was always important for me to make this boldly apparent early in my resume. At the same time, I had to make it appear to be a matter-of-fact statement, if it was to be believed, so I listed enough detail to convince anyone reading my resume that I would not make such claims if I could not prove them, since they were so easy to check: I listed a number of prominent companies and government agencies who had been my past employers or clients for whom and to whom I had written proposals that had won contracts. And to make it abundantly clear that I had no fears of being exposed as a fraud, I furnished names, addresses, and telephone numbers of people to call to verify what I reported.

On one occasion a potential employer responded to my resume and during our conversation he remarked on the futility of checking the references I had supplied. Obviously, he observed, I would have selected those references most carefully. I thereupon furnished a full list of at least fifteen past employers, clients, and customers, telling him that here was a total list for several years past, and some of these individuals really did not like me very much, but I was sure they would render an honest opinion of what they thought of my work, and never mind what they thought of my personality. I invited him to call any or all of them. He did not take me up on it. My openness convinced him that I must be telling him the truth.

By far the greatest influence in achieving that quality of credibility in a written presentation—as in any kind of presentation, for that matter—is simple honesty. It's difficult to understand why we don't resort to it more often. But because we don't, when we do we have to offer some kind of evidence that we *are* being honest. And specificity, like details (and they are so closely related that it is sometimes difficult to distinguish between them) is a most effective kind of evidence. It simply has the general impact that all but compels everyone to accept it as evidence of honesty.

SPECIFICITY AS A FACTOR

The moviemakers of Hollywood outdid the phrase-makers of Madison Avenue for years with such characterizations of their celluloid products as *stupendous, breathtaking, awe-inspiring, colossal,* and *magnificent,* each followed by at least one exclamation mark. They piled exaggeration upon hyperbole until they almost blushed themselves at their wild adjectival excesses. They were entirely oblivious to the fact that far from impressing anyone, such self-congratulation was a source of great amusement for many people.

Despite a public that is orders of magnitude more sophisticated than in those relatively early days, and despite a great deal more reserve and good sense in advertising, a glance through print advertisements in current magazines still reveals the following kinds of words and claims (direct quotes):

Great hotels	Big ... Knowledgeable ...
Fresh new styling	Convenient
Boldest, most ingenious	Superb engineering
Most advanced drivetrain	A growing corporation
One of the largest banks	*The* vodka
Exciting program	Powerful training
Handsome annual second income	Revolutionary, multilevel sales plan
	Extraordinary money-making plan

These terms are supposed to be sales arguments, and of course they are not arguments nor are they really appeals. They are claims, hyperbole, self-appraisals, adjectives of exaggeration. Whatever they are, they are not credible, nor do they contribute to credibility. Quite the contrary, they only stress the weaknesses of the sales appeals when they are used. They sound very much like someone thumping a hollow barrel: they have a pronounced hollow ring.

Now aside from the fact that one major key to achieving persuasion is to tell the reader things the reader will welcome hearing (more of that in chapters yet to come), there is the matter of achieving an atmosphere of reporting, rather than claiming. And that is one of the keys to achieving credibility.

Once, some years ago, it was my lot to present myself and a sales proposal to a federal government contracting officer to negotiate a contract the federal agency wished to enter into with us. I handed a copy of my cost proposal—which is normally a separate document when offering a proposal to a federal agency—to the contracting officer, and we sat down facing each other across a table. He glanced through my proposal and then:

"One hundred fifty percent overhead? Why the nice, round number? Why didn't you make it 149.7? I would not have questioned that. But 150? Let's make that 125, okay?"

The last question was not a question. It was an edict, and I could only nod my head and hope that my face was not as red as it felt. He was right and he was wrong. The 150 percent *was* an arbitrary number, but it was a reduction of our true overhead, not a boost in it. However, it did not appear expedient to argue the point. It would have opened a can of worms I didn't care to open.

It was, of course, foolish of us to have done that. We knew that our real overhead was excessive, and we arbitrarily cut it to be competitive enough to win. Under the circumstances, it would not have been dishonest to have made the number an odd one, as the contracting officer pointed out, and avoid the *confession* of a contrived number with, in this case, the appearance of being dishonest. Any reasonable person, detecting that the number was contrived, would have felt entirely justified in inferring that our true overhead was some figure well below that 150 percent quoted, rather than higher, as it actually was.

Honesty is not the issue here; the *appearance* of honesty is. Or, more explicitly, the appearance of *dis*honesty. When people in one company which employed me reported in their brochures and proposals that————Technical Corporation was the largest in its industry, the reader yawned and perhaps smiled indulgently as well. The claim is easy to make because it's an opinion, not a fact. There are so many different bases on which to claim being the biggest that there are probably a least a half-dozen "biggest" companies in every industry. I thought it had more meaning to simply state, in those proposals I wrote for the company, that we had forty-two offices in eighteen states and employed 4,400 people. Let the reader judge for himself or herself where we stood in relative size ranking, if, indeed, being biggest added to our chances for success in winning the contract, which itself was problematical.

The significant thing is this: my statement was acceptable as a factual report, and it is unlikely that anyone reading that statement would even question it. It had the *appearance* of veracity because obviously the numbers were not rounded off, there were no superlatives or loud claims, and no effort to either praise or appraise ourselves. If a customer receives brochures, proposals, or other sales literature from a dozen suppliers, the customer is not going to start making inquiries to determine whether you are being absolutely honest or bending the facts a bit; that would be entirely impractical. Instead, the customer is simply going to *judge* what you say on its own merits. If it *appears* to be reasonable and honest, the customer will accept it as such. Likewise, if it appears to be wildly inflated, the customer will assume that it is, and won't be greatly surprised by it, either. So common is the tendency to blow things up until they are far bigger than life, that the customer will probably examine your brochure or your resume in expectation of finding the typical breast-beating professions of greatness and will be pleasantly surprised if yours is refreshingly different. But there is another consideration than the readily apparent exaggeration of superlatives, illustrated by this anecdote:

Once, in managing a fairly large organization, I appointed as a manager to assist me by taking direct charge of operations a fine young man who had been working hard and earnestly, and who deserved some recognition and a chance to advance his career. Almost overnight he turned into an ogre. Instead of the hail fellow that everyone liked, he became the hated bull of the woods. One thing that characterized his style was his booming voice. He delivered all orders, even the merest one, in a commanding roar.

I took him aside after a couple weeks of this and talked to him: "Al," I said, "do you think that there is anyone on this staff who does not know that you are manager of operations, authorized to give orders?"

He looked surprised. "Of course not. Why?"

"Because you've raised your voice several octaves," I said. "I get the feeling that you're afraid that you won't be obeyed or that you have to shout to let everyone know that you're the boss."

He stared at me, dumbstruck, still not quite sure what I was getting at.

"Al, you're practically saying, 'Hey, I'm not sure of myself.' Al, everyone knows you're the boss, that you speak for me. They'll move just as fast if you whisper, and you'll show a great deal more self-confidence if you don't shout."

Al finally got the message. The shouting was a confession of self-doubt, of great insecurity, of great fears. And it works exactly that way in writing, too. All those claims, all those adjectives, all those "loud shouts" of superlatives are screaming the writer's self-doubts and feelings of insecurity. Self-doubters say "we're the biggest." The self-confident say "we're big enough to do the job properly. Here is what we have." It's not only the factual, reportorial *tone,* but the quiet self-assurance that makes the statements credible—makes the writer credible in general—whether it's a company writing a proposal or sales letter in pursuit of a sale, an individual writing a resume in pursuit of a job, or any individual in pursuit of anything via a written message. It was a Frenchman

(Voltaire?) who said, "Monsieur, what you are shouts so loudly that I cannot hear what you *say* you are." In very much that fashion, what you say in words may be contradicted and discredited by the subtle—but loud—implications of your style and tone. A written presentation has its own personality (style and tone), just as a person does, and that may very well outshout the language.

I had the fate to share a platform at a seminar with a gentleman for whom I have great respect. He is quite successful at his profession, he dresses well, speaks fluently in a pleasant and well-modulated voice, and made what I thought to be a fine presentation. Yet the evaluation forms completed by the audience criticized his presentation bitterly because he managed, somehow, to rub a great many of his listeners the wrong way through overuse of the pronoun "I" in his examples. Or so ran their complaints, for the most part. And, yet, I rely principally on my personal experiences for my anecdotes and examples, too, and have so far never encountered the problem my associate did. One reason is that I try to avoid *over*using that perpendicular pronoun, by assigning at least some of my anecdotes and examples to some fictitious third person. (The anecdotes are true but the names have been changed to escape the appearance of superegotism.) And in describing personal experiences, such as how successful proposals were developed, I try to use the pronoun "we," which is an aid also, in avoiding the appearance of egotism.

THE EMOTIONAL IMPACT OF LANGUAGE

We've pointed out here, and it's well established elsewhere, that emotion is far more motivating than is reason or logic. In general, most people make decisions based on emotional needs rather than on logical analysis and deduction, although reason plays a part in the process. And language—how we say things, as well as what we say—has great emotional impact on most readers. Let's consider, first of all, what words mean.

First of all, there are at least two levels of meaning generally in many of our words. We call one *denotation*, which refers to actual definition, as given in a dictionary, and the other *connotation*, which refers to a secondary or additional and implied meaning. For example, *stubborn*, *determined*, and *obstinate* are all synonyms—have similar denotations—but all have different shades of meaning or nuances, as connotations. We prefer to think of our own quality of persistence as determination, but not as obstinacy, because determination is generally an admirable trait, whereas obstinacy is not. Stubbornness is a trait that is generally between those other two and may be indicated as an admirable trait or not, according to how—in what context—it is used. So connotations are not absolutes usually, but may vary, according to surrounding circumstances and usage.

There was a time when the word *rascal* was derogatory in its use, as it is in its literal meaning, but it has lost its derogatory connotation in modern times. Still in use, when the word *rascal* is used today it is generally an affectionate reference to a mischievous child or pet. If you were to write that a certain individual is a rascal, it is unlikely that a reader would interpret that to mean that the person referred to is a scoundrel.

Our language, like every other, has its share of idioms, which are words, terms, and phrases—even complete sentences—that have special meanings and are not to be taken literally. *How are you?* is a greeting meaning hello or so nice to meet you, not an inquiry into your health. *Good-bye* was originally the idiom "God be with you," and *so long* came down to us from the Malayan *salaang* via British soldiers serving in that part of the world. On the other hand, we have many colloquialisms and expressions regarded as slang—which means that they are not entirely respectable or accepted terms—which presumably will one day be accepted as idiom, when they have stood the test of time and endured long enough to prove that they will remain with us. And we now find that "four-letter words" are admissible and almost respectable, if they are found in works considered to be literature, but the term *four-letter word* has its own meaning, as an idiom, and does not refer to all four-letter words, but only to a select group, some of which are, in fact, more than four letters long.

There are also many words that are emotional in their content generally, such as *messy, greasy, bigoted, cruel,* and *generous.* The selection of the word may itself characterize the message or convey an emotion itself. However, the arrangement of words and phrases suggests a stress or connotes a meaning beyond what the words actually say. Here, for example, are two sentences, using precisely the same words—even the same phrases—but strongly suggesting opposite meanings:

Bill is a good worker, but he drinks.
Bill drinks, but he is a good worker.

In this case, the arrangement of the words delivers two entirely different messages because the stress is changed, each sentence the opposite of the other. In each case a meaning is *implied* and implied quite strongly, through the use of that little conjunction *but*. However, if *although* is used as the conjunction, the effect is reversed:

Bill is a good worker, although he drinks.
Bill drinks, although he is a good worker.

At the same time, the emphasis is considerably weakened, especially in the second sentence of the latter pair of sentences, and it is not entirely clear whether Bill is being recommended or not. *But* is a much stronger conjunction, in implying a meaning not actually stated. If the conjunction *and* were used, there would be no implied bias in the message—no special stress:

Bill is a good worker, and he drinks.
Bill drinks, and he is a good worker.

One factor we have not yet mentioned that bears heavily on achieving credibility in writing is accuracy. Get 999 facts straight and no one will note it or remark on it. But get one fact incorrect, and you'll receive dozens of complaints from outraged readers. So while it is important to achieve accuracy, it is even more important to avoid inaccuracy, for it is the latter that will damage your credibility immediately. Ordinarily, a reader begins with a sense of faith in whatever appears in writing, based on the assumption that the material has been subjected to rigid editorial and managerial controls, and is therefore trustworthy. Finding a single glaring error, then, is an almost shattering experience, virtually a betrayal of trust, and causes the reader to thereupon lose faith totally in the entire book or article. Or whatever it is.

Once, in filling out all those endless forms necessary to get a security clearance when working on defense projects, I slipped up and got two numbers in the street address of one of my earlier residences transposed. It caused me no end of trouble. Even when

I had finally allayed their suspicions about my trustworthiness as a loyal American citizen, they were still entirely uneasy about the accuracy of any other representations I had made in my forms. It was a long time before I earned trust in that organization, and there appeared to be a lingering suspicion even then that I was probably not entirely dependable.

AIDS TO ACHIEVING CREDIBILITY

There are a number of measures the writer can resort to as aids to achieving credibility. One of these is the use of testimonials or references. In a resume, the names of past employers and individuals who can attest to your competence, honesty, diligence, and other qualifying characteristics are *references.* In advertising, it is customary to quote the words of such individuals and call such quotations or citations "testimonials." For example, if you are fortunate enough to get a customer to say something such as, "Bob Jones's service was not only excellent, he stood behind his work 100 percent," it's helpful to cite these actual words in your advertising literature. You should have the customer's permission, of course, and those words should be in your hands in writing, over the customer's signature.

Such a testimonial helps greatly, even if not "attributed"—the source not identified, that is. But if you can get that happy customer to permit you to use his or her name, so much the better because it adds further to the impact of the testimonial: the reader will be far more inclined to believe that it is a true testimonial if he or she sees a name attached to it. And if you can use the customer's address, even better, for that adds even more validity to it—makes it even more credible.

As a further step, if the customer is a prominent individual, perhaps the mayor of your town or a well-known executive, so much the better. That's why celebrities are paid so much money to make testimonials: the more prominent they are, the more credible and persuasive the testimonial.

There is a hazard, however: if you can get only one or two testimonials, it is probably better not to use them, for that makes it appear that it is a rare thing for customers to applaud what you do or sell. If you are going to use testimonials, it is usually far better to use a number of them, at least a half-dozen or so, to show that it is quite an everyday occurrence for you to get such plaudits from your satisfied customers.

A popular device is to stipulate that these are only a handful of testimonials in your files, and there are many more on file, available for inspection at any time. Where customers object to having their names publicized, a common resort of advertisers is to use initials, with the stipulation that the full letter may be examined on your own premises at any time, to assure readers that the testimonials are real.

It is, of course, best if you do not have to ask anyone for a testimonial letter, so that you can honestly report that the testimonials are unsolicited. Unfortunately, even the happiest and most enthusiastic customer is unlikely to think about writing a testimonial letter unless you suggest it to him. Most of those who can boast of many testimonial letters have at least hinted to customers that they would appreciate such letters.

Other devices used to gain credibility include citation of authorities. You will find this used in TV commercials, for example, where someone in a white coat explains that an association of dental professionals have found that fluoride helps prevent tooth decay and then goes on to explain about the fluoride in their product, or cites Census Bureau statistics to give weight to some statement.

One of the more effective ways of achieving credibility is to lead the reader along a path of reasoning in such a manner that the reader is doing most of the work of analyzing the situation and reaching the conclusion you have decided you want him or her to reach. The way to do this is to ask questions, usually in a way that makes the logical answer readily apparent, and thus you control the reader's reasoning process. But a useful variant of this is to make statements in the form of questions—ask rhetorical questions, that is. For example, in promoting a newsletter on government marketing, I used this device, along with the self-test gambit (many people love to take little self-scored tests). I had identified a number of items I thought would intrigue readers— they were provocative "insider tips" I promised to reveal—and I thought this the most effective way to present a sampling of these items. I therefore used, as one of my pieces of direct-mail sales literature, a sheet that announced itself as a test. It followed this general line, with seventeen items (questions) similar to the ones listed below:

TEST YOUR PROPOSALMANSHIP I.Q.

- How can you APPEAR to be a low bidder, even when you are not?
- How can you GUARANTEE yourself a high technical score for your proposal?
- How can you unwire a wired procurement?
- What are five basic strategies you can use in your proposal?
- How can you handle the impossible-to-price RFP to almost guarantee winning?

My promises to answer these and the other questions, plus providing other special information, lent a great deal of credibility to my presentation: those who thought they were reasonably competent at proposal writing but found themselves unable to answer most of the seventeen questions suddenly realized that they could still learn some valuable things about the subject. The promotion was highly successful, in any case, so it seems reasonable to conclude that the device was effective.

Of course, it is worth noting here, too, that most of the respondents were naturally interested in increasing their success in writing the winning proposals. They welcomed the promise of imparting specialized, "inside" information. They *wanted* to believe my promises because it was very much in their interests if I could make good on those promises. So always bear in mind when striving for ways to be highly credible in what you write that you can get a great deal of help from the reader if you can manage to motivate the reader to want to believe you.

There is another, possibly even more effective way of using the rhetorical question. Suppose I had posed those seventeen questions in a slightly different way:

WOULD YOU LIKE TO KNOW HOW TO WRITE WINNING PROPOSALS?

- Would you like to know how to APPEAR to be a low bidder, even when you are not?
- Would you like to GUARANTEE yourself a high technical score for your proposal?

- Would you like to learn how to unwire a wired procurement?
- Would you like to learn five basic strategies you can use in your proposal?
- Would you like a technique for handling the impossible-to-price RFP in a way that almost guarantees winning?

This is an even more direct way to stimulate reader interest and desire—presumably—to know the answers to these questions. It addresses the reader with a reason to want to believe in each and every item and so is possibly even more motivating than the "I.Q. Test" idea. These are truly rhetorical questions—especially the headline question—because there is no doubt how the reader must answer; therefore, it is obvious to the reader that the writer is not seeking an answer, not really asking questions, but making statements. The question form, however, is generally more effective than is a straight statement because it challenges the reader and is far more likely to evoke some kind of response.

The question format, incidentally, is particularly advisable when you believe that you are faced with special problems that make it more difficult than usual to achieve credibility, such as when you are opposed by bias or when what you have to present will probably be quite difficult to sell because it is radically new or novel or somehow flies in the face of conventional wisdom.

5

HOW TO WRITE ADVERTISING COPY

Nowhere in the world is the advertising art honed to as fine an edge as it is in the United States, where not only is a torrent of copy produced every day, but thousands of specialists labor at research tasks to discover words that will increase results by a fraction of a percentage point.

MADISON AVENUE IS MORE THAN A STREET NAME

IF THERE IS any single field in which there is a primary focus on efforts to produce the most persuasive writing, it is the advertising field. There are, by best estimate, approximately 6,000 advertising agencies offering services to the public at large, but there are many times that number of in-house organizations devoted to producing persuasive writing of many kinds—marketing and advertising departments of companies, for example, as well as sales organizations and sales-support departments. So seriously do we take advertising as a career field that thousands of youngsters spend four or more years in universities pursuing the primary goal of learning how to conduct marketing (advertising) research. (The two are difficult to separate from each other.)

Over the years advertising has become more and more sophisticated, especially with the preeminence of behavioral psychology and the use of psychology in such pursuits as *motivational research,* which attempts to learn what motivates various people in various situations and to organize the information in as scientific a manner as possible for use in improving the effectiveness of advertising. To a large degree, this—what motivates people—is the very heart of advertising, what advertising is all about. The essential goal of all advertising is to persuade people to buy or, at least, to take some step that will aid the advertiser in ultimately consummating a sale to the prospect. And of course motivation and persuasion are closely linked, if not identical.

THE ELEMENTS OF AN ADVERTISEMENT

The conventional wisdom in advertising is that an advertisement must do these things:

1. Get attention
2. Arouse interest
3. Create desire
4. Demand action

If you study advertisements and TV commercials you can easily see how these principles are put to work in most instances. On my desk now is a trade journal that is circulated among those in the marketing field, and one of the full-page advertisements inside the front cover advises the reader: PUT SOME STEAM IN YOUR SALES.

This headline is under a photograph of a man and woman clinging to the side of a locomotive from which issues a cloud of steam. The copy under the headline is far from crystal clear, but a bit of study reveals, finally, that the advertisement is by a rather well-known manufacturer of men's shirts and other clothing products, and the advertisement has as its objective urging the reader to call on the advertiser and learn how to use his allegedly effective program of premiums (gifts of his products) to salespeople to stimulate their sales efforts.

There are at least two things wrong with this advertisement. One is that the headline is only an indirect explanation of why the reader ought to be interested in what this advertisement is all about; it does not really come to grips with *how* the advertiser can help the reader stimulate sales. The second fault is that the copy is somewhat vague, and requires a bit of study to grasp the import of the message. It uses the word *steam* twice more, each time with a bit different pun—"full steam ahead," in one case, and "all steamed up," in another case—clearly straining for effect.

There is, in fact, no real strategy behind this copy: the headline and the "steam" idea are obviously contrived and "dragged in by the ears" because they have no natural or logical connection with the whole idea and main message.

Another supplier of gifts and premiums designed to motivate sales forces uses the headline POUR IT ON and a photograph of gold being poured in a puddle. It's an effective attention-getter, but it has little direct bearing on the main message and so accomplishes only that single purpose of getting attention.

On the other hand, another seller of incentive items headlines his copy: INCREASE YOUR SALES 44% WITH (NAME OF PRODUCT). This headline gets attention and arouses interest at the same time because it makes a specific offer of a much-to-be-desired direct benefit. What reader would not like to increase sales 44 percent? Even the reader who thinks the promise extravagant is likely to take a moment to read on and see why this advertiser makes such a promise.

A wise advertiser goes even further. His advertisement's headline is this: WHAT IS TRADE SHOW MARKETING? The copy consists of several questions and the advertiser's answers, providing a direct incentive to *read the advertisement.* The advertisement, in this case, carries out the most essential function of a salesperson: it functions as a consultant, aiding the prospect by providing useful information. (And the copy is highly persuasive, so we'll study it in this chapter.)

It seems futile, to me at least, to spend energy, time, and money for the sole purpose of getting attention, when it is always or nearly always possible to both get attention and arouse interest at the same time. And that means for the same expenditure of energy, time, and money. Moreover, anything that arouses interest at the same time it gets attention is likely to be far more effective in both these functions.

AROUSING INTEREST

The most important word in advertising is *you,* because the most important words to each of us are *I* and *me.* Even when we act altruistically we do so because it *makes us feel good.* The super-wealthy become philanthropists because it makes them feel noble and important. It perpetuates their names on libraries and other public-building foundations. It assures them a form of immortality in the annals of history. It adds meaning to their lives. It does many things for them, even while they are trying to convince themselves that they have absolutely no selfish motive in their charities and good works.

This is not to derogate such people and their noble acts, for there are many superwealthy people who do not use some of their surplus wealth to help others in society. But it is important to understand that we do not do things we really do not want to do or are not compelled to do. Even when we do something with great reluctance, it is because we want to do it—that is, we would rather do whatever it is than suffer the consequences of not doing it, whatever those consequences may be.

All these factors of motivation—doing something because there is some reward in doing it or because there is some penalty in not doing it—are important in advertising, therefore, because they are the direct clues to what makes one advertisement work and another fail. And there are at least these four approaches to arousing interest or persuading someone to read your advertisement:

1. The advertisement talks about how to gain something that will be of great benefit to you.
2. The advertisement talks about how to avoid something that would be most distasteful or harmful to you.
3. The advertisement itself offers information that is beneficial to know.
4. The advertisement itself offers information that represents security from a great hazard or distasteful consequence.

Here are examples of each of these, to illustrate the points made here.

An advertisement that promises to tell you how to make your next meeting the biggest success you've ever had, if you send in the coupon in the advertisement, is offering you a reward as a result of doing whatever the advertisement asks you to do.

Another advertisement headlines: SORRY. NOT INTERESTED. It furnishes a coupon for salesperson-readers to send in and learn how to henceforth avoid this discouraging response from prospects.

That copy that asked the question WHAT IS TRADE SHOW MARKETING?, and then began to answer the question in the advertisement itself, is an example of the third type of advertisement mentioned, the advertisement that itself provides a benefit of some useful information, whether the reader takes a further action or not.

The fourth type of copy is exemplified by an advertisement that headlines: THREE WAYS TO AVOID COSTLY MISTAKES. It then goes on to provide three useful tips in the advertising copy for avoiding common sales mistakes.

The idea behind those stated elements of advertising is to carry the prospect along a rising curve of involvement, from getting attention to demanding action. If we were to graph it, it might look something like Figure 1, and the rationale is along these lines:

Initially, the prospect (reader, TV viewer, radio listener, etc.) is neutral, neither pro nor con, with respect to the product or service being advertised, and presumably not interested. To get the prospect interested, it is necessary to get the prospect's attention first. But it is necessary to do something that will arouse the prospect's interest very soon after getting attention, or the prospect will move on to something else. (Ergo the advantage of doing both, getting attention and arousing interest, in the same step.)

Interest will flag if the advertisement does not keep building the prospect's interest—the interest curve must not be allowed to flatten out—and fanning it into a flame of desire to gain the promised benefit(s). Even when that is established the prospect is not yet fully committed, for surprising as it may be, by far the majority of prospects even at the point of wanting to get what the advertisement promises will not exercise even a little initiative and take the next step *unless specifically instructed to do so.* That is why good advertising *instructs* the prospect to send in the coupon, rush down to the corner drugstore, pick up the telephone, or whatever action you want to suggest.

Nothing happens instantaneously, even though some things appear to. Vehicles, even superpowerful rockets, must overcome inertia and build enough power to reach operational speed. Every journey begins with a step, even if it finally encompasses thousands of miles. Every construction job, large or small, begins with small first steps. And so it is with motivating a prospect. There is an inertia to overcome, for one thing, and what is at most only a passing interest must be nourished and encouraged until it be-

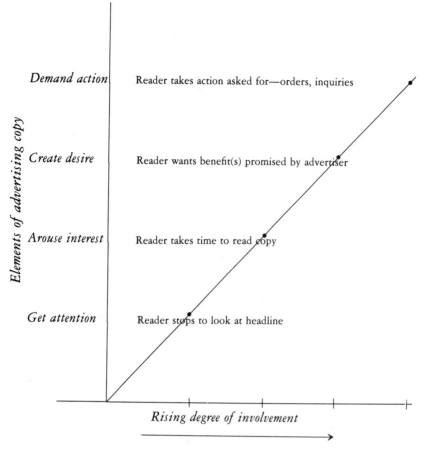

FIGURE 1. Elements of advertising versus degree of
prospect involvement

comes a basis for action. That is why advertising is separated into those discrete steps so that the entire process may be rationalized and learned.

CREATING DESIRE

Some teachers of advertising and sales techniques—really the same subject, philosophically—refer to a "desire to buy." That's a bit of an overstatement, in fact, and represents wishful thinking by the advertiser. Perhaps an advertisement does create a desire to buy ultimately, but more often than not the desire it creates, when it is a successful advertisement, is a desire for whatever benefit has been promised. Suppose, for example, that the advertisement manages to convince a female prospect that the skin cream advertised will, indeed, make her skin look years younger. Obviously, if the prospect believes the copy and wants to use the product, she will have to buy it. But she does not have a desire for the product per se; she has a desire for what that product will do or has been pledged to do. That is the meaning of the third item, create desire. And it is quite important to make that distinction, to understand precisely what that *create desire* means. It means desire for the benefit, whether the benefit is to gain something highly desirable or to avoid something highly undesirable.

DEMANDING ACTION

Perhaps *demand* is the wrong term to use here, for in practice what most advertisements do is to *suggest* action or to *instruct* the prospect in the next action to take, as illustrated a few paragraphs ago. Somehow, strange as it may seem, it is necessary to point out to the prospect that some action is necessary to gain the benefit promised. If madame wants to keep her skin young and beautiful, as promised, she must stop in her favorite drugstore or department store and buy the product. Or if it is a mail order item, it is necessary to send in the order blank with a check. Or call and have it sent out.

It is also helpful and sometimes necessary to lend the matter some urgency. Otherwise, many prospects who decide they'd like to take advantage of the offer make a mental note to do so, but never get around to it. Therefore, it is usually helpful to make "limited time" offers and resort to various other means to urge immediate action.

Humans tend strongly to take the path of least resistance, so it is also usually helpful if you give the prospect as much help as possible in taking advantage of your offer. Coupons are one such aid; many people would never manage to send an order in if they had to write a request and mail it. Self-addressed response cards, especially those that are postage paid, are also helpful in inducing prospects to act. The convenience of charge cards, so that the prospect does not have to go to the trouble of writing a check or getting a money order is still another inducement to action. And the convenience of a toll-free telephone number and the invitation to phone in an order is a great help also.

ALWAYS USE THAT PATH OF LEAST RESISTANCE

Taking advantage of people's tendency to take the path of least resistance is helpful in persuading them to act. But it is also a helpful principle in other respects, such as in guiding people's thinking, and persuading them to the viewpoint you wish them to adopt. Most of us find that thinking is a taxing endeavor, and we tend to do as little real thinking as possible for that reason. It is useful to bear that in mind, in writing copy: the more you demand of a reader in terms of real cogitation, the less likely you are to hold the reader's interest. He or she is tempted to go on to something less demanding.

This applies to many situations. Here are some situations that make demands on readers which may discourage them from going on:

- Copy that attempts to refute what has always been commonly accepted as fact by most of us.
- Copy that pursues lengthy and convoluted paths of reasoning
- Arguments that demand the retention of many points
- Copy that uses "75¢ words"
- Any tiresome or laborious copy—arguments, recitals, expositions, or other

This is not an argument against lengthy copy or large advertisements, for many of those are successful, but only against tedious, laborious, dull, and difficult copy, whether long or short.

ANOTHER PERSPECTIVE ON THE ELEMENTS OF ADVERTISING

Those four elements of advertising—*get attention, arouse interest, create desire,* and *demand action*—are real enough and describe functions that advertising must accomplish. But there are other ways to express the functions of advertising which, I believe, are more enlightening and reflect a clearer insight into what advertising must be and do, if it is to succeed. In the perspective of this approach, there are three main elements in advertising, as far as indentifying the principal functions and aims of advertising are concerned. They are these:

Promises
Proofs
Instruction

PROMISES

Every advertisement makes or at least implies one or more promises. There is the promise of great wealth, a better job, increased prestige, attraction of the opposite sex, more security, ego gratification, and thousands of other benefits. One of the advertisements we cited here promised 44-percent increase in sales. A famous and highly successful advertisement of recent years promised to teach buyers the "lazy man's way to riches." Brewers promise that drinking their beer means good times at the beach and at the local tavern. Sellers of diet aids promise slenderness and attractive figures.

In the final analysis, it is not the product that respondents to these advertisements buy; it is the promise that they buy. The seeker after riches does not want the book; he or she wants to be rich, the lazy man's way or any other way possible. The unhappy overweight individual does not want the diet aid; he or she wants to be slender and attractive. The target of the beer advertisement does not want the beer; he or she wants the fun that goes with drinking it.

Smart advertisers recognize this. They don't sell products or services; they sell promises. Buying the product or service is a necessary means to the end of gaining what the promise holds forth, a nuisance, perhaps, but a necessary one, if you want to get what was promised.

Advertising professionals generally refer to those promises as "benefits." Benefits are what are promised, so the distinction is not important, except as it affects and explains the next element of proofs, and that connection will become clearer shortly. But it is important to understand this point because in the end that is precisely what your advertisement is, a promise. In fact, however, it is even more than a promise; it is a *quid pro quo* offer; you promise that if the reader does what you ask—takes that action you call for—you will keep your promise. But you are asking the reader to act in good faith and to accept your assurance that you will make good on your promise. That can prove to be something of a problem.

We discussed credibility in the last chapter, and made the point there that credibility is something not automatically achieved, nor is it a trait of the presentation entirely, but is affected by several factors other than what the presentation says and how it says it. As far as advertising copy is concerned, these are the main factors to consider, in connection with the inherent credibility of your promise:

- Name recognition—that is, General Electric versus Jones Appliances
- What the prospect is asked to risk on the promise made— for example, $2 versus $200
- What the prospect is asked to believe—for example, better toothbrush versus totally, radically new way of cleaning teeth

Major corporations, with high name recognition, are always more credible in their claims and promises than are unknown organizations. If you manufacture a popcorn maker and try to sell it against the competition of General Electric's popcorn maker, you've got to do some heavy selling to persuade the prospect to give more credence to your promises than to General Electric's promises.

The amount of risk you ask the prospect to undertake is an important consideration. A prospect might risk a couple of dollars without having supreme faith in your promises, but is not likely to risk $200 without careful consideration of how reliable your promises are likely to be. But money is not the only risk you might ask of the prospect: a prospect might risk taking up a major pharmaceutical or drug firm on their promise that a new patent medicine will help overcome their symptoms, but taking a new patent medicine marketed by a small and unknown newcomer of a firm to the drug field appears to be a much larger risk, and the prospect is likely to hesitate over that. Or the promise of a safe and happy flight on a major airline might be accepted without hesitation, but not a similar promise from NewlyOrganized Airlines, Inc.

Asking a prospect to make a radical change in his or her accustomed way of thinking represents another obstacle to accepting your promise unhesitatingly. While the prospect might be entirely willing to give at least tentative credence to your promise of a better ketchup and actually try the product, a promise of a new kind of sauce or seasoning, based on an entirely new concept, is likely to require a good bit more study and much greater reluctance to try your new product. Most people resist change, and the more radical the change, the greater the resistance. Too, some promises appear to contradict established wisdom and ordinary experience, and so are doubly hard to give credence to. History is full of examples of that, of people rejecting new ideas simply because they appeared to contradict common experience. Thus it was that all the following, to name only a few, found themselves jeered at, denounced as fools, and otherwise vilified by the experts of their day:

Louis Pasteur, challenging the notion of spontaneous generation

Robert Fulton, inventing the steamboat

Charles Kettering, inventing the automobile self-starter

Thomas Edison, inventing the incandescent electric light

Ignaz Semmelweiss, telling doctors to wash their hands between examinations

The Wright brothers, inventing the airplane

Alexander Graham Bell, inventing the telephone

Montgomery Ward, offering customers a money-back guarantee

Gail Borden, developing evaporated/condensed milk

For these men, the only way they achieved credibility, finally, was by proving their assertions through direct demonstration of successful results. But ironically, while the public in general has always rejected and even persecuted those of vision working on important advances, there also have been a great many people who cheerfully believe in propositions that are even more absurd and, in the end, prove to be futile dreams, such as perpetual-motion machines and magic powders to turn water into gasoline, or miraculous cancer cures. And while many of these are the sincere, if wildly improbable ideas of fanatics, many are out-and-out swindles, the fraudulent schemes of Ponzi and others. And we'll explore why it is that an individual who rejects the work of Edison or Borden will eagerly choose to believe in perpetual motion, which is a direct contradiction of basic scientific laws.

PROOFS

Having made one or more promises in your advertisement, and assuming that they are promises the prospect finds reasonably attractive, you must now furnish some kind of proof or at least evidence that the promises you made are credible. But usually the proofs must be of at least two kinds:

1. Logical proof that your product or service will produce the kind of benefits you claim for it, so that the promise is believable

2. Evidence that you are a trustworthy dealer and can be relied upon to make good on your promises, delivering the goods/service, as promised, and also standing behind your guarantees

For examples of how that is done, you can study any of many TV commercials and print advertisements. Sometimes the "proof" is truly a logical explanation, but sometimes it is quite specious. A manufacturer of portable typewriters advertises "ten good reasons" for buying his product, claiming that no other electric portable has them. The proofs offered start by claiming that the product is not a typewriter, but a "total typing system," and then goes on to explain why the claim that it is a system is justified. To the critical mind, the proofs do not justify the term *system,* but they do present a number of desirable features the machine can boast of, and they do make a case of some kind for the claim of being a system.

In another print advertisement a cigarette is claimed to be the "best" cigarette, as rated by the Federal Trade Commission, on the basis of having the lowest amount of tar and nicotine. However, a competitor states in his advertising that the former is lowest only in the eighty- and eighty-five-millimeter size, whereas this advertiser has the lowest tar in the one hundred-millimeter size.

A pipe-tobacco advertiser claims that his product offers a cool smoke, and for proof he states that he blends his tobaccos especially to provide a cool smoke, which is a somewhat circular argument and less than irrefutable logic.

Several other cigarette advertisers simply claim low tar and suggest, some subtly and some quite plainly, that it's macho to smoke their brands. And perhaps that's as good a "proof" as any, because cigarette smoking is itself an irrational habit for which it is most difficult to prove any practical benefits. Therefore, the benefits must be emotional ones, such as ego gratification, and that explains the nature of the proof or the lack of it, more precisely. (These cigarette advertisements are from a magazine that is read almost exclusively by men, most of them mechanics, construction workers, and outdoors types.)

A manufacturer of telephones says in its headline that it's "an open and shut case for owning your own phone." That proves to be one of those too-too clever puns, because a photo shows the telephone open and shut—physically open and shut, that is—with open being electrically equal to lifting the telephone off the stand and shut equivalent to hanging up. The headline thus really makes no promise, except by implying that the copy will show you why you should own your own telephone. The body copy then goes on to extol the virtues of this instrument, explaining the "open and shut" feature in the process. The body copy thus doesn't really prove anything because there was really no promise made. But the copy does concentrate on all the magnificent features it claims for this instrument and reminds the reader that there are no monthly rental charges for this telephone, only a one-time purchase cost.

It isn't always easy to find proofs in these advertisements because so many of them have nothing to prove. They haven't made a promise even by implication. Many of the advertisements are simply announcements. Here are some of the items offered, with apparently no effort made to sell them, but only to announce that they are available:

Solar chronograph (watch)	Wooden toy kits
Clock components	Log-splitter wedge
Solar panels	Stair glide (electric
Aquascooter	lift)
Solar greenhouses	Library bookcase
Saw guide	Water conditioner
Sports car kits	Wristwatch

Many of these are little, one-inch advertisements, and a number are offers of catalogs and follow-up information—inquiry advertisements. As such, they do not require a great deal of hard selling, since the respondent is not asked to spend anything, but only to furnish his or her name and get a catalog or other information in return. One, for example, offers a free color catalog—and the headline is FREE, in the largest type of the advertisement—

which will describe the parts you can buy to build your own grandfather's clock. Another offers to teach the reader how to make a lot of money as a chimney sweep, and goes on to explain the big earnings and the easy life of the modern chimney sweep.

Rarely, in any case, are there serious proofs offered, although there are the claims made, over and over, as though they become more credible with repetition. Perhaps they do, for some readers, but the evidence is against it. The evidence is that most advertisements succeed well enough to show the advertiser some profit, but are far less effective than they ought to be. What most such advertisements really show is a woeful lack of imagination and resourcefulness on the part of those who wrote the copy, and we'll go back to some of these shortly and see what could have been done with them. But first, let's look at another matter: headlines, which are the traditional attention-getters of print advertising, and are still used primarily for that purpose.

HEADLINING

It's been held by many experts in advertising—Maxwell Sackheim, acknowledged "dean of mail order copywriters," for example—that the headline makes or breaks a print advertisement. The conventional wisdom of these advertising savants is that a weak headline dooms the advertisement: even strong body copy is not likely to salvage it. Conversely, a strong headline takes the load off the body copy, and even mediocre body copy can carry the day when the headline is a good one.

Here we come to that matter of whether the headline can or cannot always be used to arouse interest, as well as to attract attention. In my own opinion, I believe the answer is yes. I think a throwaway headline—one used for attention-getting only and then discarded—is a tragic waste. Worse, I think it is a confession of sorely limited copywriting talent. A resourceful and able copywriter should not have to waste copy like that, and ought to be inventive enough and creative enough to find a way to make the headline do three things:

1. Get attention
2. Arouse interest
3. Make the basic promise

Let's go on a quest for such a headline. Surely, there are some advertisements that are well enough written to meet this challenge successfully. Here is one, a modest display advertisement of only two column-inches. The headline and subhead are as follows:

ACCOUNTANTS: START YOUR OWN PRACTICE!
We'll send you The Book on how and why. *Free.*

I find this headline attention-getting because it addresses a specific reader: the accountant. It arouses interest by suggesting a benefit: the accountant's own practice. And it makes a promise to send a book free—in fact, calls it "The Book" to dramatize it. It also illustrates the book, with a title—*Programmed for Success*—showing plainly. The title is itself motivating because it makes a promise too. And as a further inducement to action, a toll-free number is supplied, so the individual can order the book by telephone without delay or cost.

Another small display advertisement offers a main headline, a subhead, a second headline, and a boldface caption or subhead to introduce the body copy, along these lines:

SAMPLE IMPORT FREE!
Shows How You Make Big Money Part Time
MAIL ORDER/IMPORT
HOME BUSINESS

The subhead introducing the body copy reads "Buy Below Wholesale." The word *free* in the main headline is the attention-getter; the word *free* apparently never loses its appeal. And the promise of being shown how to make big money part time is bound to arouse the interest of many readers. Further, the headlines make the proposition clear enough: it concerns importing and selling by mail. So the reader is not left in doubt.

An advertisement that has been running in many publications for some time—excellent evidence that it is a successful advertisement—simply headlines this:

when I planned to
RETIRE BEFORE FIFTY
this is the business that made it possible

a true story by *(name)*————

The rest of the page—a full page—is solid copy, the first-person story of the man pictured at the top of the page, explaining what the headlined story promised to tell the reader. The headline states the promise—retire before fifty—and enough readers find it attention-getting and interest-arousing to make the copy successful.

Here is another example of how an advertiser delivers his entire message in a headline and subhead:

TRAIN AT HOME FOR A BETTER CAREER
(24 ways the —— school can help improve your life)

This copy hardly needs comment. It promises a better career, improvement of the reader's life, and explains that it's a train-at-home proposition. The body copy expands on the home-study courses offered, the credentials of the school (it's very well-known and long in existence), promises that no salesperson will call if the reader sends in the coupon, and asks for brochures describing the courses of interest.

A small advertisement—about four column-inches—promises THICKER, STRONGER, LONGER HAIR—in just five to seven days, in its headline and subhead. This is an almost surefire attention-getter of women who are dissatisfied with their hair, and there appears to be a substantial number of those. It therefore makes the promise and arouses interest, as it gets attention. The body copy explains how the conditioner works, offers a guarantee, instructs the reader in how to order.

But now let's look at a few headlines that do not do the job they could do, and see how they might be improved.

A mail order firm headlines its advertisement: INCREDIBLE! It then goes on to headline its offer of $4.99 worth of selenium tablets free. The body copy explains that selenium is a trace mineral with a unique skin-saving action that keeps skin elastic and keeps the possessor of the skin looking young. The copy asks for $1.00 for postage and handling, and promises one hundred fifty-milligram selenium tablets free.

What is wrong with this headline is that while it features the word *free* boldly, it fails to tell the reader why he or she ought to be interested in the selenium tablets. Perhaps a few readers are aware of the product and believe it valuable, so that the offer is attractive. But for anyone else—and that is for most readers—the offer of free selenium tablets is of no special value.

The headline ought to have featured the promise of helping the reader maintain a youthful appearance. If *free* could be combined with that, the appeal would almost certainly be far greater than the appeal of *incredible.* Something along this line, perhaps:

TO HELP YOU KEEP THAT YOUTHFUL SKIN—
$4.99 worth of selenium tablets FREE!

A great many men and women would stop to see what that headline means, especially when the word *free* is dangled before them as well.

An industrial salvage company offers to sell an instruction manual guiding the reader in locating and salvaging various materials, which the advertiser offers to buy. The motivation is obviously an opportunity to earn money, using what the advertiser claims is little-known information. However, instead of suggesting that this is a money-making opportunity in the headline, the advertiser asks the question in the headline: THROWING AWAY $5 PER LB? This is, of course, a cryptic message, which may impel some to read it out of sheer curiosity, but then the body copy is almost equally cryptic, never identifying any of the rare materials it refers to. I would have suggested something along these lines:

WE'LL BUY SCRAP MATERIALS FROM YOU
AT $5 PER LB
and we'll tell you where and how to find it!

A manufacturer of do-it-yourself satellite receiving antennas uses its own trade name for its antenna systems as the headline and its company name as the subhead. The body copy begins by introducing the model the manufacturer advertises here. Not until then does it finally furnish some small-type body copy that informs the reader what the advertisement is all about—that the manufacturer offers an antenna dish to receive signals from satellites—and doesn't explain it even that specifically, but just states that it is a complete home satellite receiving system that the buyer can assemble as a weekend project. The best clue as to what it is is contained in a balloon at the bottom of the copy that says "fifty channels." Obviously, only initiates—those who are actively interested in such systems and perhaps seeking one of their own—would grasp what this is all about or understand enough of it to pause and read the copy. If the advertiser hopes to attract others and get them interested, he ought to approach his advertising along these lines:

RECEIVE FIFTY TV CHANNELS
Install Your Own Receiving System

Here, again, the headline makes an effort to get attention while it arouses interest by making the basic promise: get fifty TV channels. The advertiser who wrote the copy as it appears, however, thought that the names of the manufacturer's product and of its company were items to be headlined, and so obviously did not understand any of the purposes of a headline, not even that most basic purpose of commanding attention, much less those of arousing interest and making a promise to the reader.

Note there what the promise ought to be. The promise the advertiser made (finally, in his body copy) was that the reader could assemble the system himself or herself in a weekend and that he or she would save money in so doing. But that is not the promise he should have made, for that is not the main benefit. In fact, the do-it-yourself aspect is not a benefit at all, but is only a means to the benefit, which is saving money. However, in this case, that is a secondary benefit: the main benefit is getting fifty TV channels, and the secondary benefit is that the reader can do so for only $2,400 plus a weekend of his or her own labor, instead of the $7,000 to $10,000 the reader is advised it would otherwise cost him or her.

Of course, at $2,400 each, the advertiser does not have to get many orders to make the advertisement pay out. But that is not the point. Even if the advertiser gets a dozen orders from this advertisement and makes a substantial profit from those orders, the advertisement is probably a failure because it is so weak it could probably pull at least three times as many orders as it will.

Remember that the *emotional* appeals are the strongest ones. No doubt everyone likes to get a bargain and to save money by so doing. But the real drive to install such a system—the reason anyone would spend that much money on an antenna system—is to enjoy a choice of fifty channels, pulled in from *all over the world,* and stressing that aspect too, somewhere in the copy, would be a large plus. (A couple of generations ago, amateur radio operators spent large sums of money to talk to other radio amateurs all over the world, and they exchanged cards with each other to document their radio communications successes.)

FINDING THE MOST APPEALING PROMISES

If a great many advertisers fail to appeal to readers with promises in their headlines, a great many more use headlines with promises, but fail to find the best promise to use—the most appealing or most motivating promise. The case of the satellite-antenna manufacturer is only one case, although it is probably an extreme case, where the advertiser failed to even identify a probable motivation on which to base his copy. But there are several factors to think about when deciding on the motivator that the headline will feature:

1. Which of two or more possible promises is the most appealing—is most likely to "strike a nerve"?

2. How can that promise be expressed to make it most dramatic—make it likely to strike a nerve?

3. How can the promise be made most specific, and yet broad enough in its appeal to arrest the attention of many readers?

It's safe to generalize that the headline most likely to strike a nerve with the reader is that which has the greatest emotional component. Always consider this when comparing and co-evaluating alternative promises. Let's look at a few for-instances:

ACCOUNTANTS: START YOUR OWN PRACTICE was one headline we considered a few pages ago. It was not a badly done advertisement, and the headline had appeal and probably did a good job. However, the idea of starting one's own practice is still a bit abstract, and is not a *direct* emotional appeal. In fact, it is a rational appeal, which is the strongest criticism I can make of it, since it is emotion, not reason, that sells goods and services in America. The emotional component—only implied by the copy as written—of having one's own practice is *independence, more money, ego gratification, success, security,* and perhaps even a few other emotional drives. The advertiser who promises that the reader can have his or her own practice hopes that the reader translates that concept into those emotional satisfiers. But why depend on the reader to make the translation? Why not do it directly, along these lines, perhaps:

ACCOUNTANTS: ENJOY INDEPENDENCE
AND SECURITY
IN YOUR OWN PRACTICE

That is the *direct* emotional appeal, designed to strike a nerve, and it should. What human does not dream of being in the driver's seat, of being the star in his or her own field? How can anyone not like the idea of independence and security? (Even though there are some who are afraid to tackle it.)

The next advertisement we looked at began with offering a sample import free, and the promise to show the reader how to make big money part time in a home business involving mail order and importing. The emotional elements in this copy are making money part time, a dream with many people who can't quite make it on their salaries; running a business at home, an appeal to security, because we all feel more secure in our own homes and in our own familiar surroundings; and the import idea is a romantic one that appeals to many people, with its implications of exotic, faraway places. It's good copy, and I would suggest a reordering of the headlines primarily, leading with the promise of earning money in a part-time home business, with the import aspect relegated to second place. And I would offer the free import item in this manner, in a subhead: "Free Import Item, Just for Letting Us Tell You About This Opportunity."

The TRAIN AT HOME FOR A BETTER CAREER advertisement is an almost perfect duplicate of the start-your-own-practice proposition. The basic message is an excellent one, but again the reader is asked to translate that idea of a "better career" into the direct emotional motivators. That is, it is up to the reader, as far as this copy is concerned, to decide what "a better career" means. More money? More security? More job satisfaction? More ego gratification? Would it not have worked a bit better to have helped the reader identify just what "a better career" would mean, such as *more money, bigger job, professional status,* or other such more concrete term?

MALCOMMUNICATION: ITS CAUSE
AND TREATMENT

Nothing reveals more clearly than does advertising how often a prospect gets an entirely different message than the one the sender intended, even when the sender firmly believes that the original message was unmistakably clear and unambiguous. The case of the mentholated-cigarette commercial is a clear illustration of that.

The commercial showed the cigarette package in the background, with a heavy chain stretched across the screen in the foreground. The animation showed the cigarette package rushing forward and bursting through the chain, while the viewer was exhorted to "break the hot smoking habit." (By using this mentholated cigarette, of course.) Perhaps not too surprisingly, the use of the chain to exemplify breaking something was an unfortunate choice. Despite the thundering command to "break the hot smoking habit," an audience used to test the commercial swore that they had been implored to stop chain smoking. The impact of the chain, and especially the dramatic sundering of the chain as the pictured cigarette package smashed through the chain, effectively drowned out the words the audience heard and suggested that familiar chain-smoking metaphor.

Franklin D. Roosevelt reportedly said once that he believed people did not really hear what was said to them in many circumstances, such as in greetings uttered to them at social events. To test his theory and prove its validity, this report goes on, Mr. Roosevelt greeted each guest at one of the formal White House dinners with that famous Roosevelt smile, a handshake, and a murmured, "Good evening. I've just murdered my grandmother."

The report alleges that each guest smiled back and murmured something appropriate to the occasion, but not in response to what the President had really said. Obviously, each guest heard not what Roosevelt had said, but what they *expected to hear,* just as the cigarette commercial test audience heard what they expected to hear, rather than what the narrator said. It's a common enough problem, and has been noted many times in many places. In fact, in military organizations it is taken for granted that there will always be someone who has not "gotten the word" and will therefore manage to screw things up somehow. That does not mean that the instruction did not get down to the individuals who have not "gotten the word," but that at least a few individuals will always misunderstand or fail to understand even the clearest of instructions. It's a human failing to hear what we *expect* to hear and, quite often, what we *want* to hear.

The same phenomenon obtains in written communication.

People tend to read what they expect to read or want to read, instead of what has been written, even when the writing has been crystal clear and unambiguous. But when the writing has been less than crystal clear and unambiguous, the tendency to misread is of course even greater. In fact, I am firmly convinced that the famous Murphy's Law applies directly to the field of written communication and may be stated thus, when applied to written communication, as Holtz's First Law:

> Anything written that can be misunderstood will be.

The original Murphy's Law was extrapolated into a number of corollaries, and I offer this corollary to the above law, as Holtz's Second Law:

> Readers will tend to read what they want to read, what they expect to read, and what has actually been written, in that order of probability.

One way to improve the accuracy of our communication is to base it on the First Law and base our writing on it. To do this, we must always consider the First Law and try to identify all possible misinterpretations of what we have written, and try to make it as difficult to misread and misunderstand as we can. However, that is not the only measure; there are even more effective ones. And these derive from putting the Second Law to work first, and the First Law to work second. That is, write with regard to what the Second Law says, and then self-edit your draft to minimize the impact of the First Law by anticipating the ambiguities and eliminating or at least minimizing the probabilities of misreadings by rewriting.

The logic of this is entirely in keeping with all known principles of sales and advertising, and even with all known rules for success, such as those made almost immortal in Dale Carnegie's now-classic *How to Make Friends and Influence People.* And, fortunately, the principles of communicating clearly are identical with those of persuasion, especially the first rule:

> Tell readers what they want to hear.

Tell readers what they want to hear, what it *pleases* them to hear, and they will "read you loud and clear" (understand you perfectly), they will love you, and they will believe you.

Of course, the reverse is equally true: tell readers what they don't want to hear, and they will have a great deal of trouble understanding you, they will hate you, and they will tend strongly to reject what you say—to disbelieve you.

Both of these phenomena may be put to work in delivering your messages and persuading others to believe you and to do what you urge them to do. And both principles are, in fact, so used by those persons who are truly expert in the field of persuading others.

Take the world of politics, for example, as one with which most of us have at least some familiarity, as we are bombarded with political messages every two years, reaching crescendos every four years. Let's think back to some recent and earlier presidential campaigns, and how the candidates went about communicating their messages and persuading, or failing to persuade, the voters to support their candidacies.

The most recent campaign was that of Ronald Reagan versus Jimmy Carter, with results we all are well aware of now. The issues, as the candidates stated them, were not exactly clear-cut, but in general the challenger ran on his personal image, which was a good one, against the public perception of the incumbent's record of performance, which was an unfortunate one. While Carter tried hard to make the issue one of an inexperienced and unqualified challenger against his own experience of the four years now elapsing, he was really forced to run against his own record—or at least against what the public perceived as his record. And, in a large sense, he defeated himself, partly because of his shortcomings as a speaker, partly because he lacked charisma, which his opponent had some degree of, and partly because he was perceived as a hesitant and indecisive—perhaps even weak—President, whether that was true or not. (Remember, once again, it's not truth but perception or apparent truth that counts in persuasion.) Perhaps the issues counted, too, with inflation and interest rates soaring, so that at least some people were influenced by Reagan's promises to bring those down through conservative fiscal policies, but it is almost surely the poor image of Jimmy Carter as President that defeated him.

Four years earlier, Carter won as the outsider, a new broom that would come to Washington and sweep out all those entrenched interests and act for the people. How influential that argument was will never be known, for again it was a case of an incumbent President defeating himself on the basis of past actions. Primarily, that was Ford's pardon of Nixon, which many objected to violently and thought was evidence of a "deal" between the two men, and partly it was the gaffe about eastern Europe, in the debate with Carter, which reinforced the rumor that Gerald Ford was something considerably less than an intellectual.

In both these cases, then, people apparently voted *against,* rather than *for* a candidate. The public chose *not* to believe that Carter was truly the more able of the two men in 1980. And in 1976 the public refused to believe that Ford was acting sincerely for the public interest in awarding Richard Nixon a pardon.

On the other hand, despite a public debate and arguments about issues, it is likely that John F. Kennedy owed his victory in 1960 primarily to his own likable and charismatic image, which contrasted sharply with the image of Richard Nixon. However, to a large degree, Kennedy ran against Eisenhower's record by charging a "missile gap," an allegation that Eisenhower had permitted the Soviet Union to become superior to us in missile weaponry. If the public accepted and believed that argument at all, it was not because of any hard evidence, because there was none, but because of Kennedy's image. Eisenhower had been a President as respected and admired in that role as he had been in an earlier role as a victorious commanding general. Kennedy therefore wisely refrained from attacking the man and his personal record, pledging only to eliminate the missile gap.

THE EVOLUTION OF PERSUASION STRATEGY

In the cases cited here and in many others too numerous to explore, persuasion was based on either being strongly for or strongly against something; both approaches work, and it is a matter of persuasion strategy to decide which is the more likely to do the job or which offers the strongest motivation for the prospects. It is somewhat reminiscent of an earlier day when the conservative *Chicago Tribune,* under publisher Colonel "Bertie" McCormick, took such extreme positions against things that a Chicago witticism had it that anything the *Chicago Tribune* was against must be "pretty good."

There are, therefore, two basic approaches to evolving a persuasion strategy, the "for" and "against" appeals. Neither of these is superior to the other on anything like an absolute basis, but only in relation to some given set of conditions or circumstances that dictate which approach is likely to be the most advantageous. However, in either case, the factors to consider are at least the following:

Which, if either, has the "natural" advantage, such as already established public image, common prejudice, popular belief, or similar factor

Which approach can be exploited more intensely—is likely to produce the more intense emotional reactions

Which offers the greater number of exploitation opportunities

Which has the lesser possibility of backlash

Which is more difficult for competitor or opponent (if there is such) to counter

Kennedy, for example, did not have any good natural advantages in his campaign against Richard Nixon, for the retiring President Eisenhower was far too popular to attack on his record or on any other basis. On the other hand, Nixon should have enjoyed the natural advantage of having been Eisenhower's Vice-President for eight years, but he was unable to exploit this because Eisenhower refused to give Nixon any direct support. Therefore the alleged missile gap as an issue. It was not the most powerful argument in the world, but it was reasonably safe from the backlash Kennedy might have gotten had he attacked Eisenhower and his incumbent administration more directly. Basically, then, Kennedy ran on a "for" strategy of hope (the "New Frontier" and the "Camelot" themes) and upbeat promises for the future.

On the other hand, fifty years ago Franklin D. Roosevelt ran successfully on both kinds of appeal: because of the Depression already well underway, he could attack the incumbent Herbert Hoover administration for doing nothing effective about it, if not for being the cause, as many chose to believe; and he could and did also use a positive strategy, as his main appeal, of all the things he would do about it. And, of course, Roosevelt had a quite enormous natural advantage in his own striking charisma, which made all his promises somehow believable and made everyone feel that this man really *cared* about their problems and would *do something* about them. (The *perception* again.)

This is, of course, analogous to the fear and greed motivators, with the "against" appeal a fear motivator and the "for" appeal a form of greed motivator—the fear of something versus the desire for something, that is. So the headline that says ACCOUNTANTS: START YOUR OWN PRACTICE is a "for" motivation strategy, appealing to the reader's desire to gain something of value. Of course, it could easily be turned around into a negative fear motivator by using an approach along the lines of ACCOUNTANTS: PROTECT YOURSELF AGAINST LAYOFFS AND UNEMPLOYMENT, which would be against something—against layoffs and unemployment.

Perhaps in a time of economic insecurity and high levels of unemployment, the latter appeal has a natural advantage because of the fear of unemployment. The argument would exploit and utilize the general fear of losing one's job that is in everyone's mind in such times.

The RETIRE BEFORE FIFTY headline offers exactly the same kind of opportunity, where the headline might be along the lines of I BECAME LAYOFF-PROOF AND RETIRED BEFORE I WAS FIFTY. And TRAIN AT HOME FOR A BETTER CAREER could also be turned around to something such as PREPARE YOURSELF FOR AN UNEMPLOYMENT-PROOF CAREER. It's a matter of deciding which appeal will be more effective in striking a nerve and which you can exploit more successfully.

But the same philosophy applies to many other kinds of advertisements. Instead of the positive promise of THICKER, STRONGER, LONGER HAIR, the headline might have offered relief by asking a question, such as IS YOUR HAIR THIN, WEAK, SHORT? and then gone on to make the positive promises or to offer the product as a remedy. This approach has been used in many cases with great success.

The THROWING AWAY $5 PER LB? headline is a negative, "against" strategy, but suffers from that malady of being too vague to enable the reader to react strongly to the message. A more concrete fear headline might have been ARE YOU THROWING AWAY HUNDREDS OF $$ OF SALVAGEABLE SCRAP? Far better a long headline or a headline and subhead than a short headline that doesn't have much of a message in it.

Of course, the satellite antenna is also a natural for the neg-

ative approach. STILL WATCHING ONLY ONE OR TWO TV CHAN-
NELS? is one way to open the subject, and that could be followed
up with a subhead "Here's how to get fifty TV channels."

THE REAL CRUX OF STRATEGY

In advertising, as in political contests, what is really needed
is a main *issue.* Strategy is built around an issue, and although there
may be more than one issue, there ought to be only one main
issue. Every secondary issue detracts somewhat from the main
issue by diluting the appeal based on the main issue. In fact, a
hallmark of amateurism in advertising and related materials is the
tendency to protest too much—to offer too many arguments—
instead of deciding which is the most important argument and
focusing all attention on it.

The problem is often one of determining or deciding what
the main issue is—or ought to be. And therein often lies the heart
of success or failure. The following true story will illustrate this
more emphatically than any discourse of principles could:

Harry happened to bump into a former fellow employee one
day in a New York City restaurant, when Harry was in New York
on business. The friend, Mike, invited Harry to have lunch with
him and his associate, Bill.

"Harry is a crackerjack salesman," Mike explained to Bill, as
he introduced the two to each other. "He brought a lot of business
in, in the old days."

Harry protested. "Not true." He grinned. "Mike is the real
salesman. The best I've ever known. I'm really not a salesman at
all; I just happen to have some talent for psyching out the customer's problem and getting him interested in the way I propose
to solve it."

"That's the difference between us," Mike came back. "You
find the customer's problem and think up a solution. I *give* him
the problem and then offer him the solution."

Both men were right because each was exploiting whatever
his own natural advantages happened to be. Harry was analytical
and could do what he did because of that. Mike had certain services
he specialized in selling, and he called on the companies who were
almost sure to be able to use those services, and he then concentrated on convincing the prospect that he would be in serious

difficulties if he did not take advantage of those special services Mike could and did offer.

To a large degree, advertising is like that: there may or may not be an evident and obvious issue, but if there is not, one can be conjured up, with a little imagination. In fact, it is exactly that which the headline in advertising must address: the issue. For example, the issue in the accountant advertisement, as actually written, is whether the accountant will work for someone else or start his/her own practice. But the issue can be made into the accountant's own practice versus unemployment or, at least, the hazard of possible unemployment. The issues in each of the other headlines used as examples are similarly either the one suggested by the original headline or the one suggested by the changes postulated. But the change in headline is not merely a matter of writing preference; it is a matter of basing the appeal on a different issue. Let's look at a few other advertisements, however—some fresh ones—and see what we can deduce from them about the issues addressed.

The surprising thing is, when I begin to look for examples, that so many advertisements address no issues and appear to have no strategy or theme—at least nothing that I recognize as a strategy. A cigarette commercial features a musician at a xylophone and headlines THERE'S ONLY ONE WAY TO PLAY IT, which is supposed to be an argument for smoking that brand of cigarette, I suppose, but appears to me to be an almost total waste of advertising money, except for whatever benefit can be derived from simply giving the brand name a little exposure. Of course, it is admittedly difficult to find an argument for smoking cigarettes or for choosing one brand over another, except for such contrived issues as the one offering a macho image. Were I faced with the problem of finding a strategy on which to base cigarette advertisements, I would look to the one benefit a cigarette smoker gets: pleasure. And the pleasure of a cigarette (I confess to being one who quit, after many years of heavy smoking) is greatest for most cigarette smokers, I believe, with a drink or a cup of coffee. I can envision a series of print advertisements built around this idea and others, such as having a cigarette while you're together (man and woman over a drink), waiting for someone, or otherwise picturing those moments when a cigarette is most pleasurable or most useful. That's a "for" argument, as compared with the "against" argument the actual advertisement puts up—weakly—in claiming that no other cigarette gives so much taste at so low a tar-content figure. The issue—nonexistent, really, except by vague implication in the actual advertisement—would then be abstention versus pleasure, with pleasure a well-known powerful emotion, likely to overcome fears of being hazardous to one's health.

In passing, it might also be worth noting that almost without exception—the exception being those cigarettes that stress the macho image they associate with smoking their brands—cigarette advertisements are almost interchangeable in their copy, virtually all claiming low tar and great taste nevertheless.

Next, a bottle of whiskey, lying broken on the ground, label readable, and the footline (it's at the bottom of the page): HAVE YOU EVER SEEN A GROWN MAN CRY? A somewhat subtle message, telling the reader that this brand of whiskey is especially precious and breaking a bottle of it by dropping it is almost a tragedy. Almost institutional advertising; it isn't likely to persuade any-one to rush out and buy a bottle of that brand, but it does at least expose the name. Like the cigarette advertisement, it's not easy to find practical arguments for drinking whiskey. Nevertheless, why waste good advertising money by *not even try-ing*? What are the positive emotional things that can be said about whiskey? Whiskey is a drink for pleasure, the pleasure of a pleasant glow. But that's probably best left unsaid; it's a hazardous avenue to explore in print. However, whiskey is also a widespread social custom—cocktails, for example, before dinner or after a hard day at the office. Why not the issue of a harmless social drink versus the stresses of our society, espe-cially our high-stress, high-anxiety business world? Why not a photo of that man and woman who were smoking cigarettes over a cocktail in the cigarette example we just discussed, with a headline to suit—perhaps one that stresses after a hard day at the office.

That latter theme has many possibilities. Depending on the publication in which the advertisement appears, a man, woman, or both—or a crowd of men and women, for that matter—can appear with a variety of headlines, to wit:

AFTER A HARD DAY ON WALL STREET . . .
AFTER A HARD DAY IN COURT . . .

AFTER A HARD DAY IN

THE CONSTRUCTION SHACK . . .

AFTER A HARD DAY OVER THE DRAWING BOARD . . .

A subhead is also possible, to paint the message even more clearly:

RELAX WITH_____

An automobile advertisement has four headlines, each a quote from a publication praising the vehicle. Probably effective, but even so the copywriter missed the boat in at least one respect. Two of the four headlines, which are arrayed one beneath the other, testify that the car is a good one, while the other two testify that it's fun to drive. Guess which type of headline leads: that's right, one that stresses quality. Of course the first and second headlines should be the ones stressing fun to drive—the emotional appeal, addressed as directly to emotions as it is possible to address it. The issue here is hard to identify, with the copy apparently relying on the testimonials for its entire appeal. But it might well have relied on the rather subtle and probably effective issue of fun to drive versus quality, with the advertiser coming out on top no matter which way the reader sees it. The body copy goes on to expound on the car's great features. Were I writing it, I believe that I would go on in the body copy to expand, explore, and exploit the theme: great car, yes, but even more important, *fun to drive.*

Of course, even if the copywriter did not knowingly and openly address an issue, an issue is always implied, however subtly. The problem is that too often it is the wrong issue, an issue, that is, that doesn't help your copy do the job you want it to do. Here's an example of that:

An advertisement for an office copier headlines: EVEN IF IT DIDN'T TALK, IT WOULD LEAVE YOU SPEECHLESS. The headline is another of those tiresome efforts to be clever with a pun or double entendre. The immediate assumption is that the reference to the copier talking is a figure of speech. However, if you read the copy you discover that the machine has actually been designed to play a tape announcing that it's out of paper or advising you that you've forgotten to take your original out of the machine.

In so doing, the copy manages to make the issue one of a copier with an aural alarm system versus one with the conventional signal lights, a rather frivolous issue (certainly, not a prime consideration when investing several thousand dollars in a copier). It's not likely that the advertiser meant to make this the main issue, but the temptation to be clever lured him into it nevertheless.

AIDS TO IDENTIFYING/SELECTING THE ISSUE

Although there are many cases where the circumstances dictate the issue, to at least some degree, there are many cases where you can select the issue or identify the issue you should be basing your copy on. But the issue does not exist in a vacuum, distinct and/or independent of other considerations. In fact, it is closely linked to at least two other considerations: what you are really offering and what the reader wants to believe.

What you are really offering is that same question we have raised before in these pages: what business you are in and what the customer really wants to buy. If you sell cosmetics, you are in the making-people-beautiful business, and it better be beauty you are selling, if you expect people to buy from you. The reader wants to believe that your product will, indeed, make her more attractive; otherwise, there is absolutely no reason to buy your product.

But suppose you are selling a diet plan or a weight-reducing preparation: what business are you in then? Answer: same business—the making-people-beautiful business. Why else does anyone want to lose weight?

There are, in fact, a great variety of products and services you can sell people which, they fondly hope, will help them become more beautiful. It may not be obvious that the publisher of diet information and the seller of diet tablets are in the same business, but they are in the same business, at least in terms of what the customers want. But there are differences, in at least two respects, among these entrepreneurs: the sales arguments can vary considerably, although the main issue is the same—being ugly versus being beautiful. And the approach can be either negative—against being ugly, or positive—for being beautiful. Both will work, although there are variations in how they can be utilized.

Recognize, first, that there are different classes of customers for weight-reduction and dieting offers. There are those who will be attracted to the idea of mechanical devices, usually for exercising; there are those who are on a never-ending search for the perfect easy diet plan, one that will allow them to eat everything they want and still lose weight; there are those who will try any kind of patent preparation to curb appetite, burn up calories, or whatever the advertiser claims; and there are those who will either try all simultaneously or who will go from one to another, in a lifelong, fruitless search for the perfect solution.

In devising issues and appeals, those offering weight reduction can make a straight appeal, with the issue being fat and ugly versus slim and beautiful; or an appeal for whatever is being offered versus any other method for losing weight, the issue being one method versus another or the safety of the method being offered versus the hazards of any other method. And here again it is possible to be "for," stressing the benefits of the method offered, or "against," stressing the hazards of doing it any other way.

In the end, the reader is going to tend strongly to believe what he or she wants to believe. A reader who is prejudiced against "diet candy" is going to resist any offer of such a diet aid, just as anyone who hates physical exertion is going to rationalize arguments against exercising equipment or running. But it is almost always possible to take advantage of what people tend to believe or disbelieve to persuade them to what you want them to believe. Nor is that an anomaly or a contradiction, especially in advertising, for what you want the reader to believe is that what you offer is exactly what he or she needs and wants, and a really clever copywriter can use the reader's own prejudices or biases to demonstrate that as a logical conclusion.

The modus operandi, then, is first to select the end result that you can be reasonably sure every reader wants—or, at least, is not against. It is that which you must promise—the result. You must next decide how you can make that promise believable, in fact, almost impossible not to believe it. This is the issue around which you must build your strategy. After that you add the other credibility factor—your dependability as a source of supply—and the instruction, to tell the reader what to do next as the means for gaining that great benefit you promised in the beginning.

If we apply that kind of analytical reasoning to some of the advertisements we have reviewed together here, here are some of the conclusions we must come to:

The main thing being sold in that retire-before-fifty advertisement is security. Success, too, but success only as a means to security. Security is the end result promised, at least by implication in that headline and in the advertisement. It is made believable by furnishing a photograph and name of a man who reports his experience as evidence to support the advertiser's promise that anyone can do what the protagonist of that story did—build a business and retire before fifty or, at least, in ten years, as the protagonist did.

This advertiser could offer other end results, other issues, and he does in other advertisements—a solid, home-based business, a steady income, a good living, and other benefits—but the chief end result he chooses to focus on is the security of being able to retire with an income for the rest of one's life. So this is a case where the advertiser chose the issue and built his advertising strategy and copy around it.

The accountant advertisement is along the same lines, but doesn't use the issue of retirement as the main strategy. This advertiser chooses to focus on the advantages (security?) of your own business as his issue—your own business versus working for someone else—and leaves it to the reader to translate this as an appeal to gain the security of your own enterprise. Again, the advertiser chose the issue—he could have selected another, as the first one did—and his plea for believability is the book he offers free (obviously this is the follow-up direct-mail package offering whatever it is he wants to sell) and a pledge of help from experienced professionals.

What is most important in deciding on the issue, if the issue is not thrust on you but you have a choice, is the emotional appeal. The issue ought to be emotional, and the appeal will then be emotional. Security, for example, is an emotional factor. Of course, reason tells us that we ought to always seek security, but the real *drive* for security is an emotional one. And we all have that drive, but it is expressed differently in each of us, and that is a clue to how to select a proper issue. Here, for example, is how different people view security:

Some people believe that security is a matter of having the right job. A government job, for example, represents security to many people, but to others only a job in the military—army, navy, or air force—is really security. But there are many who believe that a job with any large company is security. Conversely, a job in certain trades or with certain kinds of companies is never secure—construction, for example, is a hire-and-fire (lay-off) business. Consequently, there are those who would rather earn $12,000 in a bank than $25,000 on a construction job because they perceive the job in the bank as more secure.

Some people doubt that any job is secure, but believe that their own independent business represents security. Some of these people will give up a good job to start their own enterprise, as a result of this kind of reasoning.

Some people see insecurity in their lack of highly specialized skills, and will undertake special training courses to acquire more specialized skills, in the belief that the latter will provide security.

And there are some who think that there is really no security in anything except their own wits and will to survive, and are therefore motivated by direct gain and never by visions of long-term security.

Consequently, the most motivational appeal—the most intense emotional appeal, that is—reminds the prospect of concerns about security, but does so as directly as possible. And if you want to touch all the bases, strike a nerve with most readers who are concerned about their security, you have to do it by first the generalized appeal to the emotional drive for security and then supporting arguments that address each subgroup in terms that are meaningful to each group. If, for example, you offer training in some form or other, you might devise a headline and general theme that says something such as TRAIN FOR A SECURE FUTURE. But you must then explain what you mean by "a secure future," and that means addressing all the above-described individuals. You have to explain that it is the trained individual who gets the solid, dependable job in the government or in a major corporation. It is the trained individual who doesn't need to worry greatly about a job: his or her skills make him or her independent and able to always find a job. But having skills enables one to also begin one's own enterprise, and become secure that way. And still another argument shows that the training produces an immediate boost in income, but operating an independent business can lead to wealth.

In short, then, while everyone or almost everyone has concerns about security, few will translate whatever you offer into their own terms which represent security to them. You have to do that, and you have to understand that each prospect has a different idea about it.

Every writer needs empathy, the ability to perceive the matter from the reader's viewpoint. The able writer understands that there is a universe of readers out there, with many different interests or different interpretations of what affects their interests and how their interests are affected. Good copywriters have well-developed empathic abilities and sensitivities.

ON CLEVERNESS AND SUBTLETIES

With only rare exception, advertising is no place for subtlety, and the many examples of clever plays on words are an even more futile activity than is subtlety in writing advertising copy. When you are paying as much as $5 to $10 per word—and sometimes even more—for having your advertising copy appear in some publication, cleverness can be an expensive indulgence. When you are tempted to be clever or subtle, remember that even when you are trying to be as crystal clear and unambiguous as possible, that immutable law is at work:

Anything written that can be misunderstood will be.

Imagine, then, what disasters that law works for you when your copy is clever and subtle. When you offer a window-caulking compound with the headline WINDOW DRESSING or an aerosol can of spray paint with the headline FINGER PAINT. Or an advertisement for jeans, the photograph focused on the rear pockets and the headline HOW TO PICK A POCKET. All clever ideas and all clever plays on words but not clever advertising strategies.

The problem with these advertisements and others like them—and we've looked at several other clever headlines in these pages—is that they rely on the reader reading and understanding the body copy to make any sense of the headline. And, unfortunately, there is absolutely no guarantee that the reader will even read, let alone understand, that body copy.

First of all, the headline must motivate the reader to want to read the body copy, to be interested in what the advertisement is all about. Take that WINDOW DRESSING copy, for example. The photo is of a hand holding a cartridge of caulking compound. The advertiser expects the photograph to aid the reader in understanding the cleverness of the WINDOW DRESSING headline, and to be motivated to read the body copy. Vain hope: the headline gives the reader no reason to be interested in reading further.

The FINGER PAINT copy is illustrated with a photograph of the spray can in a hand with a forefinger on the button, to show the cleverness of the headline. And HOW TO PICK A POCKET has a good sales argument in its body copy, but the headline doesn't lead to it, except by some tortuous path of reasoning, which the reader is not likely to follow, let alone be guided to and through by the headline.

Even when a reader does read the body copy of some of these too-too clever advertisements, the result is often confusion: even the ablest of readers may ask what the relationship of the headline is to the rest of the copy or what the headline has to do with anything of importance. For example, the advertisement for the copier was self-indulgence: the advertiser was so proud of his gimmick, the audio-tape alarm, that he forgot it was only a gimmick and not something really important *to the customer.* It's so easy to forget the customer when you're busy thinking up ways to pat yourself on the back and showing others how to be so clever. Straining to create a subtle or clever headline, the copywriter is now trapped into writing something ineffective in order to work that headline into the advertisement. It's a case of the tail wagging the dog: even when cleverness is a natural fallout of an effective strategy, it is a highly questionable tactic, but when it is dragged in by the ears, it is almost certainly a high-speed turnpike to disaster.

In short, then, it is safer to make it a firm rule to avoid like the plague clever plays on words, and be extremely wary of any kind of cleverness or humor. Both are deadly weapons when they don't work, and they do not work very often. Amusing readers is not the same as selling them, and is often directly contrary to your best interests as an advertiser.

SUMMARY

We've covered a lot of territory in this chapter, and if you're a bit confused at this point, let's recapitulate and sum up the key points:

1. Consider the prospect's needs and problems, and devise a strategy that addresses these directly.

2. Every good advertisement revolves around an *issue* and offers to resolve it for the reader.

3. A headline must do more than get attention; it has to arouse interest as well, and motivate the reader to read the rest of the advertisement, but it should deliver the basic promise of benefit to provide that motivation.

4. We humans are motivated primarily by our emotional needs and drives, and a good headline addresses our emotional needs and drives and makes emotional appeals—appeals that strike nerves.

5. Advertising is no place to be cute, clever, or subtle. It's a place to decide exactly where you wish to go with your copy, and go there directly.

6. Decide what is important to the customer—not to you—when you are deciding on strategy and appeals.

6

HOW TO WRITE
SALES PROPOSALS

A few years ago, proposal preparation was a routine function of a sales department, assembled principally by clerks. But today proposal writing is a sine qua non of many kinds of companies and even of entire industries.

PROPOSALS ARE NOT WHAT
THEY USED TO BE

THERE WAS A TIME when a sales proposal was little more than a bid—a quoted price—accompanied by specifications and contract terms. If the sale called for something to be built on a custom basis—a building, a machine, or some other custom-designed end product—there would probably be a drawing or two, also. But in many cases, the "specifications" really consisted of a standard printed brochure describing the product.

For example, suppose you planned to open a restaurant and you asked the various suppliers to submit proposals to satisfy your needs. A supplier of kitchen equipment would probably sketch a layout of the kitchen you have had or are having built, with indications of what equipment and fixtures go in all the spaces, and would enclose a number of brochures covering the various items, along with a price breakdown and relevant information about delivery, installation, and other such details.

Even today a request for proposals brings forth much the same kind of response in the commercial world, especially when the services or products required are more or less standard commercial items, even if they have to be assembled in a custom-designed configuration or system. However, this is no longer typical of responses to requests for proposals, except in such situations as the one hypothesized here, where the customer is buying standardized commercial items or services for relatively small and simple, routine projects. And in many situations today, such as in selling custom products and services to governments and subcontracting to major government contractors—or even in commercial sales but in pursuit of large contracts—a buyer requesting proposals expects to receive a rather formal document that presents a great deal more information than specifications, prices, and contract terms. In fact, for many businesses and even for complete industries today, proposal writing has become a major marketing activity, with marketing success depending heavily on proposal-writing skills. This is especially true of those companies that are suppliers to the government of the United States, with major emphasis on those which support the Department of Defense and all its military services.

There are many factors that have brought this change about, but probably the largest impetus to this was supplied by that same DOD—Department of Defense—as DOD began to seek high-technology companies to develop and create the modern weapons systems of the post–World War II era. It was soon painfully apparent that all our magnificent new systems—radar, rockets, high-speed jets, lasers, computers, missiles, nuclear weapons, and other such Buck Rogerish developments—were swiftly outmoded and had to be constantly replaced by new and improved generations of scientific marvels. And it was clear, also, that developing these marvelous new systems and thus keeping at least a step ahead of our Soviet competitor was a far from routine task. It required highly specialized suppliers, companies who had large and well-organized staffs of scientists and engineers, with all the ultramodern facilities for scientific research. Military procurement had reached a point where as far as weapons and other operational equipment were concerned, price was of secondary importance: technical capability was of primary importance. Hence, the selection of a contractor for any of these modern R&D (research and development) contracts must depend on some means for determining which supplier was best qualified to carry out the work successfully and produce the best result. At that point, the objective in writing a proposal was no longer trying to appear to be the lowest bidder or the fastest supplier: it was necessary to demonstrate that you were the *best* supplier. For it was soon apparent that contracts were going to those who wrote the best proposals, who may or may not have been the best contractors. And that is very much the situation today: those who write the best proposals, because they *appear* to be the best-qualified contractors, win the awards.

PERCEPTIONS OF THE CUSTOMER STILL COUNT MOST

A basic principle of marketing and advertising has already appeared in these pages several times: what the customer wishes to buy, as well as from whom, depends on what the customer perceives as the facts.

Again and again, as we discuss sales proposals and how to make them work for you—what makes one more persuasive than another—the same consideration will surface: how to control what the reader of the proposal perceives. He who controls and shapes that perception best wins the contract.

HOW MANY KINDS OF PROPOSALS

We have spoken of two general kinds of proposals in the most general of terms: the proposal that is really little more than a bid or quotation and a packet of commercial brochures, and the proposal that has as its main objective demonstrating to the customer's satisfaction that the proposer is the best-qualified contractor among all those competing for the contract. But we are not going to pursue further examination of the former document because it is not really a proposal, and it depends for persuasion almost entirely on price, so it is not really of interest here. But as to the other kind of proposal, that kind we are really interested in discussing here, we can break it down in several ways:

There are formal and informal proposals, with an informal proposal usually a "letter proposal," consisting of little more than a letter of a few pages, with costs quoted, and the formal proposal, ranging from a few pages to literally thousands of pages for major systems contracts.

There are proposals for products, and there are proposals for services.

There are proposals for commercial or standardized products and/or services, and there are proposals for highly specialized, custom-designed products and/or services.

There are solicited proposals and there are unsolicited proposals.

There are proposals for one-time projects and there are proposals for ongoing services and/or products stretching to one or more years.

And even in these several categories proposals may vary considerably. But let us consider first a U.S. government request for proposals and how a supplier might respond with a proposal of more or less typical size and scope. This will give us the basis for examining and understanding proposal writing in general.

HOW PROPOSAL REQUESTS ARE BORN

The customer we hypothesize here is one based on an actual organization in Washington, D.C., carefully disguised to permit me to take some liberties with it. But that is for a good cause: to help you understand why and how proposals come about. This is the Office of Training and Education of the Department of Public Buildings. The head of this office, Dr. Horace E. Reflex, has detected an urgent need concerning newly hired training planners. The problem is that many of these new hires were not experienced and perhaps not even fully qualified for the positions, but they were hired under official socioeconomic programs, and it's up to OTE—Dr. Reflex's office—to make satisfactory use of them.

Dr. Reflex calls in his second in command, Pete Harvey, and says, "Pete, we got the budget we asked for for the training planners' project. Let's get going and get a contract started to carry out the project."

Pete knows what he has to do. He has to prepare a statement of work to tell the proposers what has to be done, and get the contracting officer to help him get the thing going. Once Pete writes or gets someone to write that work statement, he and the contracting officer will talk and decide what kind of contract they'll offer the proposers. But they'll also have to tell the proposers in their RFP—Request for Proposals—what information is required in the proposals, how the proposals will be evaluated to find a winner, and anything else they believe the proposers need to know, if they are to respond properly.

Typically, the OTE will ask proposers to submit a proposal that covers at least the following:

The proposer's understanding of the requirement, to demonstrate that the proposer does, indeed, understand what is wanted

A discussion of the requirement which covers any anticipated problems or difficulties, what the proposer would do about these, and what approach the proposer believes is most appropriate

The proposer's specific response and program designed to satisfy the requirement, including such matters as schedules and end items to be delivered

Resumes of the principal members of the staff proposed for the project

The proposer's qualifications to handle the contract satisfactorily

OTE will evaluate each proposal submitted, awarding specific points for such items as the quality (qualifications) of the staff proposed, the proposer's qualifications as an organization, the practicality of the program proposed, and other technical matters. Cost will also be evaluated, of course, although usually as a secondary consideration.

TWO BASIC REASONS FOR PROPOSAL REQUESTS

There are two reasons or two situations that lead to government agencies issuing RFPs—requesting contractor assistance, that is, or "contracting out," as it is known in some government circles:

1. The agency has a problem that it cannot solve itself for any of many possible reasons—not enough resources, not the right kind of resources, not the kinds of specialists available, for example. Ergo, this is a problem-solving requirement.

2. The agency has a need for more staff—more "hands and feet"—than it has on its own staff. Usually, this is a requirement for a number of specialists, such as engineers, computer programmers, or technical writers.

Both requirements pose a problem the agency needs to solve by contracting out, but the agency knows how to solve the second type of problem; it simply doesn't have the resources. Moreover, the second type of requirement may be to have the contractor do something that requires that staff of specialists, but on the contractor's premises, or it may be a need for the contractor to supply the specialists to work on the customer's premises, as in the case of operating the customer's computer installation.

WHAT THE CONTRACTOR DOES WITH THE RFP

This is the usual sequence of events that takes place after a contractor receives a copy of the government's request for proposals:

1. Reads, studies RFP, makes bid/no-bid decision, drops if no-bid; organizes proposal effort if decision is to bid.
2. Proposal staff (usually an ad hoc team) analyzes RFP, decides on what customer wants/needs, formulates approach and strategy, writes proposal.
3. Contractor's management reviews, comments on draft proposal, especially costs estimates; directs final revisions.
4. Staff makes final changes, revisions, produces final copy of proposal in quantity stipulated by customer, delivers and awaits customer final decisions.

What concerns us here primarily is that item 2, so casually dismissed in a single telegraphic sentence, for that is the heart of the problem and the bulk of the work in developing a proposal. And what we are going to address is the development and writing of the proposal as an exercise in persuasive writing.

WHAT IS A PROPOSAL?

The question "What is a proposal?" elicits many answers. The one answer it does not elicit often enough, not even from those who ought to be able to supply this answer is this: a *proposal* is a sales presentation.

The objective of customers in requesting proposals is to furnish themselves a basis for deciding which is the best contractor for their purposes. The objective of the contractor in responding with a proposal is to persuade the customer that he or she is the best contractor for the purpose. While there are many aspects to proposal writing in particular and government contracting in general, we will address here only those matters that pertain more or less directly to what makes a proposal persuasive or what detracts from the persuasiveness of a proposal. We will therefore not address the mechanics of government marketing, nor the forms used in proposal preparation, but only those factors that make the proposer more or less attractive to the customer as a contractor.

Restricted to those matters, what we notice first is that proposal writing follows the identical principles of selling and advertising. The application and articulation of those principles are necessarily different because the entire situation is different, but the principles of sales persuasion are not different. People who work in government agencies react very much as anyone else does to persuasive strategies and tactics, and that is perhaps the first lesson of proposal writing, one that some individuals appear to have trouble in grasping: *people* buy for the government, and they are not different from any of the rest of us. They respond to the same kinds of appeals, and they are "turned off" by the same kinds of gaffes, in general. But they are also individuals, and what motivates one does not motivate another, and this too must be considered in writing proposals.

Answering the question posed here is therefore not quite as simple as defining a proposal as a sales presentation, for a proposal is also an offer and it is a promise, and the failure to recognize those truths is often the fatal weakness in proposals. The simple fact is that in a large sense a proposal is everything an advertisement or a sales letter is, except even more so because a proposal is sharply focused on a single offer to a single customer, rather than on a general offer to a universe of potential customers.

THE DEADLY SINS OF PROPOSAL WRITING

In most activities, it soon becomes apparent that there are certain common shortcomings—even mistakes made by individuals appear to be endemic in the field. You find the same things happening over and over, the same problems recurring regularly. And so it is with proposal writing. Here are some of the common failings that are responsible for as many as two of every three proposals written to be rejected swiftly, even after a cursory reading:

Many proposals appear to be saying, "I'm not at all sure I know exactly what it is you want, but whatever it is, if you'll just pay the price I ask I'll do whatever it is that you want done."

Failure to demonstrate a true understanding of what the customer wants is most common. And a smug assurance that whatever the problem is, the proposer will handle it runs that first problem a close second for the frequency with which it appears.

However, there is also the common problem of proposals that offer a solution for a different problem than the one the customer wants solved. That is, there are myriads of proposers who read into the RFP what they want to see there. (It isn't only customers who operate according to Holtz's First and Second Laws, expressed in the previous chapter.) And having read what they wanted to read, rather than what the customer wrote, the proposer proposes a solution to the wrong problem.

Sometimes this is because the proposer has several successful solutions up his or her sleeve, and is almost desperately seeking problems to match the solutions he or she has. It's so much easier to cope with problems you have ready-made solutions for, something like deciding to search for the coin you dropped where the light is best, rather than where you dropped it.

Whatever the cause, a surprising number of proposers do manage to misread RFPs. Of course, many RFPs are not well written, and this makes it quite easy to misread them. But that is a hazard of the game, and we'll discuss that, too, in a few minutes.

Another most common problem that is usually disastrous to a proposal's chances for success is a reluctance to be absolutely specific, for fear that commitment is unwise. Again and again, proposers deliberately—although sometimes it is almost instinctive and so not entirely a conscious act—employ somewhat evasive tactics in proposals. Their theory is that commitment is hazardous, for more than one reason: 1) The customer may not agree with what you propose, so it seems as though it would be wise to be somewhat elusive and not too specific; 2) it is sometimes difficult to forecast what you can and cannot do, so it can be hazardous to make promises that are too specific: suppose you can't deliver on those promises?; and 3) many proposers are quite uncertain about their estimates and price quotations, and so are afraid that commitment will leave them no escape routes should they underestimate something.

Somewhat akin to the foregoing idea is the tendency of some proposers to be "polypharmacal," after the fashion of some physicians (especially those of the days when the pharmacist truly compounded prescriptions, instead of soaking labels off already-compounded preparations) who wrote prescriptions with many ingredients, with the rationale that with so many things in the prescription, *something* ought to work and help the patient recover. So in writing proposals, some proposers promise just about everything, with hope that the customer will like *something* well enough to award the proposer a contract.

Another problem that plagues some proposal writers is an overdose of modesty. Or perhaps it isn't really modesty per se, but the fear that if the proposal praises the proposer too highly, it will appear to be in bad taste and prove offensive.

Even more common, however, is the tendency to go the other way and lather the proposal heavily with exaggerated claims and hyperbole, without the slightest shred of evidence that any of it is justified. In fact, some proposers seem to have gotten that old TV western gunslinger's idea backwards. He warned off those who would challenge him by explaining how deadly he was with a gun, and said calmly, "No brag; just fact." But some proposal writers appear to be offering no facts; just brag. And that is as deadly as any of the several other chronic mistakes proposal writers make.

THE BASIC *MUSTS* OF PROPOSALS

If the "deadly sins" just enumerated are what not to do, there ought to be a corresponding set of things to do, and these ought to turn out to be somewhat the inverse of the things not to do. There are, in fact, *do's* as well as *don'ts,* and they are really what the rest of this chapter is all about. Let's enumerate them briefly here before we discuss them:

• Do study the customer's requirement thoroughly before you begin to write, and be sure that you do understand exactly what he or she wants.

• Do exercise the greatest care that you address what the customer says he or she wants, not what you happen to think he or she ought to have. (There are exceptions to this, but this is the general truth.)

• Do cast off any ideas about modesty and confess your real abilities and achievements, but through presenting facts, not brag.

A current issue of a business magazine carries a short story about a man named Howard Rohrlick. He was a seller of audio-visual equipment—a salesman on a company's payroll—a few years ago. One thing about slide projectors that customers found annoying was the abrupt changes of light level at every slide change, for which there was a cure but one that was too expensive for most people; the problem was annoying but didn't justify major investment to overcome it.

Rohrlick believes in one of the most sound principles of selling ever enunciated: a salesperson ought to be a consultant, not selling things to people, but solving problems for them. And so he set about solving this problem and eventually did so, thereby launching a new venture, which is not relevant to the point made here. What is relevant is that idea of selling by helping the customer solve problems. For that is what selling is all about: in most cases, a customer is addressing a problem, with every purchase, and can usually be induced to buy whatever appears to be the best way to solve the problem of the moment.

This is true whether you are helping a customer solve the problem of hunger by inviting him or her to select his or her own steak from the refrigerated window or selling a better transistor to an electronics manufacturer to solve a technological problem of some sort. Really successful salespeople are not shown the door or dodged and evaded by their customers; they are welcomed because they always approach every sale with a "what problem can I help you solve today?" attitude. Nor is this a new idea even in these pages, for we have already discussed the importance of "I" and "me," to all customers. Being a "consultant" whenever you are attempting to persuade someone to what you believe or want the other to do is simply a way of saying, "Let's talk about *you* and *your* needs or problems." Do this and the other party will recognize you as a brilliant conversationalist, as well as a most reasonable, likable, and convincing talker. No one will find it easy to resist you, either in face-to-face conversation or in reading what you have written, if you talk about him or her.

If this is important in general advertising, it is even more so in proposal writing, for a proposal is expected to address a specific problem or need of an individual person or organization. If an individual person or organization has asked you directly to study a need or problem and propose a way to satisfy it, how can you fail to concentrate on the requestor's need? (Although a surprising number of proposal writers still find it possible to focus almost entirely on how clever and capable they are, rather than on a proposed solution to the customer's problem.)

It is therefore a must that you make the customer's need the main topic of your proposal, and make it almost painfully clear that everything in your proposal is offered in terms of how it contributes to satisfying the customer's need. Not only must you never lose sight of the need to keep your eye on the ball—the customer's need—at all times, but you must keep the customer aware of this at all times by appropriate references made frequently enough so that the customer is not permitted to think that you have at any time lost sight of the goal: satisfying his or her need.

NEEDS VERSUS PROBLEMS

The point has been made that customers issuing requests for proposals sometimes have a specific problem they need help in solving, but sometimes simply need support services. In the first instance, the RFP can only describe the problem or its symptoms. In the second situation, the RFP describes the customer's need as the customer sees it, specifying the required services, generally. To illustrate this, here are examples of the two situations:

The U.S. Postal Service had computerized its payroll on a large computer at a central facility. The problem was that the program was taking up almost a week of computer time to run, whereas it should have been able to run it in a few hours. An RFP asked for a contractor to rectify the situation, but it was left to the contractor to propose an approach—modifying the existing program versus writing a new program, for example, or whatever the proposer thought appropriate as an approach to solving the problem. The Postal Service did not venture to specify what it thought the remedy should be, but offered the proposers the problem and invited their ideas as to how to proceed to solve it.

Other examples of RFPs that describe problems to be solved, instead of more or less routine services to provide, are those that call for new technological advances, such as better weapons systems and instrumentation for space satellites, and those that ask for the design and development of training programs.

On the other hand, when a NASA center wants a contractor to assign and manage a staff to work at the center and catalog parts used in the various pieces of equipment at the center, that is a "hands and feet" kind of requirement, in which the customer can tell the proposer precisely what is needed. And this is true of many procurements, whether the staffs will work on the government's premises or on the contractor's premises. Typical of such requirements, for example, was one from an army engineering group at Fort Belvoir, Virginia, which called for "reverse engineering," which is the preparation of engineering drawings from the equipment itself, rather than from a theoretical design. Here, the customer makes the equipment available to the contractor, who disassembles it and prepares the drawings by measuring and examining the components and the assemblies.

The difference between these two kinds of requirements is that the first kind calls for the contractor literally to solve problems of one kind or another, technical or otherwise. The proposal must recognize this and describe an approach or methodology to be used to solve the problem successfully. The second kind of requirement, however, calls for a proposal that responds directly to the customer's perceived need and demonstrates the methodology proposed to do exactly what the customer wants done.

In a large sense, both are problems. If they were not, the customer would not be seeking help. The real difference is simply that the customer knows the answer to the problem of his or her needs and can tell the proposer what to do—can *specify* the solution—in the second case; whereas he or she can only describe the problem or its symptoms in the first case, and must then rely on the proposer to propose a method for finding the solution.

It is, of course, important to recognize these truths in responding to the customer with a proposal. It is particularly important that the *tone* of the proposal be appropriate, in one instance "Here is how we are going to go about finding the right answer for you," and in the other instance "Here is how we are going to go about supplying precisely what you have asked for." So in each case there is a "problem": In one case it is the problem of how best to supply exactly what the customer wants, which may not be an easy or routine requirement to satisfy. But in the other case, it entails really *two* problems: the problem the customer has dropped on us to solve, and the problem of how to organize the effort and approach the task of solving it.

So when we talk about "understanding the problem" (or failing to understand the problem, for that matter), we are not necessarily talking about a problem posed by a customer to be solved by us; we may be and often are talking about the problem of how to satisfy the requirement, even when the requirement is for some more or less routine set of services, such as writing a manual or developing a computer program. For example, if the customer wants someone to supply a dozen computer programming specialists, there is the problem of where and how to recruit the right people, if the proposer cannot supply them all from incumbent staff. And if these people are to work on the customer's premises, the problem is considerably different than it would be if these people were to work on the contractor's premises.

It is important, too, to recognize and bear in mind at all times that the very question of what is a *need* and what is a *problem* depends on a variable, a viewpoint, in fact, for a need is always a problem to someone else. A customer may perceive a need for a training program, but the individual to whom the job of producing the program is assigned has a problem immediately, and he or she may pass that problem on to a contractor, although calling it a "need" or "requirement." But that doesn't change the fact that the customer has solved his problem by changing it to a need and passing the need on as a requirement to a contractor, to whom it has now become a problem.

This may appear to be merely playing a game of semantics, toying with words, and perhaps it is in a sense. But in terms of selling—of developing a *persuasive* proposal—the distinctions are important for at least this reason: treating any requirement or need as a problem makes a number of advantages immediately available to the proposer, and in the pages to follow we'll explore why this is true and how to exploit it.

THE NEED FOR AN *ISSUE*

If there is a need for an issue in a sales or advertising presentation generally, the need is even more acute in a proposal, for the entire selling situation is sharply focused. Whereas in a general sales or advertising presentation you are generally addressing a universe of potential customers—thousands and perhaps even millions of prospects—in a sales proposal you are addressing only one prospect. If you are less than completely effective in an advertising campaign, you will not get as many orders as you could have and should have gotten, but you will get some orders, in all probability, perhaps even enough to turn a profit. But in a proposal situation, you can only win or lose; there is no second-place or third-place award. (Occasionally a proposal request may be issued with the intention of awarding more than one contract, but this is the exception; ordinarily it's an all-or-nothing proposition.)

There is one other major difference. In an advertising or general sales campaign you usually have many competitors, but they are not all direct competitors, pursuing the same prospects for the same dollars. Or, at least, if you are clever enough with your copy, you can avoid having the prospects *perceive* you as being in direct competition with others, by finding and offering some unique feature of whatever benefit promises you make. But in a proposal competition, you cannot even avoid the appearance of being in direct competition with others, for you are admittedly pursuing the same contract as your competing proposers are. This too accentuates the need for an issue on which you can base your sales strategy. In fact, if you succeed in finding the right issue, you can often demonstrate that your proposal is unique in what it offers.

WHY YOU NEED AN ISSUE

One of the deadliest mistakes a proposal writer can make is to appear to be saying, "Me, too." Again and again, especially with proposals calling for some clearly identified and specified set of services, losing proposals are those that demonstrate that their writers are as well qualified as anyone else to do the job, and base their "strategy" entirely on loud claims of superior abilities to do the job as well as anyone else can do it.

Consider this: there are a number of competitors submitting proposals. There may be only a few, three or four, or there may be many, fifty to a hundred (not at all unusual in many circumstances). If everyone bases his or her proposal on that "argument" of me-too-but-I'm-better, the best any proposer is likely to do is to "get in the hat"—to make a raffle instead of a quality competition of the situation. Obviously, that isn't good enough when you consider the expense and risk of writing a proposal, an expensive sales effort at best. You need something to distinguish your proposal, to give you an edge. You need a *strategy*. And unless there is a ready-made issue in the situation, you have to find or create an issue on which to base your strategy. Proposals win on issues, just as political choices are made on issues. Here are some examples:

The late Frank Bettger, who made himself into a crackerjack, almost legendary insurance salesman, often worked on wealthy executives who were compelled to consider taking out major insurance policies to protect their large estates, but who were, of course, being pursued by many other insurance salesmen. Bettger devised a clever strategy that enabled him to outflank his competitors, by creating an issue and offering a solution for it, to wit: he would pay his second or third call on his prospect and say something such as this: "Mr. Smith, in these uncertain times, a man in your position can't afford to be another day without the protection for his family that is available. Mr. Smith, I can do something for you that no one else in the world can do for you."

This latter pronouncement, made after a dramatic pause and with proper emphasis, never failed to startle "Mr. Smith" into blurting, "What's that?"

"I can have you covered within less than one hour, Mr. Smith," was Bettger's response. "I've arranged for your physical this morning, and the doctor is already waiting for you. If you'll get your hat and come with me, we'll attend to this entire matter in a few minutes and let you get back to your business."

The Postal Service asked for proposals to train maintenance technicians in its new bulk-mail plants, an apparently routine requirement. The successful proposer raised the issue of knowing what to train the maintenance technicians to do, since the equipment to be maintained was almost entirely of new and virtually untried design, offering a methodology for making the determinations. That proposer thereby turned what was an apparent request for routine work into a problem-solving undertaking, calling for specialized skills and abilities.

The Environmental Protection Agency requested proposals to assist its staff in the Pesticide Registration program, especially in the area of computer data processing, but not confined to that. Superficially, the project appeared to require technically specialized, but yet more or less routine services. However, the successful proposer made an issue of the difficulty of getting the right people because they were so specialized technically and professionally— computer scientists, chemists, biochemists, and other scientists— and offered as a solution a highly sophisticated and thoroughly detailed recruiting plan.

HOW TO IDENTIFY OPPORTUNITIES TO RAISE ISSUES

Identifying the need to make a study and search for an issue is relatively easy. But when the request itself entails no special problems, that is, when it appears to be a request to propose some rather well-defined and routine work or deliver some rather routine custom product, you have difficulties in devising a sales strategy on which to base your proposal. And a sales strategy is, so that we have no misunderstanding about it, an argument for awarding you the contract, for selecting your proposal as the best one. It is a reason for the customer to buy from you, and make no mistake about this: it is necessary to tell the customer why he or she should buy from you, to *sell* your proposal. So if the nature of the requirement, as explained in the request for proposals, is such that it does not itself raise or suggest an issue, you must find one or create one. You must therefore search for opportunities to raise important issues.

It is necessary that the issue be an important one, of course. A trivial issue will not do much for you. Certainly, it won't influence the customer unduly. What you need is an issue that goes to the heart of the customer's requirement and affects the probable success or failure of the entire project. The most effective issues you can raise are those that persuade the customer that success depends on resolving these issues properly. Or, at least, that something highly important about the project, such as its cost or the degree of its success, hinges on successful resolution of the issue.

Consider the three examples offered earlier:

Bettger raised the issue of the danger of delaying further, but had a solution ready and immediately available.

The proposer to the Postal Service raised the issue of possibly—even probably—training the maintenance technicians in the wrong things, and then offered a method to avoid the problem and ensure proper training.

The proposer to the Environmental Protection Agency pointed out that because so many people with such highly specialized credentials were needed, the real issue was the ability to produce these specialists. (Many would have to be made available as consultants, rather than as permanent employees.) The proposal then offered a carefully designed and persuasive plan to ensure the recruitment and availability of these people.

Finding the issue, then, entails study of what the contractor must do and what problems are most likely to be encountered. Any problem that appears to be real enough and threatens the success or some important factor of the project becomes a suitable candidate to be raised as an issue. If several problems are anticipated, that which is the most serious threat to the success of the project is the one to base the proposal on. If there are other issues—problems—to be solved, these should be subordinated to the main issue, and care must be taken that the impact of the main issue is not diluted and weakened by introducing a plethora of issues—a polypharmacal approach.

This is a fear approach, and it turns out that fear is the most often available motivator in proposals, for while success is the main objective of the requestor (naturally enough), custom projects inevitably, by their very nature, entail risks of failure. A custom project is one attempting to do something nonroutine and, quite often, something that has never been done before. The risk in undertaking to do that which has never been done before is obvious, and may be made the focal point of the persuasive arguments. That is, instead of focusing the proposal upon the certainty of success per se, it is often more effective from the persuasion viewpoint to focus the argument on the serious hazards—the risk of failure—and on methods for avoiding failure.

There are at least three good reasons for using this negative, avoidance-of-failure strategy when the opportunity presents itself:

1. Raising the specter of possible failure is a direct attack on the customer's worst fears and strikes home with enormous impact, when done convincingly enough.

2. It is usually different from what your competitors use as strategy, and so distinguishes your proposal and gets it special attention. It carefully and forcefully avoids the me-too tone.

3. It is a flank attack on any competitor who makes glib promises of success, and tries to assure the customer, quite smugly, that he or she (the proposer) can't miss and will certainly do a bang-up job. If you have done your work well in your proposal, you virtually compel the customer to study all competitive proposals closely and to entertain doubts about those which assure the customer that the proposer will encounter no problems at all.

There is at least one other excellent reason for using this strategic approach, and it is this: confessing frankly to the customer that there are hazards and these ought to be recognized and faced up to from the beginning is an honest-sounding approach, which is itself something of a rarity in proposals and selling in general. Of itself it is an impressive attack for that reason alone. And because of this, it tends to lend credibility to your proposal and, perhaps even more important, to your professed abilities to handle the problem successfully. Going into a project with your eyes open to problems and with advance contingency planning enhances your probabilities for success in the undertaking, and it is not difficult to persuade a customer to perceive and agree with this idea.

To find and develop your opportunities along these lines, then, analyze the customer's proposal request in a search for answers to these questions:

1. *Precisely* what is it that the customer wants delivered or accomplished?

2. What must we *do* to achieve that result? What are the various steps, phases, functions, targets, or other items necessary to reach the goal?

3. What are the problems we may expect to encounter in doing these things? What are the probabilities of each arising, how difficult to overcome?

4. What would be the effect of a failure to solve any of these problems? Risk to an essential of the project? To costs? To schedules and delivery dates? To overall project success itself?

5. Which is the most serious of these problems in its effect on the project? In the difficulty of avoiding it or solving it?

6. What contingency plans to avoid the problems are possible?

HOW TO DEVELOP A WINNING PROPOSAL

Despite the detail, all the foregoing is something of a preamble to the subject of how to respond to a request for proposals, which entails or should logically entail the following major steps or phases of development:

Analysis of the requirement
Evolution of approach and strategy
Outline development
Writing first draft
Review
Revision and final draft

But even before we explore these various steps, let's have a look at a typical proposal format, which is a reflection of a general strategy for proposal presentation. These are the four general sections, in generic terms:

I. INTRODUCTION

Generally contains two subsections: Who the proposer is and why he or she is responding (interest and qualifications, briefly, with notation that details appear later in proposal); and brief explanation of what proposer perceives as main requirement of customer.

II. DISCUSSION

Generally contains several subsections as expansion of the understanding of the requirement, which was summarized in the first section, and tour through analyses, leading logically to specified approach. Includes discussions of requirement; problems and issues; alternatives, pros and cons of each; approach proposed with reasons therefore; and anything else deemed necessary to *sell* proposed approach. This is the place to focus intensely on the main issue and argue to sell it.

III. PROPOSED PROGRAM

This should evolve from second section by being the logical implementation of what was proposed as an approach. This is the place to explain and specify organization, staffing, resumes, management, procedures, quality control, contingency plans, deliverable items, reports, guarantees, and whatever else is germane. Remember that credibility lies in detail, to large extent: detailed proposals are far more believable than vague and generalized ones, and offer customer reason to feel confidence in proposer. Details are evidence of know-how.

IV. QUALICATIONS OF PROPOSER

This is the place to provide details of proposer's experience, past achievements, facilities, and resources, delivering on the general promise made in the first section. Here, too, is the place for those testimonials and letters of commendation other customers have bestowed on you, and anything else you can provide as evidence of how good and dependable you are.

In some cases it is necessary to break these sections down into two or more sections each, to provide an individual section for management, approach, quality control, or other especially important area. Usually, the RFP will furnish the clues that tell you whether such additional sections are necessary. Too, the customer sometimes specifies a mandated proposal format in his request. Of course, in such cases you comply with the customer's request. However, mandated formats are much more the exception than the rule, and even mandated formats tend to run generally along the lines described here.

THE PROMISE

Since the proposal is a sales presentation and is subject to the same general rules of persuasion as is advertising or any other sales presentation, the proposal must make a promise, too, offering benefits to the customer. In this case, however, the customer has already explained his needs and by implication, at least, the benefits desired. So presumably all proposers will make the same promise and offer the same benefits in general. That, however, as we have already considered, is something to be avoided as fatal me-tooism. It is necessary to make a different and especially appealing promise than competitors do, despite responding to the same request and specified requirement.

That is implicit in the concept already covered of finding an important issue and basing the proposal on that issue, with the promise of avoiding failure in the quest for success. That is the specific promise or strategy, with the general promise/strategy that of making the customer feel *comfortable* in selecting you as the contractor because you have inspired confidence by the way you addressed the requirement and proposed your project. That is a key to success in many proposal situations: make the customer feel a bit apprehensive about all your competitors, in what they propose, while feeling comfortable and *secure* in electing you to handle the requirement.

That promise should be as closely related to the customer's expressed concerns as possible, however. If you have managed somehow to divine that the customer has a great concern over costs ("divine" because customers are often not at all frank about what really concerns them most), the promise most likely to warm his heart will be one that assures him of delivering whatever he wants at the cost stipulated, with no danger of cost overruns. Or one that promises a lower cost than he feared he would encounter, and yet gives sound evidence that the cost reduction will not compromise quality or performance.

It is therefore important to try to identify all of the customer's "worry items," especially his main one, so that you can try to raise the main issue and build your strategy around that item. Do not be misled by the fact that the customer has given you no overt clues. There are many reasons why a customer may not reveal his greatest concerns to a prospective contractor, but that is not evidence that those concerns do not exist; they almost always do. And to discover them, you may have to read between the lines of the proposal request, probe gently with questions, and otherwise undertake to get information. To a large degree the quality of your proposal depends on the quality of the information you have been able to ferret out.

There is sometimes a gulf between what the customer describes as his need or requirement and what you perceive as his true need or requirement. And you may be entirely correct in your assessment, moreover; the customer may have confused the problem with the symptoms and be describing symptoms, for example. Or he may have been led down the garden path by any of a variety of other confusion factors, and have an entirely false idea of what he needs. There is, of course, a hazard in offering to satisfy a requirement you know to be an inaccurate assessment of true need, but there is also a hazard in telling a customer that he is wrong, no matter how tactfully you say it. Yet, ordinary caution dictates that you study the customer's stated requirement carefully and render your own judgment on its validity.

Here again is an opportunity to stand out from the crowd of proposers and outshine your competitors, if you can handle this situation creatively. In fact, sometimes this is a tailor-made issue for you. For example, a customer who wished to have a training program developed in electrical-appliance repair for an audience of learners who had all been school dropouts, overlooked the fact that these learners did not have the right preparation—prerequisites—for this study: even at the simplest level, electrical training includes understanding Ohm's Law, which involves simple algebra, and appliance repair technicians must be able to read service literature and technical drawings. The successful proposer for this contract was one who raised that as an issue and then proposed a methodology for coping successfully with it. To avoid confronting the customer with the customer's obvious oversight and failure to make a realistic analysis of the need, the proposer pretended that he believed the customer had understood the problem and was seeking answers to this difficult problem. Using that approach, he was able to turn what the customer thought was a more or less routine requirement into a problem-solving one.

This is a gambit which should always be considered when you differ with the customer in his basic appraisal of his needs.

It's a tactful way of differing with the customer, while it is very much issue-oriented. And now, if the customer does not already have a worry item, the proposal gives him one and then gives him the solution for it. And once your proposal assures the customer that you were shrewd enough to read between the lines and see that this was the real problem he wanted you to address, you may be sure that the customer will never tell you that you were wrong. In a sense, you thus place the customer in a yes-yes position, where he finds it difficult to deny the validity of what you propose.

The promise you make, then, is at more than one level. On the most abstract level, it is a promise of feeling comfortable and secure because the project has been entrusted to the most capable and dependable hands, to someone who has demonstrated great insight into the true needs of the customer. On a more concrete level, it is a promise of delivering whatever the customer wants most ardently, whether that is low cost, early delivery, great dependability, close working relationship, ironclad guarantees, or whatever you perceive as the customer's most sensitive worry item—even if you have to create that latter item.

Do not make that promise in abstract language. In a proposal, as in an advertisement or sales letter, it is important to be as specific as possible. The proposal is no more a suitable place for subtlety than is the advertisement or brochure. You must make your intent as clear as possible.

The case of the F-111 airplane demonstrates that most clearly: Defense Secretary Robert McNamara wanted a common airplane for the air force and the navy. The unsuccessful proposer stressed that it was offering "an aerodynamic solution for an aerodynamic problem"—a logical approach, offering sound engineering analysis and design. The successful proposer promised "commonality" and stressed it repeatedly throughout the proposal. That was the proposer's promise, reinforced constantly, and entirely emotional because it reflected McNamara's desire and reminded him of it on every page. Logic had nothing to do with McNamara's decision, just as it rarely has anything to do with anyone's decision.

IDENTIFYING THE TRUE WANT

If you can't promise what the customer wants, for any reason—perhaps because he wants the wrong thing or has made a faulty analysis of his needs—you have to make him want what you can promise, or what you should promise. And that doesn't really mean persuading the customer to change his basic want; it means persuading the customer to change his ideas about how to satisfy his want. In fact, we've been discussing exactly that in some of the examples here. When Frank Bettger devised his successful strategy for beating his competitors in signing up an executive for an insurance policy, he was faced with an executive who wanted to be covered, but was stalling off making a decision, possibly because he wanted time to consider which was the best policy, which served his needs best, or some other consideration he hadn't clearly resolved yet even in his own mind. Bettger persuaded the man to perceive as his true want freedom of mind about the matter of protecting his assets and estate to be left to his heirs, and showed him the way to get the whole thing off his mind in less than one hour. How could the man resist that kind of appeal?

The fact is that when the customer describes a want, he is usually not describing the true want, but is describing something expected to satisfy the want. For example, when he says in his request that he wants a training program for his staff, what he really means is that he wants his staff to be capable of doing things they cannot do now or can't do well enough now. His true want is not to train his staff—that's merely how he believes he must proceed to achieve what he really wants—but to have a staff able to do certain things they can't do now or can't do as well as he wants them to now. Offer him a better way—perhaps a set of procedures that eliminates much of the training need—and you can change his mind *as long as you persuade him to see that you are satisfying his true want.* And that latter is most important: It is essential that you *sell* your proposed whatever-it-is by showing the customer that you are not trying to change his mind about what he *really* wants and needs, but showing him a better way. That's why billions of dollars have been spent by government and industry to turn payroll preparation and accounting over to computers: they are a better way to get the job done.

If this begins to resemble observations made earlier about knowing what business you are in and the importance of what the customer perceives as need and want, it's not a coincidence. It is the same thing, but now in terms of the custom requirements that are almost invariably the subject of a proposal request and proposal submissions.

The true want is the end result the customer perceives as

necessary or desirable. It is necessary that you do not become confused between end and means, but you must not permit your customer to become confused about this either. Raising the issue that is the heart of your strategy in a proposal often means *appearing* to go counter to the customer's stated desires. It is therefore at the heart of the sales strategy that you demonstrate otherwise, that you help the customer perceive his true need and your proposed better way of satisfying that need or want.

Ironically, in a field where logic must always be a runner-up to emotion, it is necessary to resort to logic in analyzing situations to identify true wants. Here, we can borrow a leaf or two from a field known as *value engineering* or *value analysis* (also *value management*) to help us make this analysis. This discipline is built around the identification of *functions*—what things, people, or systems do, as distinct from what they are. And functions are separated, when identified, into three classes:

1. The basic function, which is whatever the thing, person, or system is supposed to do, such as *make marks* (for a pencil), *type letters* (for a typist), or *process data* (for a computer system)

2. The support function(s), such as *hold lead* (for a pencil), or *read notes* (for a typist), which function is necessary to the accomplishment of the basic function

3. Secondary functions, such as *erase marks* (for the pencil), which may be useful, but have nothing to do with the basic function

Sometimes practitioners of value engineering, even those certified by the national organization as accomplished specialists in the art, have difficulty identifying or defining a basic function accurately. One way to address this problem is to examine the user's need or want. A basic function is one that somehow satisfies that need or want, reflecting the *why* of the item being examined— why it exists. There is a tendency of the beginner in value analysis, for example, to identify the basic function of a pencil as *writing.*

And there are three things wrong with that:

1. Pencils don't write; people write.

2. Pencils are used also to make drawings and other marks.

3. A function must be expressed (by the rules) with a verb and noun.

Therefore, a pencil *makes marks.* Perhaps the marks are writing, perhaps they are other kinds of marks. No matter: *makes marks* covers it all, which is why it is correct.

No adjective or adverbs are permitted, and you may use more than two words only if it is necessary to compound a noun or verb: a red crayon necessarily *makes red marks*.

The reason for the restriction is to prevent judgments and to ensure objectivity in making analyses. And that is an excellent rule to pursue when analyzing a customer's wants and needs. It is necessary to ask yourself, when evaluating the customer's stated requirement, *why?* The answer to that generally provides a direct definition of true want—basic function—or offers valuable clues to that. When the Environmental Protection Agency asked for proposals to support its Pesticide Registration program, what it really wanted was the services of many highly specialized scientists and computer data professionals. The proposer who then offered the most convincing arguments for the method of *ensuring* that all necessary talents would be supplied promptly when needed was rewarded with the contract. (In fact, the winner's honest admission that he did not have many of these people on staff, but had to recruit them, was far more reassuring to the customer than some competitors' pretensions to having the people available, when the customer knew that that was most unlikely.)

Asking yourself why and developing a sensible answer to that question is almost always an excellent beginning to identifying the customer's true wants. At the least, it results in one or more hypotheses, which may be examined and analyzed until you arrive at a satisfactory answer. But it is always necessary to ask and answer that question. Until you do, you are the captive of the customer's view of his need, which is almost invariably not a definition of need but the customer's estimate of means necessary to achieving the end. Here, to make the point clear, if it is not already, are some typical expressed requests and what they reflect in wants:

Request	*Want*
Perform reverse engineering	Documentation (final drawings)
Computer programming services	Increase computer utilization
Perform research/study	Information for RFP
New aircraft design	Stay ahead of Soviets
Perform land survey	Define boundary line
Laundry services	Clean clothes

These are fairly obvious examples; many real-life cases are not so obvious. In one case, the U.S. Air Force pressed the organization I was then employed by to get on with the production of a large volume of technical data to be published despite the fact that most of the data would be of little practical use. Tactful questioning produced the intelligence that the contract required that the publications be prepared and delivered, and the customer had decided that it was more sensible to go ahead and produce something not needed than to go through the difficult and embarrassing procedures of admitting error and modifying the contract.

In most cases, reverse engineering is necessary because engineering staff members fail to keep drawings up to date as they tinker with their designs and work the bugs out of a piece of equipment. So even the term *reverse engineering* is a cover-up—a euphemism—for correcting slipshot work and error. A federal agency's annual report is primarily a document intended to justify the agency's budget request each year. The bulk of technical training in the military services is for the purpose of maximizing the one-line availability of equipment, but the equipment is so complex and sophisticated today that it is becoming all but impossible to train technicians adequately in a single enlistment, and other means for satistying the want—minimum downtime of equipment—are being developed constantly.

It is therefore not always a matter of logical analysis to discover the customer's true want, but may require the gathering of market intelligence via other means than logical deduction. But in a great many cases it is the key to writing the winning proposal, however it is done.

STRATEGY

The idea of strategy is so closely linked to the ideas of the promise, the proofs, the needs, the problems, the wants, and the themes that they are virtually synonyms for each other. The differences are largely abstract considerations, except for the fact that we ought to be using the plural—strateg*ies*—for most successful proposals are based on several strategies, including at least these:

Technical or program strategy
Presentation strategy
Cost or pricing strategy

Each of these could easily consume a chapter of its own and still we would not have exhausted the subject of strategies for proposals. However, here is a brief explanation of each of the above strategies:

Technical or program strategy is calculated to persuade the customer to the belief that the technical design or program you propose is easily superior to any other design possible. Its pros and cons must be thoroughly explained in the discussion section of your proposal, to demonstrate whatever you wish to demonstrate—that it is the most efficient, most dependable, least costly, most innovative, fastest, or whatever you claim for it as the advantage. Naturally, this should be developed with the customer's true wants and concerns ("worry items") very much in mind.

Presentation strategy is calculated to impress the customer by such things as commanding special attention for your proposal, getting your main message delivered with maximum impact, and otherwise arranging to have your proposal and anything connected with it (your presentation) highly professional and impressive. (Remember that yours is usually only one of many, and if you can make it stand out you will have helped your cause.)

Cost or pricing strategy is calculated to make you the low bidder or the *apparent* low bidder (often possible), if that is a key consideration. If price is not of the essence, your pricing strategy may be to demonstrate that your proposal offers the best *value* or makes provision for cost control or cost reduction—whatever features you believe are most effective in winning the customer to your arguments.

Frequently, these are interrelated. If, for example, you believe that low price is the key to winning, you may find it more persuasive to explain your low price by demonstrating technical or program design features that make the low price possible, and you may even bring in presentation strategies to dramatize these features of your design and pricing. In fact, it is generally highly desirable to integrate all your strategies in this manner, making them mutually supportive.

THEME

Theme is closely linked to strategy and helps make the strategy successful. A great many proposals are written by a group of people working more as individuals than as members of a team, and the results are too often apparent in the product—a veritable "river raft" of a document, wandering incoherently wherever the currents and stray winds propel it. This is because the contributions of all the proposal writers are stitched together in some sequence, but never carefully linked and integrated to form a proposal that *appears* to have been written by one individual. Only careful editorial and management control will achieve that effect, but even then the product needs to have a *theme,* and the theme must mirror the overall strategy of the proposal. For example, when the strategy of a proposal for training of technicians in new and untried equipment was to offer a special method for predicting maintenance needs, the proposed instrumentality for the project, *failure probability analysis,* became the pervasive theme of the proposal. When the successful bidder for the TFX-111 (which became the F-111 after it became an operational aircraft) opted to use "commonality" as the theme of the proposal, the word appeared printed at the bottom of each page. The winning proposal for a contract to train semiliterate individuals in a modern skill focused attention upon the theme *nonverbal training methods.*

Fixing upon a specific theme and making the theme almost painfully obvious by continual references to it serves more than one purpose:

1. It focuses the writing effort, reminding all members of the proposal team of the main strategy and where the proposal is headed.

2. It reminds the customer repeatedly of what the proposer is offering, continually reinforcing the promises made by the proposal.

3. It crystallizes the strategy and aids everyone concerned on both ends of the effort—proposal writers and customer personnel—in *understanding* the strategy.

4. It brings coherence to what might otherwise easily become one of those river-raft proposals, by providing a unifying element.

It is helpful to find a brief phrase or even a word, if possible, such as *commonality,* to use as a reminder. A proposal in which the strategy is one connected with costs might have the theme *cost control* or *cost consciousness*. But other possible themes might be any of the following examples:

Quality assurance	Contingency planning
Guaranteed delivery	Maximum capability
Early delivery	Control
Maintainability	Precision accuracy
Qualified staff	State-of-the-art design
National coverage	Ultrahigh technology

QUALIFICATIONS OF PROPOSER

Part of the "proofs" or evidence a customer wants to see, typically, in a proposal are the credentials of both the individual staff employees who are proposed for the work to be done and the "track record" of the organization submitting the proposal. It is therefore customary to include in a proposal several resumes—those of individual employees who would be the key members of the proposed project staff—and the "resume" of the company, showing what kinds of experience the company has had. As in the case of any marketing/sales effort, the customer wants to be assured that the proposer is capable and a good contractor. In fact, there are really three kinds of evidence required in the typical proposal:

1. Evidence that the proposer understands the customer's requirement and has a practicable plan for satisfying that requirement, a plan that appears to the customer to be likely to succeed
2. Evidence that the proposer has all the necessary skills and abilities to carry out the plan successfully
3. Evidence that the proposer is a reliable contractor, with a track record of dependable performance

That first proof depends on the discussion and proposed program, as presented in the second and third proposal sections described in the recommended format outline. The second and third proofs listed above will be presented primarily in the fourth section. In that section should be at least the following items:

Description of the organization generally, including such details as when it was organized, for whom it has done work, what kinds of work, and with what results; also, organization chart and identification of key officials

Available facilities and resources, including staff and physical assets

Specific current and past projects, especially those most germane to proposed project, with names and telephone numbers of individuals who can verify claims (references, in fact)

Testimonial letters, commendations, awards, other special items

A FEW SPECIAL ITEMS

There are certain items that most proposers appear to neglect, unless the RFP demands coverage, and these items can have a great influence on the customer. They are, in fact, especially influential when the RFP has not specifically required them because then it is likely that no other proposer—your competitors—has thought to cover them. Here are the items:

1. *Management.* Most proposals cover management, but unless the RFP has made specific demands, most proposals skim through management rather quickly and provide only shallow coverage. In fact, there are at least two areas of management which ought to be considered and covered in most custom projects:

> *Technical management*—Someone must direct the specific technical work, whether it is to design a radar set or conduct a house-to-house survey. That task requires technical know-how and technical leadership, which probably includes design, troubleshooting and debugging, organization of the work team(s), analysis of results, report writing, and a host of other tasks.
>
> *General management*—This can be an entirely different kind of function and require entirely different skills than technical management does. That is, the general manager may not be suited to technical management, and the technical manager may not be a good choice for general management. General management may include recruiting, contract administration, and attending to many other details such as subcontracting, printing, monitoring in-house support services, and purchasing.

2. *Quality control.* The customer is always happy to be assured that you are aware of the need to guarantee high quality in your work and products, and is therefore pleased to find a subsection or discussion devoted to the subject of quality assurance or quality

control. (The former is a more positive term, and is therefore a little more effective in use.) However, do not make the mistake of simply promising quality assurance; explain and describe your specific procedures for assuring high quality in everything that will be done and/or produced under the proposed contract.

3. *Deliverables.* Someone has said that proposal writing is largely the art of comprehending the deliverable, and that is an apt summary. If you can truly comprehend—and that means identify, define, and/or describe—the thing that is to be delivered, you already have made a stride toward achieving all those other things we have talked about: needs, problems, wants, strategies, and promises. It is essential that your proposal is as specific as it is possible to be about exactly what you propose to deliver, whether the deliverable is a physical entity or a service. And if the deliverable is a service as represented by a physical entity—a report documenting the results of a study, for example—make that understanding abundantly clear and explain to the customer precisely what you expect to include in that report.

4. *Details.* What has been said above in connection with deliverables is a general truth for the entire proposal: the more detailed and specific it is, the more credible it will be. A superb plan that is not well explained or is presented in inadequate detail will not sell nearly as well as a plan of lesser brilliance, but with full, expository detail. And in a large sense, that is almost the last word about proposals, for it sums up a significant element that makes for success or failure in proposals—details and specificity.

7

HOW TO WRITE DIRECT-MAIL PACKAGES

Mail order is no longer carried on solely by mail. But the designer of the successful direct-mail package is still the true artisan of mail-order.

WHAT IS DIRECT MAIL?

DIRECT MAIL is that stuff you get in your mailbox just about every day—"junk mail," as many people call it: circulars, brochures, sales letters, samples, invitations to participate in contests, and the like. You can generally tell what it is before you open the envelope because most of it has at least one of these telltale signs:

- It has a printed box (called an "indicia" by those in the know) instead of a postage stamp, which says that it is postage paid or it has a precancelled stamp.
- It has a great deal of copy printed on the outside of the envelope, often in more than one color.
- It is an oversize and fat envelope, obviously stuffed full of paper.
- It has your name on a label stuck on it, instead of being written or typed directly on the envelope.

- It has your name on it in such a way that you can easily tell it was done with some kind of addressing machine.
- It is thick enough and heavy enough to be a catalog from some large mail order firm, and often you can see that it is a catalog because it has nothing around it but a paper band. (It is called a "self-mailer" because of that.)

Most of the stuff you get this way are solicitations of one sort or another:

- Efforts to sell you something or other directly, with an order form enclosed and even inviting you to use your credit card
- Appeals to donate to some sort of charity, worthy·cause, or political campaign
- Invitations to enter a contest, with the possibility of winning a great deal of money
- Invitations to get a free estimate to sell you a new car on a trade-in of your old one, put new siding on your house, or otherwise do something to help you along
- Flyers announcing the weekly specials at the supermarket, local dry cleaner, neighborhood handyman, or other such service or store.

Almost without exception all are directed to persuading you to spend money, either directly and immediately or after you have undertaken a preliminary step or two, as directed, such as coming in and submitting yourself to a sales presentation.

By far the overwhelming bulk of this mail is discarded by the recipients, a few after glancing through it, most without more of a glance than enough to verify that it is so-called junk mail. Perhaps 1 to 5 percent of the recipients actually open the envelopes and read what is inside with sincere interest. But there are so many pieces of junk mail sent out every day that even that 1, 2, or 3 percent who decide to buy what is offered represent billions of dollars in sales annually. Reliable recent figures are not generally available, but mail order is still a growth industry, with multibillion-dollar annual revenues climbing higher every year and providing a great many jobs for people at all levels, from order pickers to marketing executives, not to mention the employees of the print shops and others who supply the mail order industry with the supplies necessary to generate and mail out the tons of paper every day.

A GRAB BAG OR A CAREFULLY
DESIGNED PACKAGE?

Perhaps to the casual observer—to a typical recipient of such mail, for example—the envelope appears to have been stuffed at random with whatever the sender had readily at hand. Typically, a piece of direct mail has at least three or four items in the envelope and frequently many more. Here are the typical items you might find in a direct-mail envelope:

A sales letter of one to six pages

A brochure of almost any size and number of pages or panels

A broadside—something which unfolds to 17 × 22 inches or more

A card, again of almost any size, which is an order form, usually

A plastic card, which resembles a credit card and may have your name on it

A novelty, such as a pen, pencil, calendar, or other useful item

One or more circulars, leaflets, pamphlets, or the like

A sample of a product

A return envelope

Perhaps the mailer did, indeed, gather up and insert in the envelope whatever items came to hand or whatever he or she could get. And perhaps the mailer had the notion that the more things he or she put in the envelope, the greater the chances were that you would find something you liked there and as a result fish out your VISA card or checkbook and fire off an order. Perhaps— if the mailer was a newcomer to mail order and therefore naive; otherwise, no, the combination of items was not by chance—it was by design. It may or may not have been a good design and a good marketing strategy, but it was probably by deliberate design, with each piece calculated to reinforce the others. Believe it or not, there is a rationale to direct-mail campaigns and the design of direct-mail packages.

DIRECT-MAIL MARKETING THEORY

There is some relationship between the number of pieces enclosed in a direct-mail envelope and the number of orders a given mailing produces. In the general case, a single sales letter in an envelope, no matter how persuasively written, will not produce as good a result as a mailing which includes two or three other pieces accompanying that sales letter. The prospect wants to be coaxed, for one thing, but there is more to it than that, too. There is the simple fact that *Homo sapiens* is an infinitely variable species, and while one appeal or one argument may work better— strike a nerve with more people—than any other, no argument or appeal works with everyone. So, if you write an effectively persuasive sales letter, you will appeal to and persuade a certain number of people to do whatever it is your sales letter has implored them to do. And if you have enclosed also a powerful brochure or broadside, you will actuate a certain number of others, who were not turned on by the sales letter. And if you have a well-designed "response" card or order form in the package, you'll propel some of the undecideds—fence-sitters and procrastinators—into action.

Conventional wisdom about direct mail dictates these pieces, as the minimum:

1. A hard-hitting sales letter
2. A broadside or brochure
3. An order form, preferably a distinctive card
4. A return envelope, postage paid

For example, in my own morning mail today I received a package offering me a new electronic typewriter at a special discounted price. The manufacturer is a well-known one, the mailer a supplier, the Quill Corporation, with whom I have done business for some years. The mailing included a four-page letter from the president of the Quill Corporation; a 17- × -122-inch multicolored broadside, presenting the machine and prepared, I am sure, by the manufacturer; and an order form. It's an appealing offer, especially since I have faith in the mailer, who has always been a responsive supplier, but it would appeal to anyone who has use for a typewriter.

It's a rather typical package. In fact, if it lacks anything at all, it is merely the response envelope, whose contribution to a direct-mail appeal is not at all certain, in my mind. I am rather well convinced that anything that makes it easier for the procrastinator to act will make it more likely that he or she will act, instead of procrastinating. So in that respect, at least, such refinements as response envelopes do help. At the same time, my own experiments and tests lead me to conclude that they don't help enough to make a significant difference overall. And when you compare the slight increase in sales with the increase in cost, the contribution pales even more.

MY OWN BASIC THEORY

My own general theory about direct mail is simple: make the offer appealing enough—make the customer want what you promise badly enough, that is—and wild horses couldn't prevent him or her from getting the order in the mail or telephoning it in, if that is an option you offer. Even when I have used response envelopes, for example, I have been surprised at how many people did not use them, but found their own envelopes and used them. Instead of a return envelope, I would use the space and cost to enclose another persuasive element. Let's consider these factors:

1. A first-class stamp will carry approximately five letter-size sheets or their equivalent (in 20-pound bond or 60-pound offset paper) within that one-ounce limitation allowed. With postage at its present rate—even bulk-mail rates are high, nearly one-half that of first-class postage—it is the most expensive element in the mailing. Therefore, it makes good economic sense to me, to use every last gram of that one ounce I am allowed.

2. A return envelope, even the least expensive, will cost you $12 to $15 per 1,000, and can cost much more.

3. Another letter-size ($8^1/_2 \times 11$ inches) flyer or folder, printed on both sides in black ink, will cost you much less—from one-third to one-half the cost of that envelope, and will almost certainly do more for sales than that return envelope.

In my opinion, then, a return envelope in most cases is a free rider, a moocher, burdening your mailing without paying its own way. On the other hand, an extra flyer or leaflet can do a great deal for you. Here is an example:

I started one direct-mail campaign, in my early days in mail order, with a single letter-size flyer and a two-page sales letter, using this to respond to inquiries I received from classified advertising in a popular magazine. I was seeking orders for an item I was then offering at $6.

The response was satisfactory, although less than great. (The response from mailing to inquirers ought to be far greater than from mailing unsolicited to a list.) Knowing that I had ample room for at least another sheet or two, I developed a new brochure and added it to the mailing. The response rate more than doubled immediately. That was partly the result of the persuasiveness of the new brochure, of course, but it was also the result of adding new sales arguments and reinforcing the existing ones.

My theory encompasses all of these points:

1. Assuming reasonably effective writing—effective persuasion, that is—and an offer that prospects find reasonably appealing, the response rate is a factor of and is in some proportion to the volume of copy used. That is, it bears a direct relationship to the number of sales presentations and sales arguments you make in the mailing.

2. If your sales persuasiveness is powerful enough, you do not have to coax the respondent to order. In fact, the most powerful motivator in many cases is your promise to ship promptly, because many mail order customers are most impatient to get what they order immediately, as they could in a store, and they are put out by the practices of many mail order firms who are extremely slow in filling orders.

3. Every opportunity possible to add weight to the sales persuasion should be utilized, and the contribution of return envelopes to this is at best uncertain. No one really knows how much they contribute, if they do. At best, however, their message to a prospect is subtle: it's easy to order; I'm already addressed and ready to carry your order and check. Selling is no place for subtlety; it's a place to be crystal clear and explicit. Ergo, invest your money in the most direct sales persuasion possible.

THE OTHER SIDE OF THE COIN

It is easily possible to misunderstand this direct-mail philosophy, and I find it violated frequently in the direct-mail packages I myself receive regularly. Here are some of the most common mistakes I find:

Each piece of the package makes the same sales argument, apparently on the theory that if you say it enough times, the prospect will eventually believe it.

There are gimmicks instead of sales arguments, rather than in support and reinforcement of sales arguments.

There are elements that do not fit together, sometimes even

arguing against themselves—that is, one element contradicting another.

There are ludicrous fumbles, such as computer-addressing sales letters to make them appear personalized and coming up with a blooper that only a machine could make.

There's poor writing, in the sense of claims, claims, claims—hyperbole and superlatives—without evidence.

Materials extoll the virtues of the product or the seller, instead of focusing on the benefits to the buyer.

Let's have a look at each of these problems:

Repeating the sales argument. Using the same sales argument or same promise as the basis for each of several elements in a direct-mail package is the same thing, philosophically, as making repeated loud claims without evidence, without *backup* for those claims. In most cases, I have found, it is possible to think up many more good sales arguments than I can use, and my problem is not to find other sales arguments but to decide which ones to use. You may use more than one promise or more than one argument to support your original promise. (The latter course is generally the better one.) But when the sales letter is a virtual repeat of the other main elements—circular, flyer, brochure, broadside, etc.—and the others are almost carbon copies of each other, they tend to weaken the argument, rather than reinforce it. The idea of having these various elements is to appeal to various people, on the theory that some will be influenced more by the letter than by anything else, while the next one will find the broadside or flyer irresistible in its appeal—if the appeals are different.

Gimmicks instead of sales arguments. Too many direct-mail packages these days are relying on gimmicks, such as computer-typed letters and flyers, plastic cards resembling credit cards, and one that has become popular recently: a folded enclosure that says something such as, "Don't open this unless you have decided not to buy." The theory is, of course, that the respondent's curiosity will be provoked so that he or she is unable to resist opening that little brochure or letter-ette and reading it avidly. Perhaps. In my own case, I probably did read the "Please read this only if you have decided not to buy our product" folder the first time or two I saw one. But I have long since taken to muttering to myself, when confronted with one of these now badly overused gimmicks,

"I won't buy and I won't open you," as I discard the entire package. I found the whole idea somewhat banal, to begin with, although I admit it may have worked for those who used it early on, and perhaps is still working. (I freely admit that my reactions are probably not typical.)

In any case, if you plan to use a gimmick, use one that supports your sales presentation. The fake credit card gimmick may be appropriate to some sales presentations, but I can't think of many cases in which it supports or reinforces—or even dramatizes—a sales argument. (Most of the time I have seen this device used, it was an appeal by an insurance company, and I am not yet certain what the implied connection was between the card and insurance.) On the other hand, it might be a helpful device if used to offer loans, mortgages, or other finances-related service or product because of its obvious connection with credit and spending. Or perhaps to support an appeal to buy items commonly bought on terms, such as an automobile or home remodeling.

Elements that do not fit together. There are various ways to assemble a direct-mail package, but no matter what method is used it should result in an integrated package—a package in which the parts fit together. Direct mail must be a system, not merely a random collection of items.

Most people consider the sales letter to be the keystone of the package, and hope that the respondent will read the letter first. There is, however, no way to ensure that absolutely, despite the mailer's schemes for doing so, such as inserting the pieces in a pattern designed to make the letter appear first. But we are dealing with that infinitely variable sample, *Homo erectus,* and some will inevitably read the broadside or brochure first, while others will immediately seek out the order form to learn the price, and still others will turn to some other element of the package than the letter.

That being the case, as it is, making the parts fit together means pursuing at least two objectives: 1) designing each element in some manner calculated to make the reader want to read the other elements—to want to know "the rest of the story"; and 2) making the various elements *mutually* supportive—integrated, on the one hand, yet each independent or complete enough in itself to be self-supporting as an appeal and a motivator to read the other elements.

Relatively few direct-mail packages achieve these goals and, in fact, few appear to have been designed with these goals in mind.

Ludicrous fumbles. A computer addressed a fat envelope of sales arguments and appeals to "Herman Holtz Publications," which was perfectly reasonable, since I was trading under that name at the time. The sales letter, however, was addressed to "Mr. Publications," which not only tickled my funny bone, but made the mailer appear ludicrous. How could anyone take such a mailing seriously, I asked myself, when the mailer did something so ridiculous?

Of course, that is the hazard of using a computer. When Peter Drucker, the noted management consultant and author on the subject, denounced the computer as a moron, he knew what he was talking about. Computers are machines, and only the superstitious and the sadly uninformed think that they are anything more than that. Computers do not think. Even humans do not always think, or they wouldn't permit a computer to destroy their dignity and, with it their credibility as this computer did when it called me "Mr. Publications."

In these days of mass mailings and mass everything else, such bloopers are more and more common. Envelopes addressed to me have carried form letters addressed to someone else, a giveaway that it was a mass-circulated form letter, of course. That completely destroyed and nullified the effort to make the letter appear to have been meant for me and me only, and it must have had the same effect on everyone else who received their copy addressed to someone else.

The last two common faults mentioned, poor writing of sales copy and focusing on the wrong things in the copy have been thoroughly discussed before, and we won't take time to review those discussions again. However, since we have probed into the "don'ts"—the common mistakes of direct-mail copy and package design—it's now time to look at some of the "do's"—how to design and prepare effective direct-mail packages, packages that work because they were designed intelligently, not because of the lucky accident that so often is the sole reason for success.

A BASIC DESIGN

Every design, if it's to make sense, must have a primary objective. That's as true in designing a direct-mail package as it is in designing an airplane, a computer program, or a building. Otherwise, what results is not a design or a system but a random assortment of elements that came together by chance, and the effectiveness of how the final product works is also purely by chance.

In general terms, the objective of any direct-mail package is to persuade the recipient to do something—submit an order, make a contribution, come into the automobile showroom, visit the beauty parlor, vote for the candidate, or whatever the mailer wants the addressee to do. So the primary objective is always whatever that desire of yours is—what you want the respondent to do— and you must have that objective clearly defined before you can even begin to think about how to design a package to accomplish that. Be sure that you define that objective specifically—not in such general terms as *respond,* but in the explicit terms of *make contribution, register Republican,* or *send in order.*

Once you have done that, you can begin to concentrate on a strategy—how you will persuade or induce the addressee to do what you want him or her to do. Again, you know the general requirements: make a promise of something you believe the recipient will find most attractive, provide evidence that the promise will be kept if the recipient does what you ask. So the next step in the process and the first step in devising a persuasive strategy is to determine what the promise will be but again in explicit terms.

Once you have done that and you know precisely what it is that you will promise, you must think about how to back up that promise—how to prove that you can and will keep the promise, if the respondent does what you ask.

The basic strategy, then, consists of identifying something you believe the respondent will find a most attractive benefit (your promise), and then of ways of convincing the respondent that it will happen, that your promise is not an empty one. But that latter element of the strategy, proving that the promise is solid and dependable, may itself consist of several parts. Let's take a typical case, as an example. This one is a package from a magazine, *Personal Computing,* soliciting my subscription. The package contains these typical elements:

A four-page (11 × 17 inches, folded to letter size) sales letter
A multicolored brochure, 8¹/₂ × 11 inches, folded to fit a
 #10 envelope

An order blank

A postage-paid return envelope

An outer envelope with envelope copy and a die-cut gimmick

The letter, which is addressed "Dear Reader," begins by explaining the advantages of owning a personal computer and then explaining how the magazine can help me by showing me how to make my personal computer work for me. It promises that the magazine is written in everyday, jargon-free language that I can easily understand. But if I already own a personal computer, the letter then goes on, I'm even better off because the magazine is for people who don't really care how a computer works but only what it can do. It continues selling both the advantages of owning a personal computer and the corollary advantages of reading the magazine for guidance and information. And it also advises me that if I don't need to be sold any further, I can skip pages two and three and go directly to page four, where I'll learn of the fantastic risk-free trial offer.

The die cut on the outer envelope is circular, about the size of a half-dollar, and it permits the recipient to see a "token" through it. The token can be separated from its nest on a flap of the order form and inserted in a die-cut slot on the order form, thereby making the customer eligible to get a first issue free.

Obviously, one can have that first issue free whether one does that mumbo jumbo with the "token" or not. The purpose in going to all that extra expense of die-cutting and thinking up that gimmick and gimmicky offer is to persuade the respondent to believe that the offer is really fantastic, and requires only a little extra effort. Somehow, such things appear to work, for some reason, but I strongly suspect that the cost of the gimmick (die-cutting is quite expensive) would not be justified by the added response if a fair test was run. Meanwhile, the general promise is that a personal computer is a great boon in many ways, and the magazine is almost a must to help you buy the right personal computer and use it most effectively. And for evidence, as far as the letter is concerned, a case history is cited, and logical arguments are used to amplify that. However, the promise of a free issue and the lower-than-newsstand price are stressed heavily. Close examination reveals that the first issue is truly free only if you choose not to continue your subscription. In that case, you can cancel and owe nothing for that first issue; otherwise, you pay the invoice when it arrives, and you get (apparently; the copy is not as explicit as it could be about this) eleven more issues, the balance of a one-year subscription. In that event, you did not get that first issue free, but paid for it. (Nevertheless, I subscribed!)

The brochure is attractive. It includes a replica of that token printed on its front cover, reports that the computer is an "extention" (*sic*) of a business person's brain, but outside of that one blooper of a misspelled word, it's a well-done brochure. It does pick up the risk-free trial offer and refers the reader to the order form, while offering several expensively illustrated arguments for both owning a personal computer and subscribing to the magazine.

One mistake the designer of this package made, however, was to use a dark brown paper for the letter, making it rather difficult to read. Especially difficult to read was the typeset lead-in copy, which was printed in brown ink of a somewhat darker shade than that of the paper. Other copy was typed, printed in black ink.

PROMISES AND MOTIVATORS

It strikes me that it may have been a mistake to dwell so much on selling the reader the advantages of owning a personal computer. It is not the function of this magazine to sell computers, but rather to report on and instruct readers about those small computers now referred to as "personal computers." Were I doing that copy I would focus primarily on what the magazine offers in the way of information and what that information does directly for the reader. In fact, one tactic that was not used here, but probably would have been highly effective, would have been fear motivation. And that would be a legitimate enough argument because small computers are now at the stage where TV was shortly after it was introduced to the general public about 1948: the market was flooded with an almost uncountable number of makes of TV receivers, and many of them were of extremely poor design and some even dangerous to operate. And when the market finally began to shake down, the pattern was familiar: dozens of TV manufacturers who had sprung up overnight vanished as suddenly, and with them the source for at least some of the parts. (This happened also with automobiles through the twenties, thirties, forties, and even later years.) This is certain to happen in small computers, too, and is a distinct hazard to anyone buying a small computer; at least, it is something to consider, and the magazine would not be crying "Wolf" if it warned readers of that hazard and offered advice to readers on minimizing the danger of getting stuck with a computer for which parts may not be readily obtainable in the not-too-distant future. I suspect that this approach would produce good results; fear motivations, when based in fact, work quite well.

Too, as far as I have been able to determine, no one has employed this approach in selling magazines generally or computer magazines especially. Instead, this package described here has a distinct "me, too" flavor, offering that same tired, old formula of arguing that it's cheaper by subscription than on the newsstand, and the customer can cancel and get a refund of unfulfilled portion of the subscription at any time. And the first issue free is not exactly a new and original idea, either, but has also been done almost to death.

The newsmagazines are offering this argument constantly in TV commercials. There now reposes on my desk a "desk encyclopedia" in three volumes, as a result of my wife gifting me with a subscription to one of those newsmagazines. Another is currently offering a business-card-size pocket calculator with a subscription, and the third leading newsmagazine is offering a desktop digital timepiece as a reward for letting the publisher mail you its magazine every week.

Unfortunately, whatever originality and creativity the average designer of marketing promotions has—especially with such tried-and-true standards as magazines—seems to be most often applied to developing marketing gimmicks: tokens, watches, calculators, free issues, atlases, and other giveaways. Such campaigns have the effect of asking customers to choose between bonus gifts, rather than between products. The marketing effort is therefore applied to selling the giveaway, rather than the product, with the promise evidently focused entirely on the giveaway, rather than on what the product will do for the buyer.

One newsmagazine, for example, concentrates its appeal (when it isn't plugging the giveaway item for all it's worth) on its claimed magnificent coverage—worldwide reportage, marvelous stories, great photographs—even on you-are-there promises and promises to keep you well informed. But it fails to tell prospects *why* they ought to be well informed, evidently assuming that everyone automatically *wants* to be well informed. That's assuming facts not in evidence; not everyone has an inherent desire to know what's going on everywhere in the world. In fact, there are many people who don't want to know about all the trouble in the world, and deliberately insulate and shield themselves from the news every day. A smart marketer will stop and think about what arguments he or she should offer prospects for permitting the magazine to keep the prospect so well informed. That is where some creativity could be used by copywriters with a bit of imagination. Examples:

Are you left out of conversations because you are not "up" on what's happening in the world? (Imagine the opportunities to dramatize this on TV, with the viewer identifying with some poor soul sitting in a corner, left out of things at the cocktail party, at the lunch table, at various other gatherings of friends and family.)

Does your boss think you're a dodo? (Same thread, but far more serious, as potential threat to one's career. Great opportunities for dramatization.)

Are you tongue-tied when you meet that special girl or guy because you don't keep up with current events—books, movies, plays, and critics' opinions, for example? (More opportunities for dramatizations.)

With approaches such as these, you don't even need much in the way of proof or evidence. This is a fear motivation, for one thing, and fear motivations often require far less evidence than do other kinds of motivations. But there is little question that reading any of the leading newsmagazines will keep one informed; the argument here is not that the magazine will keep one informed, but that it is necessary to be informed.

This argument works well for other kinds of magazines, too. Even those that specialize in gossip and "inside stories" about prominent people could use a fresh idea now and then. They focus their appeal generally on the typical and characteristic desire of many of us to be "on the inside" and to learn about the private lives of prominent people. But we also need to have things to talk about in our social and business contacts, and powerful appeals can be made in this connection.

But it need not always be a fear appeal. While it is true enough that fear works well and is a legitimate argument for the need to keep oneself well informed about what's happening in the world, there is the more positive argument of what it does for one's social and business life to be a good conversationalist, with many bright things to say and the ability to present an image of being an alert and well-informed individual.

One of the classic advertisements, which ran without change (successfully, that is) for some forty years, was headlined: DO YOU MAKE THESE MISTAKES IN ENGLISH?

It was, of course, a fear appeal, similar to the modern "ring around the collar" commercial; both strike a nerve in the person who is frightened by the fear of being publicly embarrassed. Human nature has not changed; picture a victim of ignorance being laughed at by others because he or she never heard of Afghanistan or doesn't know what the NASA shuttle is, and you strike a nerve in many people. People will generally go to great lengths to avoid being embarrassed.

Basic and key to the package design, then, is the strategy underlying the promise, and never mind the proof, for the moment. The more appealing and more motivating the promise, the less important and less necessary the proof is. That is, they are in inverse proportion: if the promise is such that the prospect *wants* to believe badly enough, he or she simply does not demand a great deal of proof. And, of course, as in some of the hypothetical cases just considered, proof is not truly necessary, for the truths are self-evident.

STEPS IN SELECTING THE PROMISE AND MOTIVATIONAL STRATEGY

An interesting point to consider here is just that fact that some kinds of promises and motivators require little or no evidence to validate them; the prospect accepts the promise as one that will be delivered on, either because the prospect wants badly to believe the promise or because the promise simply points out or reminds the prospect of something commonly accepted by everyone. In many cases, both conditions apply, as in some of those just discussed.

Because this is true, it is wise to think deeply about this when deciding what to promise, whether something you have good evidence for and believe you can prove, or something that requires little or no proof. Obviously, you have a great advantage immediately if you can promise something that requires no proof but will be accepted readily. This should be given a first priority in your quest for a promise and motivator, and is the first goal to which to apply your creative imagination and originality.

A good first step is to research what your direct competitors are doing. In many, perhaps most cases, you'll find them doing pretty much the same thing. Somehow, that appears to happen in a great many businesses: competitors tend to imitate each other, and apparently no one questions whether what they are doing is right, but only whether this is what some successful competitors are doing. That is taken as evidence that what they are doing is the right way, as though there were only one right way to do anything.

In any case, once the standard pattern is identified, an excellent next step is to study this methodology with a what's-wrong-with-this-approach? analysis. This begins with the *assumption* that the approach is a bad one or, at least, not the best one possible. Almost invariably, what "everyone is doing" is a bad approach, if for no other reason than it is probably obsolescent from overuse. It is almost invariably long past time for a change.

Pay particular attention, when making this analysis, to precisely what the promise (or major promise, since many campaigns make more than one promise) is. Exactly what does the approach promise to do, and what is the focal point of its appeal?

As in the case of the newsmagazines, you may very well find that the presentation exhorts the reader to do or be something without offering a sound reason for so doing or being, on the assumption (evidently) that the respondent ought to recognize the doing or being as beneficial. That is itself an immediate cue to step up the explanation or rationale of the promise to a more immediate reward, because the original promise-reward is a bit too subtle, too abstract, requiring the respondent to make an analysis and infer the direct benefit. It won't happen; prospects rarely are that accommodating. If you want a prospect to perceive the benefit of your promise, make your promise and its benefits crystal clear. Don't even promise to make your reader beautiful or attractive, when you can promise to make your prospect attract handsome men or beautiful women. Certainly, a young woman can readily translate being beautiful into attracting handsome young men and making other women envious, but you are far more likely to strike a nerve when you make the translation for them and say it directly.

Try this out on yourself:

Would you like to be affluent?

Would you prefer to be wealthy?

Or would you rather have lots of money?

But would you prefer to be able to go wherever you want, live however you want, buy whatever you wish, and do as you please the rest of your life?

Or maybe it would please you more to have a Park Avenue condominium, a Rolls-Royce or two, a yacht, a winter home in Palm Beach or Majorca, and a few servants to run and fetch for you?

Note the steadily increasing concreteness of the promise, from the abstract idea of "affluence" to the delicious images of what you could really do with a great deal of money. It's those latter mouth-watering images that strike a nerve and make a prospect want to believe.

The fear motivation has an analogous phylogeny:

Are you content to be a have-not all your life?

Will you settle for having none of the good things of life?

Are you going to live in fear of old age and poverty?

Will you be forced to manage on the meager Social Security benefits?

Will you wind up in an old-age home, on public welfare, in your dotage?

"Have-not" is somewhat abstract, of course, and may not mean to your reader what it means to you. But living on public welfare and in an old-age home supported by taxes is clear as a bell, is it not? The image is frightening, for many, far more than that abstract "have-not" notion.

According to those reputed to know, we think in words, symbols, and numbers with the left side of our brains, and in images, impressions, and feelings with the right side of our brains. Whatever the case, images make a deeper impression on us *emotionally* than do words and numbers, and any emotional impact is greater, generally, than is an intellectual one. So the promise/ motivator most likely to strike a nerve—make a deep impression, that is—is bound to be the one that comes across to the respondent as an *image,* rather than as a set of words. For words are themselves mere abstractions—symbols the reader must translate into images. However, as a writer, you can *help* the reader make that translation, and in so doing add significantly—even enormously—to the impact your words have.

That, in fact, is the essential difference between offering a reader the promise of great wealth and offering expensive automobiles and luxurious homes. Instead of assuming or hoping that the reader will translate that promise of great wealth into expensive automobiles, luxurious homes, vacations, or whatever you think most appealing, make the translation yourself. Offer the *specific* benefits instead of the abstraction that the reader must interpret and translate.

You may therefore begin to devise a strategy by identifying all the promises you can reasonably make and setting them forth in more or less abstract terms, such as these:

Wealth
Security
Love
Prestige
Honors
Position
Beauty
Happiness

Select the term(s) most descriptive of what you believe you can promise, and go to the next level of definition, such as these examples:

Wealth = money, possessions, warm sense of security . . . (select one)

Security = money, college degree, better job . . .

Love = find the right woman/man, attract the opposite sex . . .

Prestige = be the boss, be looked up to . . .

Honors = be chosen Salesman or Saleswoman of the Year, join the Million Dollar Roundtable . . .

Go on from here, with whatever you have selected, to the specific benefits you can paint images of. You can't word-paint an image of wealth or money, except as symbols, but you can word-paint holidays in Hawaii, jet flights to Switzerland, sailboating in Newport, and other things people can do with wealth.

This applies to all the other items. Security may translate into a college degree in some field, for some people, but you are still dealing with a more or less abstract idea here. Better paint a picture of the reader as an engineer, lawyer, doctor, accountant, or whatever you wish security and college degrees to represent. Or if you are selling vocational training and correspondence courses, picture whatever skills and jobs are appropriate there. But always stress the security idea—the abundance of jobs and opportunities for the trained person, with pictures of what a good job means.

THE PREMISE

All arguments, including sales arguments, are based on premises. A premise is simply an assumption with which you believe the other party will agree. For example, we assume that everyone would like to be wealthy; therefore we don't argue the merits of having a great deal of money, but only the merits of a plan for acquiring a great deal of money. We assume that every woman would prefer to be beautiful and agrees that slim is better than fat, so we don't argue those things, but we assume that they are desirable results.

Again and again, we can find copywriters wasting time and money arguing premises, trying to persuade people to believe what they already believe. However, we find also that some copywriters go the opposite way and assume that certain ideas are acceptable premises when they are not universally accepted. That is, some copywriters allow themselves to be trapped by mythology, under the mistaken notion that everyone agrees on such ideas as these:

Democrats are all liberals and are for working people.

Republicans are more responsible fiscally than are Democrats.

All millionaires are philanthropists.

Everyone wants to keep up with the news and be well informed.

If it's in print it must be true.

Foreign goods are superior to American goods.

Foreign goods are inferior to American goods.

Orientals are all small people.

Americans are all friendly people.

Be careful in selecting a premise on which to base your promises and strategies that it is, indeed, a notion that enough people accept to qualify it as a suitable premise. However, if you can select a suitable premise, you have the advantages noted earlier of requiring little or no evidence that your promise represents something desirable and even, in some cases, that your product will produce that result. If, for example, your premise is that your correspondence course in electronics will open a new career for the reader, you will require little proof that this is so: a great many—most informed people—will accept this readily. What you need evidence for, presumably, is that your course of study will impart that skill promised.

Take note of some of the advertisements for diets and diet aids: instead of focusing on how their product or system works, they focus on the advantages of losing weight. Now of course no one will argue that it's desirable to lose weight, if you're overweight (as so many of us are in America). So if you argue that, it is either because you haven't thought out your persuasion strategy very well, or because you have no good arguments for your product or system, and hope to conceal that in a smoke screen of the benefits of losing weight.

In short, don't lose sight of what it is that you are trying to sell: you are not selling the basic premise, if it is a premise that most of us accept. What you are selling or trying to sell, in a great many cases, is the *second* premise, for every well-structured argument has two premises, the basic one and a second one. For example, let us suppose that you are trying to sell a diet-aiding pill of some kind:

First premise: It's desirable to lose weight.

Second premise: This pill will help you to lose weight.

(Conclusion: Buy this pill and benefit by becoming thinner.)

In this case, you have to work at proving that second premise— that this pill helps one to lose weight. And the evidence can be any of several kinds:

Medical testimony, especially explanations of how the pill's chemistry works

Testimonials from satisfied users, who swear that the pill works

Testimonials from doctors who testify that the pill works and is safe

Logical arguments or arguments that appear to be logical

Before and after photographs (in the class of testimonials)

GETTING TO YES

One rule of thumb often taught people in sales courses is that a good tactic in making a sales presentation is to get the customer saying yes, on the theory that saying yes becomes habit-forming and makes it easier to get the customer to say yes when

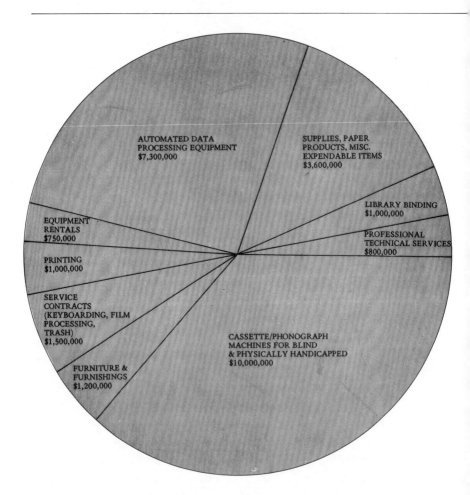

**Distribution of
Expenditures for
Supplies,
Equipment
and
Materials
During a
Typical
Fiscal Year**

AUTOMATED DATA
PROCESSING EQUIPMENT
$7,300,000

SUPPLIES, PAPER
PRODUCTS, MISC.
EXPENDABLE ITEMS
$3,600,000

LIBRARY BINDING
$1,000,000

EQUIPMENT
RENTALS
$750,000

PROFESSIONAL
TECHNICAL SERVICES
$800,000

PRINTING
$1,000,000

SERVICE
CONTRACTS
(KEYBOARDING, FILM
PROCESSING,
TRASH)
$1,500,000

CASSETTE/PHONOGRAPH
MACHINES FOR BLIND
& PHYSICALLY HANDICAPPED
$10,000,000

FURNITURE &
FURNISHINGS
$1,200,000

FIGURE 2. Pie chart of Library of Congress expenditures

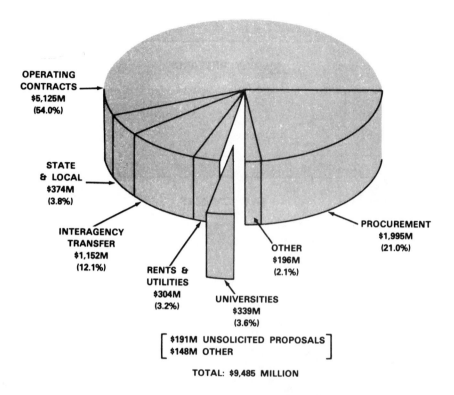

OPERATING
CONTRACTS
$5,125M
(54.0%)

STATE
& LOCAL
$374M
(3.8%)

INTERAGENCY
TRANSFER
$1,152M
(12.1%)

RENTS &
UTILITIES
$304M
(3.2%)

UNIVERSITIES
$339M
(3.6%)

OTHER
$196M
(2.1%)

PROCUREMENT
$1,995M
(21.0%)

[$191M UNSOLICITED PROPOSALS]
[$148M OTHER]

TOTAL: $9,485 MILLION

FIGURE 3. Department of Defense pie chart of expenditures

you ask for the order. And, so goes this theory, it doesn't really matter too much what you get yes answers to, at first, as long as you get them. Therefore, you lead the customer on in saying yes, at first, through questions the customer finds no problem in responding to in the affirmative. For example:

Of course, it is better for your health to be at your right weight, don't you agree? Don't the doctors tell us that thin people have a much better and longer life expectancy than overweight people do?

And don't we *feel* better when we know that we are thin and attractive, and we can bend over to tie our shoelaces without grunting?

Total DOT Grant Programs

($ in thousands)

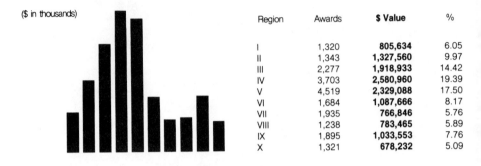

Region	Awards	$ Value	%
I	1,320	805,634	6.05
II	1,343	1,327,560	9.97
III	2,277	1,918,933	14.42
IV	3,703	2,580,960	19.39
V	4,519	2,329,088	17.50
VI	1,684	1,087,666	8.17
VII	1,935	766,846	5.76
VIII	1,238	783,465	5.89
IX	1,895	1,033,553	7.76
X	1,321	678,232	5.09

Airport Development/Planning Program

($ in thousands)

Region	Awards	$ Value	%
I	62	20,477	3.17
II	80	64,193	9.94
III	86	39,905	6.18
IV	185	115,972	17.96
V	134	81,305	12.59
VI	185	71,284	11.04
VII	65	42,045	6.51
VIII	83	49,877	7.72
IX	129	105,618	16.35
X	91	55,178	8.54

Federal-Aid Highway Program

($ in thousands)

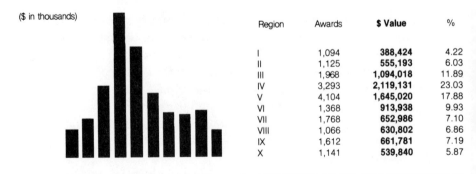

Region	Awards	$ Value	%
I	1,094	388,424	4.22
II	1,125	555,193	6.03
III	1,968	1,094,018	11.89
IV	3,293	2,119,131	23.03
V	4,104	1,645,020	17.88
VI	1,368	913,938	9.93
VII	1,768	652,986	7.10
VIII	1,066	630,802	6.86
IX	1,612	661,781	7.19
X	1,141	539,840	5.87

FIGURE 4. Department of Transportation bar charts

FIGURE 5. Sample page of clip art

Now wouldn't you find it easy to diet if you could diet without ever being the least bit hungry? And, especially, if you knew that you were still getting all the vitamins and minerals that you need for good health?

Of course, the only way you can be sure is to try this product, is it not? Unless you try it, you'll never know whether you missed the greatest opportunity ever to lose weight the comfortable, safe, easy way, will you?

So don't you agree that it makes good sense to give this thing a try, at least? Especially when the cost is so small?

Note the technique of starting with questions that are based on premises that we can accept easily—who would quarrel with those first ones—and gradually approaching the critical question of trying our product. And it's done in writing almost exactly as it is in face-to-face presentations. The question technique is not used widely enough, although its effectiveness is well established. Here, for example, are a couple of items from a direct-mail piece I received recently, offering me calendars imprinted with my name as advertising specialties:

> What's the cost of your regular Christmas card? How much time do you spend filling out each card?

Unfortunately, the writer abandoned the technique at this point and began to make declarative statements instead:

> Now you can save all that time and send a greeting that will be appreciated immediately and used all year long with this fine personalized calendar in a handsome mailing envelope.

That latter is a fine argument for the calendar, and could be quite persuasive, if presented with more impact. The question technique should have been continued, and the headline (AVOID CHRISTMAS CARD WASTE) should have reflected that excellent argument, with something along the lines of SEND A "CHRISTMAS CARD" THAT LASTS ALL YEAR or SEND A "CHRISTMAS CARD" FOR EVERY MONTH OF THE YEAR. It should have been pointed out more effectively than it was that the calendar is an excellent way to get the customer to keep your name hanging on the wall in plain sight all year long. The main theme, expressed at the beginning and reinforced later, was to avoid the "waste" of greeting cards this Christmas by sending calendars. Wrong theme: avoiding waste is simply not that much of a motivation. A perpetual advertisement hanging on the customer's wall would be a far more appealing benefit, and could have been played up in the copy. (Note the false premise that the reader would agree with 1) that it was highly desirable to avoid wasting time, paper, and money, as alleged in the letter; 2) that Christmas cards were such a waste; and 3) that mailing calendars instead of Christmas cards equals avoiding the waste. What the copywriter evidently (presumably, that is, for there is no way to be sure of this) referred to as "waste" was the short life of the Christmas card as advertising matter. Unfortunately, it is unlikely that many readers will make the connection and grasp what the copywriter means because it takes a few minutes' reflection, at the least, to grasp this none-too-clear reference, and people reading direct-mail literature will not dwell long over it. You've only a few seconds to make your point, as a rule, in communicating with a reader via advertising material of any kind, and you won't manage it if you are not painfully clear.

In fact, I think that I would have tied in the idea of the year-long advertising message with the graffiti idea, using some such slogan as WRITE YOUR NAME ON THE CUSTOMER'S WALL and bringing in some suitable graphics to get attention, while tying in the message. That's the right kind of gimmick, incidentally—one that relates directly to your main theme or strategy.

WRITING THE SALES LETTER

Aside from the basics of persuasive writing, there are a few mechanical principles about modern sales letters, and there are two schools or philosophies about how to write a sales letter:

1. One school holds that it ought to appear to be a letter, and preferably not a printed form letter, but one written individually and personally. In today's environment, it is possible to do this, using either of two methods:

- A mechanical individual typing of each letter, using a computer or memory typewriter to type each letter anew
- Offset printing the letter and typing in the individual's name and address. A variant of this, commonly used, is to offset-print the letter, with a general salutation, such as "Dear friend," and not try too hard to make the letter appear a personal one. (Almost everyone today will recognize that this is a printed, form letter.)

2. The other school holds that since there are not that many advantages in making the letter appear to be individually written, in any case, and since most people today are wise enough and sophisticated enough to recognize such a letter for what it is, why not forget about even trying to make it appear a personal letter and go all out with advertising. Therefore, this school makes it a letter, nominally, but uses a variety of advertising devices that are clearly advertising devices.

The second school of thought is by far the most widely pursued in the direct-mail profession. Sales letters today are prepared on a typewriter, generally, but bear no salutations, have headlines that may be typed or typeset, and use other advertising graphics to make their points. At the same time, since it is supposed to be a letter and not a brochure or broadside, and the letter is signed, despite not being addressed to anyone, an effort is generally made to adopt a person-to-person tone, such as one might expect in direct correspondence. Sales letters are generally in first- and second-person, not third-person, therefore. Write a sales letter to the reader, as though you had had a personal inquiry from that reader and were explaining to him or her just what it is that you offer. Make references to the other elements in the package, too, and urge the reader to study those also, for more details, photos, special offers, or whatever appeals you believe will help.

The letter lays out the basic proposition for the reader, and attempts to establish a person-to-person relationship. The letter should (presumably) reflect something of the personality of the signer of that letter. It should be sincere sounding, but should also follow the basic rules of advertising and sales persuasion. Many writers of sales letters work hard at trying to close the sale with the letter, but that is a logical error, for this reason: if the sale could be closed with the content of the letter, the other elements in the package would be superfluous and a waste of money. Since that is obviously not the presumption in designing the package, but it is intended and desired that the reader should read the sales letter first, it is logical to make it the mission of the sales letter to persuade the recipient to read the other items—brochure, broadside, order form, and other items, if any exist. So a proper approach for a sales letter is to introduce the proposition generally, point the reader toward the other items and persuade him or her to read them, and *not even try to close the sale with the letter.* That would be a definite mistake, and here is why:

As they say in show business, save something for the encore. If you give your sales effort your best shot in the letter and go all-out there in a try for the sale, you all but destroy the impact of the other items. That is because an all-out sales try in the letter is likely to bring the customer to decision there and then, which means that the customer then will not even look at the rest of the package. (Why should he or she, if he or she has made a decision already?) Therefore, it is inescapably logical that the main objective of the sales letter is something other than making or breaking the sale—it must be to serve as both introduction and persuader to look the entire package over carefully. The most effective sales letters do exactly this because the writers know what the proper *objectives* of the sales letters are.

THE BROCHURE

Whether the other key piece of the package is actually a brochure, a broadside, a circular, a flyer, or some other piece, we'll refer to it here as a "brochure" because the philosophy generally is the same: it is generally the main selling effort. It is here that the copywriter typically pulls out the stops and goes for the jugular: the sale. Here is where the product is pictured, if it is something that must be illustrated graphically, and the heaviest sales argument is presented. However, the need for persuasive writing is no less acute here than it is anywhere else. The cause-and-effect relationship of "understanding" and "belief" is still murky enough so that they are virtually inseparable: it is necessary to strive for both.

Most writers do not use graphic illustrations nearly enough, but tend to rely on words alone. And most people tend to mistrust anything they do not understand very well, so it is essential that you bring the reader to at least *think* he or she understands what you are getting at. Moreover, if you can actually create a direct image of some sort through a drawing or photograph, it is far more direct and far more effective than painting that picture with words, as advocated earlier. And that is even more true when you must deal with an abstraction that cannot be translated directly into a concrete example. In that case, it is generally necessary to resort to an *analogy,* to help the reader understand your point.

Newspapers furnish a good example of this in the charts they use to show readers what an increase of 5 percent in unemployment represents. They use bar charts, generally, although they often substitute drawings of objects or people—workers, soldiers, women, tanks, airplanes, trucks, tank cars, or other such people and things—as the "bars" in the charts, adjusting their sizes to reflect ratios. That is, if they wish to show that one-half of all blue-collar workers are covered by retirement plans, the figure of a worker for those covered will be one-half the size of another figure, intended to represent all blue-collar workers. Using such devices, newspapers often print charts to show our military strength versus that of the Soviet Union, and make other such graphic models to help readers see the relationship.

Pie charts are also used often, for such purposes as to show how the government divides its budget. Figure 2 (page 174) is one example of such a chart. (This is a delineation of the Library of Congress budget.) A variant of this is shown in Figure 3 (page 175), also a pie chart, although it looks more like a wheel of cheese being cut into segments. This is a Department of Defense budget presentation, and perhaps the cheese is symbolic, but it is actually an improvement over the two-dimensional pie chart because it is far easier to grasp the analogy when it is presented in three dimensions, as in the "cheese chart." And Figure 4 (page 176) presents several Department of Transportation bar charts, showing how it has spent some of its budget. In this case, the bar charts illustrate the relative magnitude of numbers presented alongside the bar charts, a most effective technique.

Cartoon figures are often helpful in persuading readers to read on, to plow their way through what may appear to be a formidable block of text. Cartoon figures represent fun and light reading, generally, and usually make the blocks of text appear far less formidable. It is possible to get such material—cartoons and other such graphic aids—at very small cost by buying what is known as "clip art." These are collections of such drawings in reproducible form, and in purchasing them you also buy the right to use them in any publication without infringing on anyone's copyright. Figure 5 (page 177) is an example of such material, taken from a widely circulated book called *klip, klip, klip-art.* The figure reproduces only a single one of approximately twenty-five pages, which include cartoons, headlines, borders, order forms, and various other useful graphic devices, in addition to the many cartoon figures.

MISCELLANEOUS SITUATIONS AND REQUIREMENTS

Almost every day is "Persuasion Day" for most of us in our contacts with others, making purchases, seeking jobs, negotiating with children, and otherwise carrying out all the daily functions of modern life.

ALMOST ALL SITUATIONS ARE SALES SITUATIONS

A SALES MANAGER to whom I reported, in earlier days, pointed out that every time two people have any kind of an exchange a sale is made. At the least, one persuades the other to believe or do something, or the other persuades the first one to accept a refusal to do or believe that something. And that is a fundamental fact of life, whether we are talking about seeking a job, making a speech, urging the youngest in the family to brush his or her teeth and hang up his or her coat, or waiting on a customer in a retail store. Some of these daily situations require formal preparation of written instruments—resumes, letters, speeches, situations-wanted or help-wanted advertisements, newsletters, and many other specialized products of the pen. In these penultimate pages of this book we are going to have a look at various and sundry such situations and their needs, and discuss those writings the situations require. One of the most common—and for many of us, the most important—such situation is that of job hunting. In today's business environment, almost everyone seeking a job must have a resume.

JOB HUNTING AND RESUMES

There was a time, and it was not too many years ago, when the only people who needed resumes when they were seeking jobs were those who didn't hold "jobs" at all; they were seekers after "positions" or "situations"—executives and professional people, primarily, who were not paid wages, but who received a salary. (Perhaps a somewhat subtle distinction, but a real enough distinction, nevertheless.)

That has changed. Probably the chief reason for the change has been the explosion of technology (a root cause), which has brought about the age of specialization: hardly anyone today would dare to claim to "do anything" or base a job search on an offer to "do anything." Employers no longer want people who make that offer or claim; they want specialists. (However, many an individual hired as a specialist finds himself or herself actually doing anything and everything *after* being hired.)

In some areas, this has been carried out to excess—almost to an absurd degree. For example, a television receiver has several "I.F." (intermediate frequency) stages (circuits), which are virtually identical in design. Still, it was not unusual in the early days for a different engineer to be assigned to the design of each of these separately, and for that engineer to specialize in that single design year after year, as though that engineer were not eminently capable of designing many other circuits.

This modern-day belief that everyone must specialize and that generalists are obsolete is a prejudice, of course. But it is as difficult to overcome by frontal assault as are all prejudices: direct assault on the prejudice only hardens it and polarizes positions further. If it is to be attacked at all, the attack must be an oblique one, one that does not appear to be an attack at all. However, it is far better to avoid the battle entirely, since at best the chances of winning it are relatively slim. That is, as far as generalization versus specialization is concerned, it is far better to represent yourself as a specialist of some sort, even if you are a specialist in generalities!

That is not quite as ludicrous as it sounds. In the field of medicine, there are virtually no general practitioners today, other than some veterans of older days who think they are too old to change. In fact, the closest one comes to being a general practitioner today is to be an internist. However, the general practitioner is sorely missed in the medical profession, as well as by the public at large. The disappearance of the general practitioner has left a large gap in the array of medical specialties. And action has been taken to close that gap by restoring the general practitioner, except that he and she will now be a new specialist, practicing that newly invented specialty of "family medicine." And complete training programs have been set up to train physicians in "family practice." (Note the careful avoidance of restoring the term *general practitioner,* in recognition of the fact that most young physicians would reject it, another evidence of prejudice against terms.)

You can borrow a leaf from this approach in your own resume and job pursuit, by making a virtue of necessity: devise a good title for yourself and make a specialty out of whatever it is that you offer to do for an employer.

What will you do for an employer? That latter remark and the first line of this paragraph is the entire key to an effective resume. An employer is a customer to whom you are trying to sell your services on a more or less permanent basis, for regular salary plus other emoluments—bonuses, paid time off, insurance, stock options, or whatever the employer offers employees. What you are really trying to do, in seeking a job, is to trade your services—what you can *do* for an employer—for an acceptable payment. The employer has the advantage that any customer has: usually, a customer can choose among a number of options, seeking to find the one that appears to offer the most for the money, the most satisfactory service or product, or for whatever reason appears to be the most advantageous among the options available. The employer may have a fixed salary scheduled for the job, no matter who is hired, or may wish to negotiate and try to strike an individual bargain. Therefore, the price you ask may or may not be a key factor in his decision. But whether it is or not, the first consideration is always what you have to offer: what you can *do* for the employer.

What is a resume?   Bearing the foregoing in mind, it should not be difficult to perceive that a resume is a sales presentation. And as such, it ought to be based on those same persuasive principles we have talked about in earlier pages in discussing other kinds of sales presentations:

1. The promise—what you can/will do for the employer
2. The evidence/proof that you can/will deliver on your promise
   a. Evidence that you understand the employer's typical needs
   b. Evidence that you are capable of satisfying those needs
   c. Evidence that you are *in other respects* a good employee
   d. Evidence that you can make a substantial *contribution* to the job

Of course, in applying the principles of sales presentations and persuasive writing to resumes, some special adaptation is necessary. Let's consider the items listed above.

The promise.   Every employer—and that term is a generic one, and may refer to owner, manager, personnel chief, foreman, or anyone who happens to represent the ownership/management responsibility of the company—has problems. A for-profit company always has problems of profit and loss, for example (and that is probably the foremost and most important problem in most companies). No company turns an invariable profit on everything it does. Every company has losses in various operations at various times, and the goal overall is to turn enough profit overall to absorb and surmount the setbacks of operations that did not go right. Ergo, anything you can offer that translates as contributory to profits—greater sales, more efficient operation, stop-loss methods, or anything else that benefits the bottom line—will get attention. (Of course, it will probably be skeptical attention, and you'll have to work hard at providing the evidence.)

Some of the things you promise will not bear directly on the bottom line, but will, nevertheless, offer the employer help in making something work more smoothly, with less trouble, and—especially—at less cost. That latter is always a powerful, appealing promise: there is probably nothing quite as attention-getting and motivating to an employer reading a resume as some solid evidence that the subject of that resume will provide bottom-line benefits by reducing costs. This is especially true in these days, when costs appear to be nearly impossible to control. Anything you offer will be more effective if you relate it to cost reduction, or even to cost control.

As a second choice—and it is not always possible to link what you do directly with costs and profits, admittedly—focus on anything else you can promise to do for an employer, and think of this in terms of problems you can solve or overcome, or any other benefits you can think of. But the solving of a problem or two is usually the best course, because all employers have a basketful of problems, and are always interested in reducing the load.

The evidence. Evidence, in a resume, takes two or three forms. Education and/or other training is one kind of evidence that you can do what you say you can do. Experience is another and stronger evidence, especially if you can show a close linkage of that experience with the prospective employer's needs. The explanations and presentations you make in your resume may also show, of themselves (that is, by the proper use of terms and explanation; that in itself reveals true understanding of the problem), proof that you know what you are doing and can deliver. And, of course, if your former employers and other references bear out what you claim, the evidence will be strong enough.

Resume formats. There is no universal format for a resume, despite what some books on the subject say. In fact, because most employers find themselves faced with many resumes to choose from, as a rule, it is beneficial if your resume does not resemble most of the others. There is definite benefit in making your resume distinctive—not garish or outlandish, however, but thoroughly businesslike—so that it does stand out from the others. But the important thing is what your resume says. Here, first of all, is the information that ought *normally* (there are exceptions, for certain exceptional cases) to be in your resume:

Education and/or other training, scholastic achievements, honors

Relevant work experience

Noteworthy honors, awards

Specific achievements, especially in work experience

The above are not in any particular order because they can be presented in any order, according to individual circumstances. If you are a recent graduate and have no specific work experience relevant to the position you seek, you are all but compelled to begin with education: it's the only thing you have to offer as qualifications.

On the other hand, if you have some substantial work experience, it's a mistake, usually, to begin with education; the work experience is more germane and more important.

If you have some specific, noteworthy work achievements— a patent, the design of a system that worked wonders for a past employer, a remarkable sales record, or other such, it's important to somehow make the prospective employer aware of that as soon as possible. The rest of your qualifications can wait.

In short, you must decide what your strongest asset is—*asset* meaning qualifications for the job you seek (not for anything else)— and trot that out first. And you should select or design a resume format that enables you to do exactly that.

In my own case, for example, I have the good fortune to have won many millions of dollars' worth of contracts with proposals I have written for others. You may be sure that my resumes featured that accomplishment up front when I was seeking positions where that achievement was relevant to the job I was after. I deliberately devised resume formats that enabled me to do just that.

Banalities and other common mistakes to be avoided. Here are things to avoid as you would nuclear fallout:

1. Claims of being an "idea man" (or woman). Terribly overdone, makes readers of resumes yawn, was not effective even when a new idea. Amazingly, almost everyone thinks he or she is a person of many original ideas, when the reverse is true: relatively few people come up with really original or creative ideas.

2. Protestations of being hardworking, conscientious, loyal, and similarly virtuous. Just a claim, not evidence, also stimulates yawns.

3. Statement that you're looking for challenges. Also terribly trite and besides no one cares what *you* want; what are you *offering?*

4. Totally irrelevant personal data, such as religious preferences, spouse's and children's names, hobbies, age, weight, color of hair, and other such. Only rarely is any personal data relevant even remotely. Such data rarely helps, often hurts your case. Safer to leave it out, keep resume as brief as possible, use available space for things that contribute.

5. Statement of "objective." Risky thing to state, unless carefully slanted to employer's interest. But also totally unnecessary. Employer really doesn't care about your objective, but only about what you can do for company.

6. Any statements that are mere claims—hyperbole and superlatives—that you can't support with evidence. (When you have the evidence, you don't need to make claims; just provide the evidence.)

Do's to balance the don't's. Here are some things you should definitely do in preparing your resume:

1. Arrange all information in order of importance, and importance means in order of how much the item contributes to selling yourself to the employer.

2. Avoid generalities—especially avoid those superlatives and other adjectives. Stick with nouns and verbs, focus primarily on your relevant achievements, back the statements up with evidence, provide *details*. As in proposals, details are convincing, persuasive, lend credibility. Anyone can generalize and philosophize; the presence of illuminating details suggests strongly that you are telling the truth and you know what you are talking about.

3. Stick with those items that are totally relevant. How fast you ran the 440 in college or how good a philatelist you are is not likely to have much relevance to most jobs. But neither is solving a shipping problem for a past employer relevant if you are seeking an entry-level job as an electronics engineer.

4. Be brief while you still do not neglect to provide all necessary detail. In fact, use telegraphic style, which eliminates articles and conjunctions, is thereby brisk and businesslike, a good effect to achieve.

5. Be clear about what you want—what kind of job, that is. Be sure, too, that your resume is compatible with what you seek. Don't expect the employer to study your resume and decide where you will fit into the organization; it won't happen, ordinarily. *You* have to decide what you are after and where/how you can contribute most effectively. But you must let the reader of your resume know what you think about this.

It's quite amazing how many job seekers fail completely to give even a hint of the kind of job they seek and/or believe themselves best qualified for. Obviously, their hope is that by not declaring themselves to be candidates for any specific kind of job they will maximize their chances of being considered for one job or another. Unfortunately, it's not an effective strategy.

Who should write your resume? There are a number of companies who will write your resume for you, and there are many moonlighters also who offer such a service. Prices vary enormously, from as little as $10 to $25, at the bottom of the scale, to as much as $1,000 and even more, at the top of the scale. Yet, despite these gargantuan prices, it is doubtful that anyone is better qualified to write your resume than you are.

In any case, a number of sample resumes, including "before" and "after" examples, follow, to guide you in devising your own best format. Some of the resumes shown here were invented; others are of real people and therefore have certain key names and other identification blocked out. The illustrations and borders used in some of the samples are all "clip art," available in most art-supply stores. (See Figures 6 through 12.)

Study these examples, with respect to what has been said here. You'll find some contradictions—for example, many of the writers listed "objectives"—but in most cases the exceptions to the rule were justified or, at least, were such that they did not harm the resume materially.

Note especially that each of these managed to be one-page resumes, even those of highly experienced, high-level corporate executives. Bear this in mind, when you consider how long your resume should be: the purpose of your resume is not to elicit a job offer directly, for it certainly cannot do that. What you seek is an interview. Therefore, your resume ought not to tell the whole story and ought to somehow make it clear that it is necessary to interview you to get the rest of the story. Ergo, the ideal resume is a "teaser," providing just enough of and the right kind of information to arouse the reader's interest and impel him or her to call and say, "Please come in and let's talk. I want to know more about you and what it's going to take to get you on our team." You need detail, but too much detail can be ruinous to your chances. Like they say in show biz, exit leaving them wanting more.

Broadcast letters. Job hunters often use what some specialists call "broadcast letters." These are letters printed in quantity and sent out together with the resume, in the hope that it will

```
                    TYPICAL  "BEFORE"  RESUME
```

Peter Mardin   Married (Wife, Sara Jane)
765 15th Street   Two children, Sandra Lee, 5
Potauk, N.Y.   and Thomas Woodridge, 9
007-0007

OBJECTIVE: Position of responsibility and challenge, where I can use my
natural resourcefulness and develop new ideas for a far-seeing employer.
Interest in people and people-oriented activities, talent for leadership,
decisive personality.

EDUCATION:

    Political History, 2 years, Vayzmirh University, 1961-63.
    Computer programming, Software Systems Center, 1964.
    West Plotnik High School, Academic course, 1960-64.

PROFESSIONAL EXPERIENCE

    1971 to Present: Systems analyst, Automated Information, Inc., designing
    business and management information systems on custom basis for clients.

    1967 to 71: Computer programmer, Automated Information, Inc., implement-
    ing system designs in COBOL for Honeywell 200 and IBM 360.

    1965 to 67: Computer operator, Automated Information, Inc., operating
    in-house H-200 and H-1200 for service bureau operated by company.

OTHER WORK EXPERIENCE:

    Harvey's Hardware, 1962-64, part-time, while attending high school. Kept
    stock, made deliveries, waited on customers.

    Telephone solicitor for the Dandy Department Stores while attending
    college.

MEMBERSHIPS:

    Member American Computer Programmer and System Analysts National Society
    (ACP&SANS).

    Member Potauk Civic League and Potauk Parent-Teachers Association.

MISCELLANEOUS:

    Member National Honor Society in high school, graduated third in class.

    Hobbies include skiing and chess.

FIGURE 6. Traditional resume style ("before")

Peter Mardin
765 15th Street
Potauk, N.Y.
007-0007
COMPUTER-SOFTWARE DESIGNER

SUMMARY: 10 years computer experience, presently solving technical problems
in software design, leading team of five. Cited and awarded bonuses
three times by employer for outstanding contributions in design
leading to estimated 2-years' savings of $1,300,000. Know Honey-
well, UNIVAC, and IBM equipment, languages.

OBJECTIVE: MANAGEMENT POSITION.

PROFESSIONAL HISTORY:

1965 to present: Automated Information, Inc. Presently Systems Analyst
(since 1971), having been promoted from programmer, with beginning experience as computer operator).

Principally called upon to solve special problems in system design.
Designed all systems currently used by our own service bureau division.
Designed MIS for several clients, wrote successful proposals for over
$14,000,000 in last two years.

Have designed systems for use in educational establishments also, for
IBM 1500.

Innovations in design resulted in documented cost savings of over $400,000
in past year. Methods used have become company's proprietary information
and provided the company a large competitive advantage. Company comptroller
projects current-year's cost reduction at over $900,000, as a result of using
these innovative ideas.

EDUCATION includes two years college and diploma course at Software Systems
Center.

PUBLICATIONS: Technical papers in software systems design for professional
journals (list available on request).

FIGURE 7. Resume redesigned, reformatted

```
                        John Henry Jones
                        3722 N. Oak Drive
                        Puscatawket, NH
                        336-7707

EDUCATION:        BBA, major in Accounting, 1965, PDQ University
                  MBA, major Financial Management, 1967, XYZ University

EXPERIENCE:       1970 - Present.  J.K. Smith Tool & Die Manufacturers, Inc.
                  Office Manager, responsible for payroll, purchasing, account-
                  ing, supervising three clerks and secretary.

                  1968 - 70 Brown Shoe Company, shoe wholesalers. Made up
                  payroll for 12 people, keep inventory, records, processing,
                  payables and receivables.

                  1967 - 68 Association for Business Development, Director
                  of Public Relations.  Wrote news releases, brochures, news-
                  letters and handled membership correcpondence.

HOBBIES:          Skiing, swimming, reading Civil War History, chess,
                  gardening

MEMBERSHIPS:      Podunk Men's Club, Baptist Christian Association, Young
                  Republican's Club

PERSONAL:         Age:  31.  Married, two children:  Brian, age 8 and Marilyn
                  age 4.  Own home
```

FIGURE 8. Another "before" example of a resume

support, reinforce, and somehow add to the impact of the resume.

Whether a broadcast letter does this or not is moot, in my opinion. (And I have been the employer ploughing through large stacks of resumes, trying to find some that showed promise.) In fact, in a company large enough to have a personnel officer, that individual will probably discard the letter or, at best, file it away, and send only the resume on to the appropriate manager for review. So the individual who actually makes the decisions is not likely to even see your broadcast letter in most cases.

It is my opinion that if you use such a letter, it should not travel together with the resume. It can, instead, either precede or follow the resume, to wit:

1. Preceding a resume, it may arouse enough interest to provoke the employer to specifically request your resume. If so, you have made a giant stride toward an interview. At least, you

JOHN H. JONES
3722 North Oak Drive
Puscatawket, New Hampshire 02307
Telephone: (514) 336-7707

POSITIONS SOUGHT:
Comptroller
Financial Manager
Treasurer or equivalent

SUMMARY OF
QUALIFICATIONS:

Financial/Accounting executive (BBA and MBA), 6 years experience.
Have successfully handled management of accounting, inventory,
purchasing, financial controls; earlier experience in Public
Relations. Have successfully accommodated 40 percent increase
in workload in past two years without increasing staff, cut
material costs 6 percent through new purchasing policies I developed on my own initiative.

EXPERIENCE:

1971 - Present

OFFICE MANAGER

J.K. Smith Tool & Die Manufacturers, Inc.
Staff is 3 clerks and secretary. I prepare payroll for 29
people (salaried and hourly). I handled other payables of
$36,000/year. I bill $1,200,000/year, for which I handle all
credit and collections. And I purchase about $65,000/year in
raw materials.

Sales have increased from $850,000 to $1,200,000, with a corresponding increase in work force and all other functions. I have
managed to handle the increase in my workload without adding to
my original staff. I also developed a new competitive bidding
system for buying raw materials that has reduced costs of materials
by 6 percent.

1968 - 1970

ACCOUNTANT

Brown Shoe Company (Wholesalers)
I did all accounting including inventory, payroll, credit and
collections. Before I joined company, they were unable to process
payables in less than 30 days or to pursue collections on receivables less than 45 days overdue. Within 3 months I was paying all
bills in time to take discounts, saving the company nearly $70,000
per year.

I also pursued receivables more than 10 days overdue and reduced
overdue receivables to an insignificant amount (which enabled me
to put the company in a cash position to take advantage of cash
discounts). I also improved the inventory system to alarm management about slow-moving stock. This again helped our cash flow.

1967 - 1968

**DIRECTOR OF
PUBLIC RELATIONS**

Association for Business Development
I wrote all news releases, brochures, the association newsletter,
and all correspondence with the membership. I succeeded in getting
85 percent of our news releases published locally, and had nearly
20 percent of them put on the wire for national coverage.

My activities increased membership from 211 to 380 during my stay.

EDUCATION:

BBA, Accounting, PDQ University
MBA, Financial Management, XYZ University

FIGURE 9. Another "after" example of a resume

can address your resume directly to the hiring manager, avoiding the often dead-end stop at the personnel office. Moreover, your resume will then get special attention. Caution: your letter must be quite strong to do this. (Of course, you can always follow up with your resume if your letter has evoked no response.)

2. Following your resume, it may help to draw attention to your resume, if it is strong enough, perhaps persuading the hiring manager to have another and closer look at your resume.

3. Instead of a resume, if you choose to so use your letter, it will soon enough indicate whether it is likely that a resume would draw any interest. That is, if there is no response to your letter, it seems likely that you would be wasting postage to send that company a copy of your resume.

There is one advantage in using such a letter: it is different, and may therefore draw a bit more attention than a resume would. Moreover, you can be fairly sure that if you learn the name of the hiring manager relevant to your wants and address your letter to that manager, your letter will reach him or her and be read, whereas if the manager opens an envelope and a resume pops out, the resume may be promptly dispatched to the personnel office without so much as a glance at the name on it.

Broadcast letters, then, can be helpful if used wisely and not merely to say, "Here is my resume. Please read it and hire me."

NEWS RELEASES

News releases are written by individuals seeking publicity, which should not surprise anyone. What is probably not quite as obvious or as well-known is that by far the overwhelming majority of news releases are barely out of the envelopes which carried them before they have been redeposited in the well-known "circular files"—wastebaskets—so abundantly in evidence in editorial offices. And what may be even more surprising to the uninitiated is that the chief reason for the prompt rejection of well over 90 percent of all news releases is not poor writing. Quite the contrary, most releases are quite literate and clear. What ails most and leads to their early demise is simply that there is no earthly reason for the editor who receives them to publish them: they are simply not newsworthy, to use that term in a rather broad sense, for the news

PROFESSIONAL BACKGROUND

Wilmington, Delaware 19808
302 ███ Home
215 ███ Office

General manager
Sales/Manufacturing/Finance
BSE, MBA, PE

ACCOMPLISHMENTS:

Turned three companies around. Increased profitability of another company by 900%, and increased another's sales from $5,000,000 to $28,000,000. 21 years in general management, sales, and finance; manufacturing and services: pollution control, steel castings, wire and cable, reinforced plastics, explosives, concrete, construction, and land development. Designed aggressive marketing programs, accountability and incentive systems, and directed operations. Work well with people.

6/75
to
Present

President and Chairman, ███ Corporation, Philadelphia, Pa. Pollution control services for steel mills, refineries, utilities and chemical plants. Liquid and solid waste removal. Heavy-duty vacuum cleaning; high pressure water blasting; tank cleaning. Reorganized immediately, increased efficiency and obtained six major new customers to bring company into black after first six months. $23 million sales. 626 people.

6/73
to
6/75

Executive Vice-President, ███ Casting Company, New Castle, Delaware. Carbon and low-alloy steel castings sold to over 200 industrial users. Complete P/L responsibility; managed all aspects of sales, operations, administration and financial control; 365 employees; $11,000,000 sales. Doubled sales and production and turned previous 3 years' losses ($490,000, $640,000, $880,000) into 2 years' profits ($985,000, $1,895,000). Director and stockholder.

7/71
to
6/73

Vice-President and General Manager, ███ Jamaica (Division of ███ International Corp.) The largest land development operation in the Caribbean: construction and management of two resort hotels (1,050 rooms), housing projects, condominiums, roads and utilities. Also managed the security and agriculture divisions. $120 million capital projects. 1,245 employees. Increased profitability 900% the first year, 290% more the second year.

2/62
to
7/71

Plant Manager, ███ Incorporated, Wilmington, Del., Super-Temp Wire and Cable Division. Managed 836 people in this $38,000,000 division, which had lost $600,000 in the previous 12 months. My first year produced $3,600,000 profit, second year, $5,800,000. Venture Planning Manager for New Enterprise Department (two successful acquisitions). Sales Manager, Reinforced Plastic Products, raising sales from $5,000,000 to $28,000,000 in 2 years. Division Controller, Plastics Division. Project Engineering Manager, Polaris missile manufacturing. Also contributed special marketing and computerized accounting and financial analysis projects.

6/57
to
2/62

Sales Manager, ███ Industries, Inc., Kingston, N.J.: ready-mix concrete and crushed stone. Had also been Sales Engineer and Project Engineer in charge of new plant construction and mix design, testing and quality control.

6/55
to
6/57

Construction Project Engineer, ███ & Company, New York, N.Y. Worked on construction of $60 million polyethylene plant and Polymer Chemicals Division administrative/marketing offices and R & D laboratories. (Earned MBA at night during this time)

EDUCATION: BSE, Princeton University 1955. Civil Engineering, structural design, construction materials, management; basic engineering sciences. Industrial engineering. Economics

MBA, Graduate School of Business, New York University, 1957. General management, marketing, corporate finance, accounting and personnel.

PERSONAL: 43, married, 1 child. Excellent references.

FIGURE 10. Typeset one-page resume, featuring achievements

MICHAEL ▮▮▮▮▮▮▮

▮▮▮▮▮▮▮▮▮▮▮▮▮▮▮▮▮▮▮   *(703)* ▮▮▮▮▮▮ *(home)*
Arlington, VA. 22201   *(202) 5▮▮-▮▮▮▮ (office)*

OBJECTIVE: ECONOMIC RESEARCH ANALYST/ASSOCIATE POSITION

> Extensive experience in proposal development with major
> consulting firm; contributed to several successful pro-
> posals. Conceived and developed expanded research capa-
> bility for firm (on own initiative) by establishing inter-
> library loan system. Currently performing variety of
> investigative functions (interviews, records, research,
> surveys, studies) in field of "import injuries" for
> Department of Labor.

I: EXPERIENCE SUMMARY

Economist, U.S. Department of Labor, February 1976 to present.

Economic investigations in response to petitions, seeking to determine whether
imports are causing separations of U.S. workers. Study records, interview and/
or survey company and union officials, firm's customers, and others with relevant knowledge.

Analyze and interpret data on employment, production, and sales of firm whose
operations are being investigated.

Prepare reports and recommendations based on the investigations and studies.

Research Associate, ▮▮▮▮▮▮▮▮▮▮▮▮▮▮▮▮▮▮▮ *June 1975 to February 1976.*

Developed inter-library loan system enabling   to borrow from various libraries (including Congressional Library) to aid research. Conducted many literature searches in various subject areas (e.g., bilingual education, child abuse
and neglect, Indian alcoholism). Sought out Congressional Committee reports,
hearings, bills, laws, and other Washington-area information sources.

Wrote sections of successful proposals for large contracts (most recent over
$3,300,000). Found consultant experts and subject matter authorities and
secured their approvals to be available for proposed projects.

II: EDUCATION

Currently in Master's program Georgetown University (evenings).
B.A. Economics and History (magna cum laude) State University of New York at Albany.
*Economics Statistics: probability theory, sampling, hypothesis testing, regression
analysis. Operations Research: linear programming & inventory, transportation,
and PERT models. Computer Sciences: programming in FORTRAN & BASIC.*

III: REFERENCES

Dr. ▮▮▮▮▮▮▮▮, Executive Vice-President, ▮▮▮▮▮▮▮▮▮▮▮▮▮▮▮

Mr. ▮▮▮▮▮▮▮, President, ▮▮▮▮▮▮▮▮▮ Corporation

Dr. ▮▮▮▮▮▮▮▮▮, Senior Vice-President, ▮▮▮▮▮▮▮▮▮ Corporation

All above may be reached at (301) ▮▮▮▮▮.

FIGURE 11. Resume with proper "objective" statement

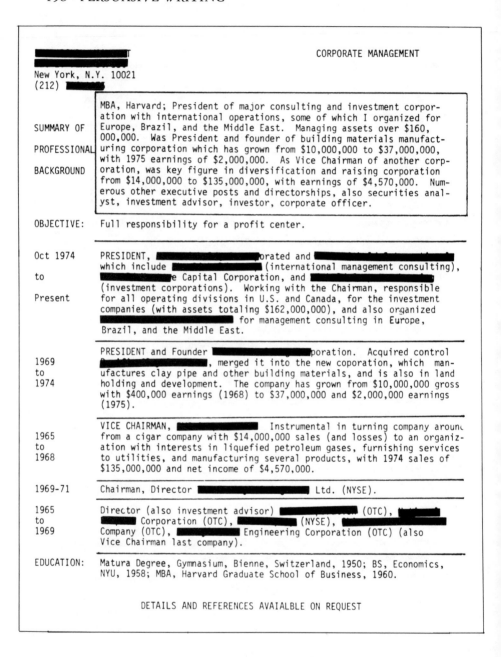

CORPORATE MANAGEMENT

New York, N.Y. 10021
(212) ███

SUMMARY OF PROFESSIONAL BACKGROUND

MBA, Harvard; President of major consulting and investment corporation with international operations, some of which I organized for Europe, Brazil, and the Middle East. Managing assets over $160,000,000. Was President and founder of building materials manufacturing corporation which has grown from $10,000,000 to $37,000,000, with 1975 earnings of $2,000,000. As Vice Chairman of another corporation, was key figure in diversification and raising corporation from $14,000,000 to $135,000,000, with earnings of $4,570,000. Numerous other executive posts and directorships, also securities analyst, investment advisor, investor, corporate officer.

OBJECTIVE: Full responsibility for a profit center.

Oct 1974 to Present

PRESIDENT, ███████████orated and ███████████ which include ███████████ (international management consulting), ███████████e Capital Corporation, and ███████████ (investment corporations). Working with the Chairman, responsible for all operating divisions in U.S. and Canada, for the investment companies (with assets totaling $162,000,000), and also organized ███████████ for management consulting in Europe, Brazil, and the Middle East.

1969 to 1974

PRESIDENT and Founder ███████████poration. Acquired control ███████████, merged it into the new coporation, which manufactures clay pipe and other building materials, and is also in land holding and development. The company has grown from $10,000,000 gross with $400,000 earnings (1968) to $37,000,000 and $2,000,000 earnings (1975).

1965 to 1968

VICE CHAIRMAN, ███████████ Instrumental in turning company around from a cigar company with $14,000,000 sales (and losses) to an organization with interests in liquefied petroleum gases, furnishing services to utilities, and manufacturing several products, with 1974 sales of $135,000,000 and net income of $4,570,000.

1969-71

Chairman, Director ███████████ Ltd. (NYSE).

1965 to 1969

Director (also investment advisor) ███████████ (OTC), ███████████ Corporation (OTC), ███████████ (NYSE), ███████████ Company (OTC), ███████████ Engineering Corporation (OTC) (also Vice Chairman last company).

EDUCATION: Matura Degree, Gymnasium, Bienne, Switzerland, 1950; BS, Economics, NYU, 1958; MBA, Harvard Graduate School of Business, 1960.

DETAILS AND REFERENCES AVAIALBLE ON REQUEST

FIGURE 12. Resume of top executive, with relevant objective statement

14 October 1982   Contact: Mindy Cooper
Release # 8463   215/299-5470 Days
                                               215/449-3254 Evenings

JOHN LOVE, JR., RECEIVES
ASTM AWARD

PHILADELPHIA, PA--John Love, Jr., professor of mechani-

cal and aerospace engineering at the University of

Missouri, Columbia, Missouri, was named a 1982 recipient

of the Award of Merit by ASTM, the internationally

recognized standards-writing organization.

    Love, a resident of Columbia, was honored on

10-13 October 1982 during ceremonies hosted by ASTM

Committee E-38 on Resource Recovery in Dearborn,

Michigan. Love was cited for his dedication and

management of the development of ten standards and test

methods for refuse derived fuels, and for service since

1974 as founding chairman of Subcommittee E38.01 on

Energy.

FIGURE 13. A more or less typical news release

release does not have to be literally news to be newsworthy. In
fact, *news release* is only one of several terms applied to this piece
of paper. It is known as a *press release, publicity release,* and simply
release, also, and some of those other terms are far more descriptive
of what it really is than is *news release.* Let's look at one as an
example. (See Figure 13.)

    This is the first page of a release that covered more than two
pages. The word *more* at the bottom of the page tells the reader

that there is more to come. The final page has the symbol—30—
to indicate that it is the final page.

This is typical newspaper practice. "More" was used traditionally on copy coming "over the wire"—the teletype machine—
to let the editor know that there was more to the story, yet to
come. The —30— symbol was an old telegrapher's symbol for
"end of transmission." However, also in common practice to indicate the end of the story is the word *end* and the symbol ###.

In the case of this release, it is possible that Philadelphia
newspapers will pick up the release and use it because the ASTM
(American Society for Testing and Materials) is located in Philadelphia. It is most likely that periodicals in Columbia, Missouri,
and especially any circulating on the campus of the University of
Missouri will use this item because it is of local interest there.

Whether anyone else publishing information and news for
general consumption would be interested is problematical, although it will surely be useful information for any publications
catering to people in science and industry. The release should
therefore be directed to such publications.

Note these features on this release, which appears to have
been prepared by someone thoroughly experienced in the art:

1. The source is clearly identified, but suffers in that it uses
only the initials ASTM, without identifying the words they stand for.

2. It gives a release date and a release number. The number
is for reference, in case someone calls to inquire about the item
and wants to get more information.

3. A "contact" is given, for that same reason—as a source to
answer questions and provide more information. Note that both
a day and night number are given, a wise precaution, since someone may call from another time zone, or from a morning newspaper. (People on morning newspapers work late at night.)

4. It has a headline.

5. It has generous margins for the use of the editor in marking
the copy up for typesetting and insertion, as well as for general
editing to match the publication's style. (All publications have their
own styles, and the wise writer of releases makes it as easy as
possible for the editor to edit the release according to his or her
own style.)

There are two criticisms that can be made and would be made

by some people familiar with releases and news-writing practices:

The head takes up too much of the paper, restricts the white space left for editing, to at least some extent.

Some editors don't like releases to have their own headlines; they prefer to write their own heads, and would rather not have one even suggested to them.

Figure 14 illustrates another release. This one is on the organization's letterhead, is dated but does not list a release date. Presumably, therefore, it may be released immediately, but in that case it ought to say "For immediate release." And with the mailing date listed, by the time it arrives the editor may decide that it is stale news and discard it promptly. Moreover, it fails to say *more* at the bottom, although this release did have a second page, with the symbol —30— used to designate the end of the story. The most glaring fault is that the copy is single spaced, making it all but impossible for the editor to mark the copy up effectively. This is a most definite no-no in writing releases, and is almost sure to prove a fatal fault.

Figure 15 is a crisp, one-page release which uses a headline that summarizes the story immediately, and a text that gets to the point. It does not have a contact listed at the head of the release, but does present one in the last lines of the text. It calls itself a "press announcement," still another euphemism for "publicity release," which is what these really are—efforts to gain publicity.

Whether they succeed in this or not—that is, whether the newspaper, newsletter, and magazine editors to whom these are sent choose to use the releases or not—depends on whether the release is itself persuasive or not. Again, we are looking at a situation in which we are trying to sell something. The editor is going to use the release only if he or she believes that it is newsworthy— will be of interest to readers. And a release can fall into any of several categories and categorical situations, such as these:

Not newsworthy and unabashed try for free advertising, giving nothing in return. Definitely no.

Good material, will interest, inform, amuse readers. Use.

Mediocre material. May be used, if it arrives on a "dull day"— when the editor does not have a great deal of good material and is almost desperate for something to plug a hole in the next issue. Otherwise, the piece won't make it.

**Coalition
for
Common
Sense
in
Government
Procurement**

1990 M Street, N.W. Suite 570
Washington, D.C. 20036
(202) 331-0975

Board of Directors

Stephen D. Channer
*Business & Institutional Furniture
Manufacturer's Association*

John P. Luke
National Micrographics Association

John H. Fitch
*National Association of Wholesaler-
Distributors*

Bruce M. McLellan
National Office Products Association

Joseph T. Morris
*National Association of Photographic
Manufacturers, Inc.*

Kenton H. Pattie
National Audio-Visual Association

Adrian H. Pembroke
Business Products Council Association

Forrest I. Rettgers
National Association of Manufacturers

Michael J. Timbers
Chairman (Past President)

Officers

Paul J. Caggiano
President

Gloria C. Gamble
Executive Vice President

Counsel

Robert D. Wallick
Steptoe & Johnson

Regional Representatives

Colorado
Michael J. Timbers
Information Handling Services

Florida
Kurt F. Enfield
Enfield's Miami Photo, Inc.

Illinois
James R. Fleming
Ansley Business Materials, Inc.

Massachusetts
John E. Shirey
Wright Line

Minnesota
Jon R. Grunseth
Economics Laboratory

Utah
Adrian H. Pembroke
A. H. Pembroke Company

Washington, D.C.
Arthur D. Caulfield
Olympia USA, Inc.

NEWS RELEASE

July 14, 1982

Contact: Gloria Gamble
           (202) 331-0975

COALITION REJECTS GOVERNMENT'S EFFORTS TO

BURDEN FEDERAL GOVERNMENT SUPPLIERS WITH PROFIT

LIMITATIONS AND INCREASED CONTRACT DATA REQUIREMENTS

WASHINGTON, D.C. -- Through the General Services Administration, the government is threatening to dictate the profits suppliers to the Federal Government can make when they contract to sell to the government. Further, the government is threatening to impose additional paperwork and reporting burdens on those firms interested in selling to the government.

The COALITION FOR COMMON SENSE IN GOVERNMENT PROCUREMENT submitted a firm position objecting to a number of proposed policy changes the General Services Administration (GSA) has presented to industry on a procurement system that benefits agencies throughout the government, all over the country.

The proposed policies affect the multiple award schedule contracting system which is designed to allow federal government agencies to buy small quantities of commercial, off-the-shelf items quickly, mostly from local businesses, and at a discount off their commercial prices. After GSA negotiates these contracts, establishing standard terms and conditions and preferred prices, federal government user agencies then order their small needs directly from the multiple award schedule contractors. The agencies are required, under procurement regulations, to order the lowest priced items to meet their needs. However, no orders from the government are promised to contractors just because they have a multiple award schedule contract.

The Coalition objects to unreasonable and unbusinesslike policies that GSA is fostering in its proposal. These policies would require contractors to give the government the same prices for its "onesy-and-twosy" orders that contractors give to their large volume customers in spite of the drastic differences between the two customers' contractual arrangements and purchasing practices. In order

FIGURE 14. "How not to" example of a news release

National Conference on

LOCAL
NETWORKS
**Designing and Implementing
Applications for the '80s**
November 17-19, 1982
Washington, D.C.

**PRESS ANNOUNCEMENT
For Immediate Release**

CONFERENCE FOCUSES ON DESIGN AND IMPLEMENTATION OF
LOCAL COMMUNICATIONS NETWORKS

Washington, D.C.: An indepth look at designing and
implementing information systems using local networks will be the
theme of the National Conference on Local Networks, to be held at
the International Hotel, Washington, D.C. on November 17-19, 1982.

Emphasis of the three-day meeting will be on practical evaluation
of the advantages and limitations of local networks for different
applications, including how local networks fit into an overall
communications strategy. National experts will provide a wide range
of experiences with respect to designing, installing and managing such
networks.

Two full days will be devoted to presentations on such topics as
comparisons of baseband and broadband networks; evaluating voice and
data networks; network design, management, and security; performing
communication assessments; establishing communications strategies;
using fiber optics; and selling a communications strategy in the
organization. Three preconference Workshops will provide
opportunities for indepth studies on integration of voice and data;
data communications for local networks; and choosing a communications
strategy.

A special feature of the Conference will be an exhibit of
hardware, software and services for local networks.

Infosystems, the Information Systems Magazine for Management,
is sponsoring this Conference to draw together user information on
local networks and to assist those who will be faced with making MIS
and data communications decisions in the near future.

For further information, contact the Conference Manager, U.S.
Professional Development Institute, 12611 Davan Drive, Silver Spring,
MD 20904. Telephone: (301) 622-5696.

###

FIGURE 15. Another flawed example of a news release

WHAT IS "NEWSWORTHY"?

As you read a few pages ago, a release does not have to be literally news to be used in a newspaper or other publication. Editors use material that amuses, entertains, and interests readers for other reasons than that it is truly news. The editor knows very well that when you send in a news release you are looking for publicity—free advertising. That's allowable, however, if you are furnishing worthy material because it costs the publication money to collect and/or buy the material it uses; therefore, useful material is a fair exchange for publicity or free advertising. It's a quid pro quo: you trade with the editor. If you understand that, you'll see why you have to make it worth the editor's time to give you that publicity; it can't be a one-way street.

All you really must do is apply the same principles we have been talking about throughout these pages: make the other party an attractive offer. At the same time, be as professional as you can by double spacing, providing generous margins, identifying a contact, and writing succinctly. And here are a few tips on how to make a newsletter on even a relatively dull subject reasonably newsworthy:

Try to capture interest at once by using the most striking idea or piece of information in the lead—even in the headline. Take that Figure 13 release, for example: The headline says JOHN LOVE, JR. RECEIVES ASTM AWARD. Newspaper editors are busy people. Even a Missouri newspaper editor might trash this release if he or she did not read beyond the headline. But if the headline had read UNIVERSITY OF MISSOURI PROFESSOR HONORED WITH ASTM AWARD, the editor would have known immediately *why* he or she should have been interested. And with energy so much in the news and such a worry item today, it would have been a good idea to have mentioned early in the story or even in the headline that the work for which the award was made concerned energy. Other possible leads (depending on where the release is to be sent) could have been focused on any of several other information items in the release.

The release presented in the next figure focused on the organization that issued the release, when it should have focused on what the government is trying to do to suppliers. The latter is far more newsworthy—a far better "peg" on which to hang the story. Readers are likely to be far more interested in what the government does than in what the Coalition thinks of it.

Figure 15 presents a businesslike release, and yet even that could have been greatly improved, as far as getting attention and arousing interest are concerned. For one thing, the first few sentences are rather vague and rambling. Instead of talking about the theme of the conference, it might have better explained what benefits attendees will derive by being there. What will they learn? What will they be able to do as a result of what they learn? Just who are the "national experts" who are promised.

Here, as we have seen again and again, vague generalizations destroy credibility and persuasiveness. If this release furnishes a compelling reason for anyone to attend this conference, the reader will have to deduce that by analyzing the release and, probably, by making some telephone calls. Of course, only those with a direct interest are likely to go to that trouble, and not too many of those, either. You simply can't ask readers to do all the work of finding out what it is you are trying to tell them, and the key is *specific detail* here, as it is elsewhere.

Of course, editors know this very well, and an editor who wants to use such a release badly enough may go to the trouble of writing or calling—calling, more likely, for a busy editor—to get the needed detail to make the story worth running. But of course only an editor who either wants this story very badly or who has a dire need to fill some holes in an upcoming issue is going to go to that much trouble.

If you were to apply the classic news-writing standard of *who, what, when, where, why,* and *how* to this "press announcement," you would see the trouble immediately: *what, when, where* are revealed in the lead sentence, but *who* is not explained until the next to last paragraph, and *why* and *how* are explained only in those vague terms already mentioned. Moreover, *who* should include the names of individuals—those "national experts." *But not one individual is named anywhere in this release.*

And that is why most releases are a waste of time and money. The tragedy is that it is not really that difficult to write an acceptable release, one that will please editors and find its way into final print in a number of periodicals.

SPEECHES

Speech writing is a highly specialized art, admittedly, and yet it is not really that difficult to learn. However, there is one peculiarity about speech writing you must take into account: a given speech must be written for the person who is to deliver it. The speech that is a tremendous success when delivered by one speaker can be a disastrous flop when delivered by another speaker—even though both speakers are perfectly competent public speakers.

Speaking is a highly individualized art, and almost every public speaker has had to undergo a great deal of self-training to find his or her most successful style, organization, mode of delivery, gestures, expressions, and other such things. It's like telling a funny story: it can be a great hit and evoke gales of hilarity when delivered by one speaker, and be met by nothing but deadpan silence when another speaker tells the story.

There are a few general rules, however, to be observed, no matter who is to deliver the speech:

1. Be wary of tongue-tripping words and combinations of words. Read the script aloud to yourself, as you go. What appears easy to say may or may not be so easy when speaking on your feet.

2. Stay away from cute and tricky devices, such as strings of words with the same initial letters, words that rhyme with each other, and homonyms—words that sound alike but have entirely different meanings, such as *meet* and *meat,* or *bear* and *bare.* And even words that are spelled alike and have different meanings, such as *bear,* meaning the animal, and *bear,* meaning carry or endure. The distinctions are not always apparent when such words are used in speeches and can be grossly misunderstood by an audience or even make the speaker appear ludicrous.

3. Avoid unusual words and jawbreakers, which may or may not give the speaker trouble, but will be "over the heads" of many in the audience. Use the simplest words and synonyms possible.

4. Be most wary of attempts at humor unless the speaker can handle it well. Humor can be deadly in its backfire, if the speaker is not entirely up to using it well. (And even then it sometimes falls flat and embarrasses the speaker.)

5. Keep the sentences short and paragraph frequently. It's much easier on the speaker that way, even if he or she is reading the speech.

6. Don't suggest gestures. Let the speaker decide on that. (Speakers should and generally do rehearse and mark up their manuscript with guidance notes.)

It's best if you know the speaker and can work closely with him or her, but if you follow these guidelines, you won't go far astray in any event—not even if you are writing your own speeches.

SPECIALIZED ADVERTISEMENTS

Small advertisements, both classified and display, are used successfully by individuals, small businesses, and even large businesses. In principle, a small advertisement is no different from a large one. In practice, there are at least a few differences, owing to the fact that what is termed here a "small" advertisement does not afford room for the features of larger advertisements. In fact, it might be more accurate to refer to some of these specialized small advertisements as "announcements," rather than as advertisements. In any case, we are referring here to display advertisements of not more than one column-inch and classified advertisements of only a few lines—again not more than one inch, which in most major media means fourteen lines at most.

Such advertisements are necessarily specialized because there is not a great deal of sales argument possible in such a limited amount of space. Therefore, such advertisements are suitable only for use as inquiry advertising—to draw inquiries so that you can respond with direct-mail literature packages: to offer items for only a dollar or two, the most you can expect to sell successfully with such a small advertisement; and to announce items or services that will all but sell themselves by the mere fact of their availability.

The essential need in this latter class is clarity more than anything else—once you have established that the item or service does not, in fact, need a great deal of selling. Here are examples of such notices:

Free search for the out-of-print book. Any author, any title. No obligation.

Quick cash. Borrow by mail. Easy credit on your signature.

Free report. Tells how you can start a business at home, in your spare time, without investment. Send self-addressed, stamped envelope for full details.

Such notices as these draw a response because they cater to the reader's desires and/or assure the reader at the same time that there is no obligation. Words such as *free* and *easy* never lose their appeal, quite evidently; there are always many people who want to believe them.

On the other hand, there are many small notices that work well simply because there are many people who need what the notice offers, but have some fears about the matter. Take, for example, the case of individuals who need resumes and want some professional help to get their resumes written. They know that in some cases the fees are much higher than they can afford, and they are fearful of walking into or even calling anyone who has a prominent advertisement because the mere fact of a large advertisement suggests a large company and a large fee. So they look for either the small company or the moonlighting individual, and in this case the bulk of the persuasion is accomplished simply by demonstrating that the advertiser is, in fact, a moonlighter. Here are examples of such advertisements:

> Resumes by professional writer. Low rates. Call evenings. Tel: _____

> Resumes written by personnel specialist. Personal service, fast results. Call _____.

The fact that many people deliberately seek out small, classified advertisers in the hope and expectation that they will thus get more moderate prices than they would have from the larger organizations is not lost on larger businesses. Many of them utilize this psychology to their advantage by running small, classified advertising to reach this class of customers and to convey the impression of smallness. (Yes, there are those who prefer doing business with large companies, but there are also those who reason that the reverse is preferable.) Here, for example, is such advertising:

> Typewriter, portable, like-new condition. Must see to appreciate. Very low price. Call _____.

This advertisement appears to be one inserted by an individual who has either no longer any use for the typewriter or who needs money badly enough to sacrifice it cheaply. That notion is supported by the fact of a telephone number without a street address. The reader who calls this number is invited down to see the typewriter and discovers (if he or she didn't discover that during the telephone conversation) that the address is that of a dealer of some sort, who has many typewriters to sell, and perhaps other things as well. In fact, such dealers often run a half-dozen or more such advertisements every day, each notice offering a different item at an allegedly low price.

Many seeking jobs insert "positions wanted" advertisements in the classified columns of their daily newspaper, and some even use small display advertisements. Some will get results simply because they offer to accept positions that are relatively hard to fill, even in times of high unemployment, such as domestic service and even secretarial jobs. Such advertisements tend to read somewhat as follows:

> Administrator/secretary, self-starter, take-charge type, flexible hours, word-processing experience, take shorthand.

As in the case of a resume, the key to success in such advertising lies not in making claims, but in reporting facts—facts of what you can and will do for an employer. The claims to being a self-starter and a take-charge type in this advertisement are just that: claims; there is no way to verify them except by calling references, and even then you cannot be sure that the references are not just being kind to the individual seeking a job. On the other hand, experience in word processing and the ability to take shorthand appear to be factual reporting, and will be accepted as such, at least until proved to be not true.

In a small advertisement—and a one-inch advertisement rarely permits you more than about fifty words, even packed tightly—every word counts. Here it is more important than ever that you stick to reporting items in such a manner that they will be accepted as facts, and not scowled at as self-applauding claims. It is also essential that you make every word count by using telegraphic style and eliminating those free-riding articles, conjunctions, and adjectives that contribute little or nothing.

Again and again, however, when you study such advertisements, you find the same mistakes as those made in resumes: claims of being hard-working, industrious, loyal, full of great ideas, problem solvers, seekers after challenges, and badly in need of a job.

NEWSLETTERS AND OTHER SPECIAL
PROMOTIONAL ITEMS

Estimates of the number of newsletters in existence in the United States vary so widely that it is all but impossible to be sure what the total is. It is safe to say, however, that there are many thousands of them. (One number which appears to be reasonably accurate to me is 30,000.) By and large, the majority of these newsletters are for-profit enterprises, and while a great many of them are small and even home-based, part-time ventures by individuals, a great many are big business. (A few years ago, a publisher of several newsletters in the Washington, D.C. area sold out to a major publisher for a reported $15 million.) But there is a special class of newsletters of interest here: that class of newsletters published primarily for the purpose of supporting the marketing and sales activity of a for-profit organization, or as a publicity vehicle for a government or nonprofit organization. Essentially, the objective is the same in both cases, with the newsletter designed to support another activity, rather than to be an enterprise in itself.

There are many such publications in existence, some of them published fairly frequently (monthly or even weekly), some of them relatively infrequently (bimonthly, quarterly, semiannually, and even occasionally, which means whenever the mood strikes). Some of them are fairly well disguised as bona fide newsletters which happen to carry a few notices and advertisements for their publisher's other interests: others are unabashedly advertising and sales-promotional efforts.

Obviously, if you go too far in the latter direction, you defeat the very purpose of your effort to increase the readership of your advertising and sales literature. Of course, the idea of creating a newsletter for promotional purposes is to persuade the recipient to read it—including reading your advertising/promotional copy. Therefore, such a newsletter ought to include at least some information worth reading, sandwiched among your advertisements. Ideally, it ought to be the other way around, with advertising and sales copy sandwiched among legitimate news items and features—at least, it ought to *appear* to be that way.

Figure 16 illustrates such a newsletter. This one was the official publication of a now-defunct organization, and was intended primarily to attract new members, who would then buy various items and services sold by the organization. That the organization eventually discontinued its existence was due simply to the fact that it did not return profits satisfactorily, and the founder of the organization decided to turn his efforts elsewhere.

Figure 17 is the front page of a newsletter I designed some years ago, when I was offering a number of my own small reports. This was an eight-page product, with ample advertising in its inner pages. (It is my belief that with such a newsletter, there should be no advertising on the cover.) Note the address box at the bottom of the front page, making it possible to mail the item without an envelope, as a self-mailer and what the Postal Service calls a "flat."

Note that both these newsletters are addressed to specific audiences (writers and aspiring writers, on the one hand, and those seeking to earn money in their own enterprises, on the other hand). In both cases, the letters begin by offering what is intended to be useful information. (Newsletters do not necessarily deal in news per se.) This is what is intended to persuade the recipients to read the publication from cover to cover. Inside, most of the stories are "jumped"—started on one page and continued elsewhere, on later pages. There are two objectives in doing this:

1. It enables the publisher to crowd all the most appealing and attractive headlines or captions in the early pages, where most readers—even casual browsers—are likely to see them and want to read them.

2. It persuades readers to turn to back pages, where the stories are continued and advertising appears on the pages.

The latter is important. Some fairly recent advertising research has shown that full-page advertisements often do not "pull" as well as those occupying less than a full page because readers skip over them, whereas they see advertisements on pages where they are reading editorial matter.

Probably for best results, advertising should literally be sandwiched between editorial items, as suggested earlier, and never bunched up. That maximizes the probability that readers will see, read, and note the advertising notices and promotional items.

Note, too, that one of these two examples is formally typeset, while the other is composed by typewriter. Typesetting offers the advantage that it generally permits more copy to be crowded into a given amount of space—probably about 20 percent more, as compared with typewritten copy, and even more if the publisher

The
Writers/Publishers Digest

VOL. 1, NO. 1 — FEBRUARY 1979   National Writers Syndicate

Helping You to Market Your Ideas, Information and Processes Through the Written Page

NWS PURPOSE STATEMENT
Welcome New Subscribers!

The purpose of the National Writers Syndicate (NWS) is developing writers, their projects and the respective markets that their projects fall into. Whether or not you are a seasoned book or newsletter writer, or a "rookie" staff writer looking to break into mail order, writing for the government, newsletter, film strips, plays, how-to's, or anything pertaining to the printed page, you will find help with NWS. Our focus is people; our objective is to help you sell every word you write, members helping members, helping you find the help you need—when you need it—be it marketing, typesetting, editing, re-writing, printing, advertising, breaking into new markets, developing new contacts and friendships for the purpose of you both going together on a joint venture or a project, or simply finding money sources. We will be covering it all—taking you, I trust informally, from beginning of a project (via case histories) and a few neat ideas of marketing you can "steal" for your own project, to developing your own consulting services.

INSIDE
THIS ISSUE

THE TWO HALLMARKS OF
THE SUCCESSFUL WRITER

by Herman R. Holtz
President and Publisher of Government Marketing News, Inc.

I once knew a budding author (we were both 17) with whom I had many violent disagreements about writing. I believed in writing for the market—writing what would sell. He claimed to be indifferent to what would sell, but was dedicated to writing what was in his soul, whether it sold or not.

Now, more than a few years later, he has been the author of short stories which won critical acclaim (although very little money), two novels (as far as I know), and a non-fiction book about Hollywood. None of his books has ever been more than a modest success. And the fact that he chose to write an expose-type thing about Hollywood ought to reflect his disappointment that the world was not waiting for his "messages" with fame and fortune. It's the sort of writing he would have disdained—sneered at contempuously—when we were 17 and were going to conquer the world of letters.

Professing to be indifferent to whether your work sells or not is the worst kind of self-deceit. The mere fact that you offer your manuscript to a publisher is pretty good evidence that you do want it published. And what you get paid for the manuscript is pretty good evidence of what someone else believes it to be worth! If you get paid in a free subscription....

There are two things a writer must learn eventually, and the earlier one learns these, the easier the path to success. These are the two messages:
1) Success in writing is not different from success in other professions and other enterprises. It rarely comes quickly. (Those "overnight successes" you read about generally have happened overnight only after long years of obscurity and struggle!) It takes patience, courage, persistence, and faith—faith in yourself and faith in your work. It's the faith that lends you the courage to overcome disappointments and struggle on.

FIGURE 16. A newsletter used for promotional purposes by an organization

Money Making Tips

news and ideas for enterprising people

Editor: Herman Holtz

PUBLISHER'S DECLARATION

This newsletter is dedicated to serving the interests of the very small entrepeneur--the men and women who launch their enterprises with little or no capital and operate at minimum overhead, so that risk is almost zero, and the entrepeneur gets to keep most of the gross profit realized. Our purpose is to bring such readers as much sound information, business offers, ideas, and help as we can provide, and to serve, also, as a medium for exchange among such small entrepeneurs for their mutual benefit.

We will not accept paid advertising, although we reserve the right to list our own offerings to those who need the help our reports and services can provide. But we will accept news releases and general information submitted by readers, if we believe publishing the information is in the interest of our readers generally.

THE JOYS OF SELF-EMPLOYMENT

Nearly two years ago we closed our own downtown Washington (DC) offices and re-opened our offices in our own home in suburban Maryland. (We had lots of room here.) In so doing, we got rid of about $1,800 a month in operating expenses with-out suffering one penny's loss in business. We also did away with the laborious automobile trip through traffic every morning and evening, and gained about three hours a day to work at our business. But the greatest joy was discovering that we were no longer "in business," enslaved to office hours and a daily regimen, but were now self-employed, living like country squires! We set our own hours, usually according to how busy we happen to be, and do generally what we like, often fitting our office hours to other conveniences, rather than the reverse. Of course, it's also most pleasant to be able to keep most of whatever profits we manage to make on our operations, instead of paying out some 40% (two day's work!) to landlords, parking lots, telephone companies, city government, and other "partners."

Not every business can be run out of your own home, but a great many can. If yours can, we heartily recommend it. (Of course, you also get to write off some of your home expense as a business deduction on your income tax, as an added bonus.)

I find being "self-employed," rather than "in business," is like semi-retirement. At least it feels that way!

HERMAN HOLTZ PUBLICATIONS
P. O. BOX 6067
SILVER SPRING, MD 20906

 **First** Class

FIGURE 17. Newsletter designed to promote sales of reports

chooses to use a condensed type. Some publishers believe, too, that typesetting offers the advantage of being more polished and professional looking, and it certainly does present that image. However, whether that is or is not an advantage is moot, when it comes to newsletters. There is a large school of thought on the subject that holds with typewriter composition because those who believe this way are of the opinion that a newsletter should not be too polished and professional looking. Quite the contrary, say this group of publishers, a newsletter ought to give that impression of spontaneity that can be far better achieved with typewritten copy than with typeset copy. And to some degree, the same kind of thinking that we discussed with regard to small advertisements applies here: many customers are somewhat suspicious of too-successful an appearance, and fear of doing business with those who appear too prosperous. Even some highly successful news-letters, such as the Gallagher reports, are printed directly from typed copy.

Make no mistake about this: it has nothing to do with costs or schedule pressure, but only with psychological impact. It is quite easy to have a small typesetting machine in your own office today and produce professionally typeset copy with it, as rapidly and as inexpensively as you would by typewriter. But the reader has no way of knowing that, and senses that typewritten copy is later information and has more of a person-to-person impact than does the more formal typeset text.

The advertising copy you insert in your own newsletter need be no different from the copy you would insert in any publication, and it can be of any size. It should not, of course (as already noted) dominate the newsletter, if you wish to persuade readers to read it thoroughly. Otherwise, it is no longer a newsletter, but is a direct-mail advertising package with a bit of editorial matter scattered throughout.

It is also possible to conceal and disguise your advertising in your own newsletter by running features and service articles (principally, how-to-do-it pieces) which promote sales. For example, if you sell books, reports, or other such information items, you can review several of these in each issue of your newsletter and supply cost and ordering information on each. But you can also do this for products, in the manner of the slick-paper magazines, which run "new product" columns in their publications.

You may wish to run some kind of contest, as a sales promotion, and the newsletter is, of course, an excellent vehicle for this.

You may want to promote a product by publishing an article describing some common problem and explaining several ways of solving it, one of which is by buying and using something you sell.

You may run articles about your own organization as a kind of institutional advertising, to promote confidence in your organization.

You can do a feature in each issue on a different one of the items you offer or a different service you offer, explaining it in great depth, which is often an excellent approach to selling anything: prospects are much more attracted to that which has become familiar and which they understand and feel somewhat at home and at ease with.

All of these, because they appear as straight editorial matter, are far more believable and persuasive than they are when they appear as paid advertising.

While many publishers of these promotional newsletters offer free subscriptions and mail copies by the thousands, others charge small, usually nominal fees, enough to cover direct costs of printing and postage. And a great many pursue a compromise between these two ideas, in this manner:

In the early stages, free subscriptions are given to everyone on a suitable mailing list or inquiry advertisements are run, offering sample copies. And in many cases, if the newsletter is being published by someone already well established in business, free subscriptions are given to established customers.

Later, those who have never responded to any of the advertisements or promotional copy are dropped from the free or "complimentary" subscription list or are asked to pay some fee—$5 or $10, usually—for a "regular" subscription. However, you may choose to ask everyone, eventually, to pay at least some nominal sum for a subscription.

One large advantage of running such a newsletter is that it is an almost ideal vehicle for inquiry advertisements. You can legitimately offer free subscriptions or at least free sample copies of your newsletter in small classified advertisements, at very little cost, and get quite good results usually. There is relatively little skepticism on the part of even sophisticated readers of your advertisement, for one thing; it's quite believable that a newsletter publisher will give free sample copies. A free copy of a newsletter is also quite attractive to a great many people. Therefore, such advertisements generally produce rather good results.

Another thing you can do with such a newsletter, if you have not gone overboard in making it an advertising vehicle, is to exchange complimentary subscriptions with other newsletter publishers. Or even if other newsletter publishers do not want to make such a trade, you may choose to send them copies of your newsletter anyway, because they may and probably will pick up items from your newsletter and report on them, occasionally, adding to your coverage in much the same way a news release does. But you can greatly increase this kind of expanded coverage, too, by offering to swap items with other newsletter publishers. That is, you each grant the other the right to quote freely from each other's publication.

This is not exactly an uncommon arrangement between newsletter publishers, but there is still a better way for you, since you want the greatest amount of coverage you can get, and you are really not that interested in using others' copy. Instead of offering a mutual swap, you announce boldly in your newsletter—in every issue, as standard boilerplate—that anyone may use the material in his or her own publication provided that he or she makes attribution—identifies the source and credits you or your newsletter as that source. If you do this, you can mail out your newsletter freely to other newsletter publishers whose readership is likely to be suitable as prospective customers, but you need not limit yourself to other newsletter publishers. You can mail freely to magazine publishers and even to newspaper editors, if you choose. You can, in short, use your newsletter also as a news release, and if you have designed it skillfully enough and included enough of the right kind of material, you will get a great deal of coverage beyond your own subscription list. (You might even want to select a title for your newsletter that suggests this, such as *Joe Brown's Monthly News Digest,* or *The Sizzle Company's Monthly Food Tips.*)

Some who offer a free copy of their newsletter (including some of those whose business is newsletter publishing) do not send a true sample copy of their newsletter (if, indeed, they really have a newsletter!). Instead, they send what purports to be a copy of their newsletter, but is really a direct-mail advertising package, with all the elements—sales letter, brochure/broadside, "special offer" flyer, and order form—incorporated in what is represented to be a sample of the newsletter. In fact, in such cases, the advertiser rarely offers *anything* that is not pure and unabashed advertising copy, which is clearly misleading and perhaps even fraudulent.

My personal feeling is that this is self-defeating in at least two ways. For one, if you do this you lose the benefits of the true newsletter, as just described: it is a rare customer who is so unsophisticated that he or she does not recognize that what you have sent on is pure advertising matter. And, for another, you may very well arouse the resentment of the recipient, who feels victimized and will therefore not do business with you. You have not, in truth, demonstrated that you are very honest, when you do this, have you? You have, in fact, given the respondent good reason to mistrust you.

I know personally of some who do this, and they send the same "sample copy" to inquirers year after year. They do not even have the grace to rewrite their copy occasionally. At least one is truly a newsletter publisher—that is his business—and he could easily send a true sample copy with suitable advertising literature enclosed, or at least make up a special sample that does include some legitimate, useful editorial material. But he chooses to go on deceiving those who send him their requests for sample copies.

SPECIAL PROMOTIONAL MATERIALS

The secret of success in periodical publishing lies primarily in being able to achieve and maintain a large enough number of readers to justify high advertising rates. And to do that, most publishers find, it is risky to rely entirely on newsstand sales. (Moreover, newsstand sales entail a great deal of waste, with returns and other problems.) Ultimately, it comes down to establishing a satisfactory number of subscribers and achieving a satisfactory renewal rate.

That explains the almost frantic effort to get your subscription, in the first place, and even more frantic efforts to keep it—to persuade you to renew your subscription. (Perhaps you've noticed that?) Since I subscribe to a fairly large number of publications, for business purposes, and often subscribe to a new one for only a single year, because I need to use it in connection with gathering information for a new project, I am in perhaps a better than average position to judge this. Hardly a week goes by that I don't get almost pathetic appeals to renew my expired or about-to-expire subscription. In fact, it is not unusual for me to begin getting such notices as much as six to eight months before my subscription is due to expire. Periodical publishers obviously do not believe in waiting until the last minute. The latest one to arrive on my desk is from a business magazine I try to read regularly. It includes three pieces: a sales letter, an order form, and a return envelope, prepaid, of course.

The sales letter says HOT POTATO! in large type—about 24-point or about one-third inch—printed in bold red ink. It explains the order form, which has a green border, like a bond, and is entitled "Renewal Saving Certificate," offering what is alleged to be a special rate. The "hot potato" idea is rationalized thus: the saving certificate is the hot potato because I can't hold onto it for long, since it has an expiration date about three weeks hence, although my current subscription has three months yet to run. The certificate, which is just the right size to fit into the response envelope, does everything for me: I need only check off whether I want to be billed or am enclosing payment and whether I want to take advantage of the savings with a one-, two-, or three-year subscription renewal. The publisher will do everything else, including billing me. And the card assures me that my credit rating (with them, anyway!) is better even than AAA; it's AAAA.

The outer envelope that carried the package had two windows, one through which my name and address (on the order form) showed, the other a small one through which the "due" date showed. And under that latter small window was printed in rather bold type: EXPIRE NOTICE, intended, no doubt, to alarm me and send shivers up and down my spine.

All in all, it's an appealing package, however, although not a very original one. I'll renew because I want to continue reading the publication, not because the package was that attractive to me. (I am not typical, fortunately for this publisher.) However, it could have and would have probably been far more appealing and much more motivating if the appeal had given me some hints or even broader indications of articles, reports, or other information projected for future issues. Most periodical publishers have material scheduled for many months into the future (some of my own articles have not seen print for a year or more after their purchase by magazine editors), so that should not be a problem. But, like others, this publisher relies on that same formula of basing the appeal on saving money, and goes to any extremes necessary to sell that, instead of selling the product. Suppose that creative originality were applied to the product itself and to selling the product; would that not probably work wonders for the publisher?

Seminars are big business today and carry a substantial price tag, in most cases—as much as $200 per day for each registrant, and sometimes even more. It is understandable that it requires special appeals to induce people to pay such fees. Figure 18 shows the front panels of two small brochures designed to promote seminar attendances. Note that each features its main appeals on the front cover—what the attendee will learn that will be of benefit enough to justify the time and expense required to attend the session.

Another special device is the card that fits a standard rotary or flip-file, such as illustrated in Figure 19. This particular card is issued by a nonprofit—government—organization, the Massachusetts Department of Commerce Business Service Center in Boston. It's an organization designed to support small business generally and minority-owned business especially, and it issued a number of pieces of literature to explain the program and its services, and to persuade respondents to use the toll-free number and call whenever they needed some assistance. The card was designed to be of more than ordinary use by being die-cut to fit into the typical rotary or flip-file, but that did not restrict its use for the recipient who didn't have such a file: it was still useful as a separate and independent card.

There are, of course, a great many such advertising novelties available, and you can also invent your own or have some useful but inexpensive item imprinted with your own name and advertising message—calendars, rulers, memo pads, pens, pencils, key holders, money clips, business-card cases, and wall posters, to name only a few. All are persuaders of one sort or another, if only by the virtue of repetition until they have made your name a familiar one—which makes the customer comfortable with it—or because of the convenience of being able to find your name and telephone number quickly.

UNITED BUSINESS INSTITUTE

presents
A Procurement Seminar

Pricing and Negotiation of Government Contracts

- Pricing for Victory
- Pricing for Profit
- Winning while losing (and vice versa)
- Regulations and You

Washington, D.C. Metro-Area

Tuesday, July 28, 1981
9:00 am. to 5:30 p.m.
WESTPARK HOTEL
Tysons Corner
8401 Westpark Dr., McLean, VA
(I-495 Exit 10W off VA Rte. 7)

OR

Thursday, August 6, 1981
9:00 a.m. to 5:30 p.m.
HOLIDAY INN - SILVER SPRING
8777 Georgia Avenue
Silver Spring, MD

ATTEND THE MOST CONVENIENT SESSION
TELEPHONE: (301) 423-3200

NWS

How To Make Money Writing

Learn how to start your own publishing company with your book or newsletter — or, sell your book or idea to a major publisher.

If you've ever thought of writing as a career or just a profitable hobby, here is the most practical, useful, and revealing seminar/workshop you've ever attended. Brought to you by:

THE NATIONAL WRITERS SYNDICATE

*and three of Washington's most successful newsletter and book publishers who started their businesses virtually off their kitchen tables. (One had gross sales for February 1980 in excess of $50,000 — **one month, and growing!** — and began 18 months ago with beginning capital of only $6,000!)*

MAY 24, 1980
8:00 a.m. to 5:00 p.m. + + +
Ramada Inn — Tysons Corner
Beltway (I-495) and Rt. 7
Falls Church, Virginia
Seating definitely limited.
First Come — First Served.

FIGURE 18. Two brochures (front panels) announcing seminars

FIGURE 19. Example of one advertising specialty

A FEW SPECIAL, PERSONAL SITUATIONS

Occasionally, even as private citizens and ordinary consumers, we have reason to write letters attempting to persuade others to some course of action or some belief. For example, a gentleman of my own acquaintance, employed by the District of Columbia (city) government, came to me for help one day several years ago. It seems that he was being unfairly treated, in his opinion, in being subjected to frequent changes in both his work-shift assignments and his post-of-duty assignments. He had written a letter of complaint to his superior on the job, and had been rewarded with what appeared to be a somewhat irrelevant response, which offered no relief at all. He wanted to respond with another letter, but was unsure how to proceed.

After studying the original two pieces of correspondence, I suggested that we write a higher authority and point out both the irrelevance of the superior's response and the continuing injustice this employee was being subjected to. I drafted a letter, which did just that, and had the gentleman send it off with enough copies to others to ensure that the matter was thoroughly documented and would be in enough files so that it could not be conveniently mislaid.

The results were as hoped for: the employee's various complaints were adjusted to his satisfaction, whether because the simple injustice of the situation became apparent or because of the pressure applied fairly subtly was not clear, nor was it important. The results were all that really mattered.

As suggested at the beginning of this book, "persuasion" is sometimes closer to coercion or pressure, but that does not mean that the method is any the less honorable or effective than is intellectual persuasion. In many cases, especially in this society of the past few decades, pressure is not only necessary but is thoroughly justified. In fact, a popular book on the subject of how to complain successfully recounted numerous cases.

Not too long ago, I had some problems with a TV receiver, which I had bought locally from a national chain of department stores. I also had some trouble getting adequate service from this store. After several weeks of frustration, I sent a letter off to the company's chief executive officer, at the company's home office in Chicago, explaining that while I was a happy customer—indeed, the company has usually been fine to do business with—I was most unhappy over this situation. Within a week or two I was getting telephone calls from the manager of that store and the store soon straightened out my problems.

Locally, there is a TV program on our channel 7 station called "Seven on Your Side." A local newscaster, Paul Berry, helps viewers straighten out such problems as the one I have just recounted— gets them refunds and or other satisfaction, as the case requires or justifies. Sometimes a telephone call or a personal visit is required by Paul Berry, but more often than not, a simple letter does the trick, and probably the individual could have done as much for himself or herself, had it occurred to him or her.

In such cases as these, "persuasion" often means nothing more nor less than going high enough in an organization. Even in the military service, a letter sent to the right party straightened out more than one problem I encountered, such as difficulty in getting reimbursed for travel expenses, in one case. What appeared to be insurmountably difficult at the company and battalion level suddenly became easy to solve when orders came back from a general with whom a complaint was lodged.

In such situations as these, it is necessary to identify and use the right pressure points. Often the right pressure point is a high level in the organization, whether it is a company or a government agency, but that is not always the case. Once, years ago, as a civil service employee of the federal government, I found it necessary to bring political pressure to bear. The federal executives—including a cabinet officer, in fact—who were involved were sure that I had political influence when they found a United States senator breathing down their necks about this matter. But the fact was that I had written appeals to both senators from my state, and one became interested enough to help me. (Of course, I tried to be persuasive in my letter by pointing out that I was a veteran—it was not too long after World War II—which I knew would appeal to this senator, who was himself a reserve officer.) In any case, even gentle pressure from the senator had a salubrious effect, and we soon resolved my problem.

In short, *who* you write to may be even more important than what you say in your letter, although your letter ought to appeal to the individual. Think, then, about what is most likely to motivate that individual to whom your letter is addressed. (Perhaps Paul Berry's battles in behalf of his viewers and fans is aided by the fear of adverse publicity for his antagonists, for example.)

9

ROUNDUP

Give the reader sound reasons for wanting to be persuaded, and persuaded he or she will be.

SITUATIONS MAY CHANGE, BASIC PRINCIPLES DO NOT

EVEN AFTER THESE many pages of explanations, revelations, discussions, and examples of the many situations calling for written persuasion and the many instruments used to persuade others in writing, we are dealing with the same principle in every case:

1. First, you must know precisely what you want the reader to do as a result of reading whatever you have written.
2. Then you must decide exactly what will make that reader *want* to do what you want him or her to do—the motivator.
3. Then you must provide that motivation—a promise of something.
4. Then you must provide the evidence that you can and will keep your end of the bargain—the promise.

Necessarily, the bulk of this book has been devoted to advertising and sales materials, for that is where the bulk of our business energies are directed in this country, and for which by far the bulk of our writing effort is expended. But, as I have tried to point out from time to time in these pages, we are all salesmen and saleswomen, selling our ideas and our personal services to employers, if nothing else. And we are also all writers, to at least some extent—if only in writing our own resumes and letters applying for jobs, in writing letters of complaint, and in writing anything that has as its purpose persuading someone else to do or believe something.

It is readily apparent, if only from watching the Paul Berry "Seven on Your Side" program referred to in the last chapter, that by far the vast majority of our citizens do not know how to take either protective or corrective measures, even when they have been clearly victimized unfairly. Paul Berry manages to find acceptable remedies for most of them, and he goes about doing so in a highly efficient and commendable way. So it is not with any thought of demeaning his work or minimizing his real accomplishments in behalf of his "clients" that I must observe that in probably a majority of the cases, the victim could have and should have at least attempted the same measures. In at least some of the cases, they would not have had to call on Berry at all. Remember this basic principle too about achieving persuasion:

Persuasion is essentially motivating someone to do or believe something, but there are both positive and negative motivations—hope of a gainful consequence and fear of a disastrous one.

In short, there is nothing wrong with fear as a motivator, and in every situation you ought to use whatever appears to be the most effective measure or, at least, the most credible promise/threat you can make. In a recent book project I sought certain information from a procurement official in each of the fifty states. At first, I found a rather indifferent response to my requests. But I soon learned to mark each letter of request in this manner: "cc: Governor's Office." That increased the response considerably, and in only a relatively few cases did I have to actually enlist the governor's assistance. (Although I did, in fact, do so in a few cases. When I did, I pointed out to the governor that it would be most unfair to him and to his great state to be inadequately represented in the forthcoming book, which would certainly be on the desks of many of his constituents.)

IT COMES DOWN TO SELF-INTEREST

All these situations point up the same thing: what motivates most people in most situations is self-interest, nothing more and nothing less. Even altruism is motivated by self-interest—the need to feel noble or proud, or possibly to atone for the guilt of being wealthy in the midst of poverty.

There are two ways to address self-interest: one is to appeal to self-interest needs of which the other is already aware; the other is to help the other party become aware of how and where his or her self-interest is involved. My letters to governors succeeded because I made sure that they understood what failure to be fairly represented would mean: it was a fear motivation I employed, although suggested in a positive way. Why did I choose that motivational strategy instead of a positive one of possibly pointing out that the governor owed it to his constituents, etc.? Simply for this reason: my rationale was that I was not credible as a vote-getting force, nor even as a force for enhancing the governor's public image. On the other hand, he could be hurting his public image and possibly losing votes if he did not compel his procurement official to cooperate. I thought the negative promise (threat, that is) far more *credible* than would be any positive promise I could make.

CREDIBILITY

That latter item makes the next point in persuasion: it is necessary to employ a credible threat or promise, or to somehow make it credible. In some cases, one may be inherently more credible than the other, but in many cases you have to decide which you can offer better evidence for—which, that is, you can make a more credible case for.

That is one reason that writing a letter or some other document offers you advantages over making a verbal presentation: the written presentation affords you time to think things out, to marshal arguments, to research sources, and to present your entire case coldly and unemotionally and without interruption. It also gives you the time to consider how much evidence you can gather for each type of appeal—positive and negative—and judge which is the more credible promise (or threat).

WHAT OTHERS WANT TO BELIEVE

Credibility also depends, however, on what the other party wants to believe. Even the most colossal bluff is credible if the other party chooses to believe it, and we find people believing the most astonishing things—including all kinds of supernatural phenomena—with exceedingly little evidence for the beliefs. So the art of persuasion depends also on knowing or sensing accurately what others want to believe.

A number of people have become quite wealthy trading on this tendency of many people to believe what they want to believe. Most get-rich-quick schemes are so based, for example. The victims want so badly to be rich that they are eager to believe in any scheme that promises riches, and they will accept a great deal of sophistical argument as proof. A number of books, for example, argue that if you manage to make yourself believe that you are indeed a great success, you will soon be one. Of course, the idea is contrary to our everyday human experience, and we've no evidence that it is true except the repeated assurance of the authors of these books. Still, it's tempting to believe that if you merely assure yourself many times a day that you are a success and form the right mental pictures of yourself as a success, you will eventually become one.

This is not to suggest that you should deliberately deceive readers, exploit human fears, or take advantage of the gullible. It is, however, important to understand that we each of us live in our own reality—each of us, that is, has our own vision of reality, and our agreements on what reality is are not much more than agreements in principle, quite often. Our differences in perception of what is real surface constantly in our disagreements over politics, religion, economics, social standards, and just about every other subject that occupies our minds and commands our attention. It is necessary, therefore, to understand the other's reality, as well as our own, if we are to communicate at all, much less persuade others to do or believe as we wish them to do and believe.

In short, then, everyone's reality is a reflection of what he or she wants to believe, chooses to believe. It may be your reality that the Republicans represent fiscal stability and responsibility, while another is absolutely certain that his or her 20/20 insight proves definitely that Republicans are entirely irresponsible fiscally. You may see life in general as a series of marvelous opportunities, while another person sees it as an unending trap for the ordinary citizen, and a third party sees it as a fat bird to be plucked. It's been said, in fact, that to the person who thinks, the world is a comedy; while to the person who feels, it's a tragedy. Obviously, then, the argument that works well with the person who feels is not likely to go far with the person who thinks.

A few years ago I attended one of those famous diamond auctions on the Atlantic City boardwalk. At the beginning, a gentleman came forth and explained to all of us seated there that diamonds were probably the world's most secure investment: it was all but impossible to lose a dime in diamonds, and almost certain that one's worth would increase if he or she bought and held a few of the famous gem stones. Once everyone understood those basic truths, the auction began.

The first piece offered was a ring. We were advised that it belonged to a gentleman who was of some European nobility and who had recently fallen on hard times. This forced him to sacrifice this fabulous ring, but it offered some fortunate individual seated there in that room the opportunity to profit greatly from the poor Prince's misfortune. The bidding began; the ring was finally sold to the fortunate gentleman who was the highest bidder.

At no time did it occur to anyone to inquire how it was that the Prince was losing so much money on his diamond ring when, we had only minutes earlier been assured, it was nearly impossible to lose money in diamonds? So powerful is the will to believe that which it is so pleasant to believe that the paradox was not evident to anyone else in that room, apparently. Obviously, everyone assumed that the poor Prince was the exception to the rule. Or perhaps he was too ignorant to know that he couldn't lose money in diamonds.

Obviously, even cold logic cannot prevail against the desire to believe. What the other party prefers or chooses to believe is your strongest asset, in any effort to persuade, if you can devise a way to harness that desire to your own ends, to make that desire help you in presenting what you wish to present. Therefore, it is important, as a first step, to ascertain or at least make a good estimate of what the other party wants to believe. In general terms, you may safely assume that all other parties are generally interested in acquiring wealth, becoming more secure, being loved, admired, and/or respected, and otherwise being blessed by all the good things that can happen to us in life. If you can somehow reasonably hold out the promise of one or more of those things happening as a result of doing or believing whatever it is you wish them to do or believe, there is an excellent chance that you will strike oil.

However, there is more to it than that. The promise will get some attention, and in some circumstances will be accepted readily and swiftly. But it is quite possible, also, that you will need to *sell* your promise—provide some evidence to make your promise credible.

EVIDENCE AND CREDIBILITY

Evidence is whatever another will accept as evidence. In a court of law there are "rules of evidence," and allegations must meet and comply with those rules to be acceptable as evidence. In persuasion in other activities than law, evidence is whatever others find credible enough to accept. And that does not mean it must be logical, either, as we have just seen.

One of the bits of evidence that apparently a great many people find convincing in the various get-rich-quick offers is the claim of the offeror that he became extremely wealthy by doing what he is now going to share with you for a small sum. The rationale is that if he did it, you can do it. Why he is interested in selling his secrets for a few dollars when he knows how to get rich easily is not explained, usually, and no one appears to want to be bothered with such unimportant nitpicking. The offeror goes to some pains to "prove" that he is as rich as he says he is—one device is an affidavit signed by the offeror's accountant, swearing that the offeror is as rich as he claims to be. Usually, however, it doesn't testify as to *how* the offeror acquired his wealth. But again, as far as the eager-to-believe victim is concerned, that's not important: why shouldn't this rich man who has now gone beyond the need for more money share his good fortune with less-fortunate brethren?

Ironically, it is not necessary to use this powerful factor of the will to believe in a negative way, to fleece victims. It can be as rewarding used honestly, to make honest sales. What is important here is to understand the basic drives, the *need* most people have to believe certain things. Sometimes it's called "hope," and life would soon become unbearable if we could not engender hope in ourselves.

USING THE PRINCIPLES

The principles work in virtually all things. They work in creating advertising and sales literature of all kinds—print advertising, radio and TV commercials, direct-mail literature packages, proposals, resumes, sales letters, letters of applications, letters of complaint. They work because everybody wants something, and people will yield to whatever appears to be the best opportunity to get the things they want. A customer will pay money to feel better, look better, be loved, be respected, feel happier, be more secure. An employer will hire you if you convince him that you can benefit his business or help him solve problems in carrying out whatever his mission is. An official will adjust your complaint or comply with your request if you show evidence that it is better to do so than to refuse.

Bear in mind at all times that each of these exchanges is a *negotiation* or at least an offer to conduct a negotiation:

With customers: the benefits I promise in exchange for your money.

With employers: the valuable services I offer in exchange for a salary plus.

With officials: no further trouble for you in exchange for adjusting my complaint.

Approach these as negotiations, not as favors you seek. Approach these in the philosophy that you've something to offer that is of great value to the other party, and you must negotiate the best trade possible. Approach these understanding that the other party may not understand, at first, the value of what you are offering—or the hazards of not listening to what you have to say. Recognize that you may have to do a great deal of explaining before negotiations can begin. You and the other party must, after all, understand each other clearly before you can even begin to discuss any kind of trade.

COMMUNICATION

If you wish to truly communicate with every reader, you must be almost painfully blunt. It is necessary that the reader grasp not only the meaning of your words and sentences, but your total *intent*. Anything less is flawed communication, and you can hardly persuade anyone unless you have delivered the message.

These are days of euphemisms. We say "mortician," instead of "undertaker"; "sanitation worker," instead of "garbage man"; "custodian," instead of "janitor." There is not much harm in most of these, for communication does not suffer. But it is necessary to be sure that communication does not suffer; some of these terms we use are pure jargon, and communication does suffer. I once had a serious dispute with my insurance company because I did not know that it meant "payment" when it wrote "premium."

It is not always necessary to find the shortest word, to make your meaning clear. In fact, the length of the word is irrelevant. What is relevant to clarity of meaning and communication in general is how commonly the word is used. Only a few minutes with even a small dictionary will uncover short words that few know the meaning of, and long words that are in everyday use among us all. Here are a few examples:

covet	cylinder
cyton	debatable
erose	escalator
induit	industrialize
sopor	specialist

Here are synonyms or definitions for that left-hand column:

covet: desire
cyton: body of nerve cell
erose: uneven, ragged
induit: grant, privilege
sopor: lethargy

It is necessary to judge which words are in common, everyday use—which words, that is, will be understood easily by all readers. Use not the shortest words, but the most common words, short or long. There is one purpose and one purpose only in writing anything: that is to communicate information, ideas, images, messages to others. Any writing that fails to deliver to the reader that information, idea, image, or message intended by the writer is failed communication, and the writer must accept responsibility for the failure: the responsibility for communication does not fall on the reader; it falls on the writer.

INDEX